IMAGES
of America

THE 1958 COLFAX TORNADO

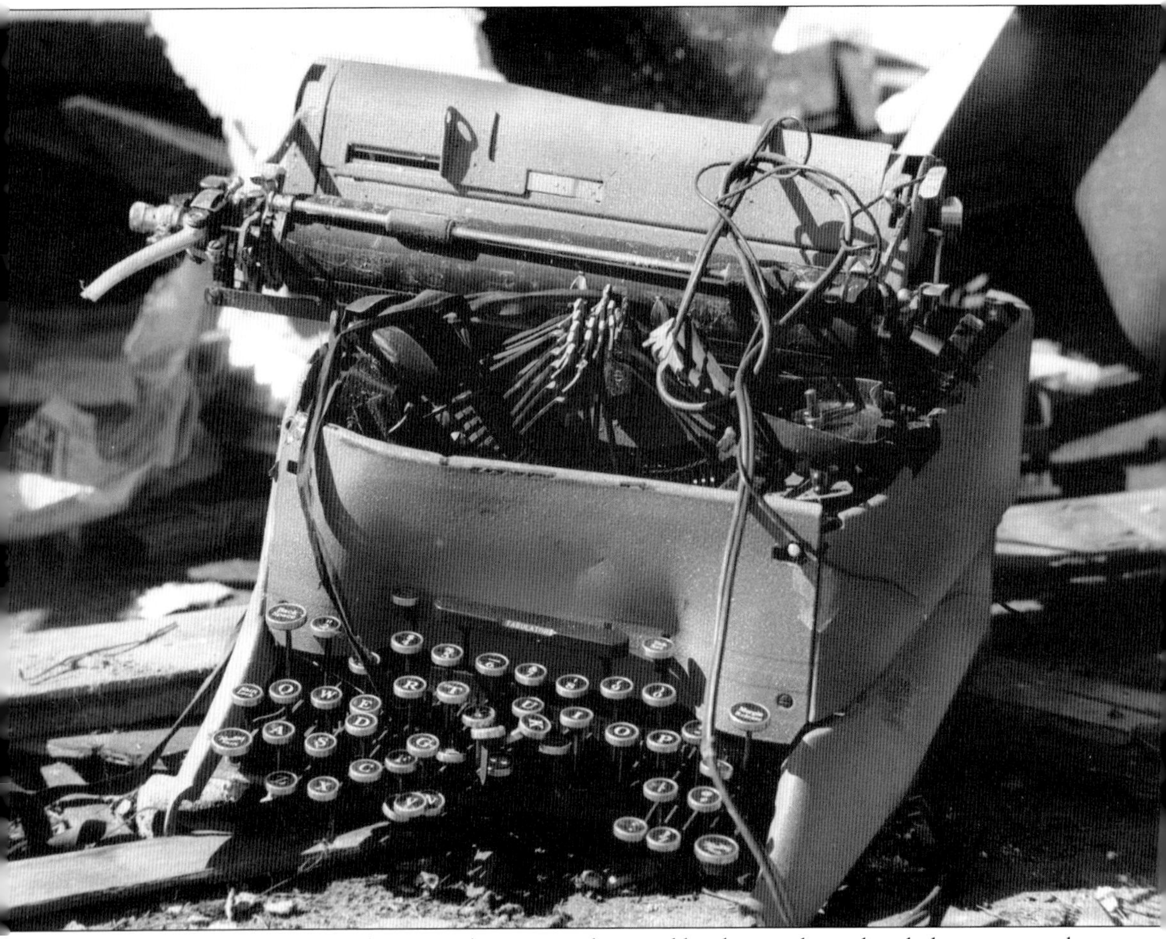

This typewriter rode out the storm, being tossed around by the winds, and ended up in a nearby field. It is unlikely it was able to be salvaged. There is a story of a mother and her two children who took shelter in the basement of their home when the tornado hit. The mother remembered looking up at the sky at one point and seeing her home about 30 feet in the air above them, and then it just exploded. (Author's collection.)

On the Cover: People look through the remains of the Arthur Hovland home just east of the Burling home on the north side of town. They were looking for personal effects and anything that was salvageable. The Clarence and Minda Burling home in the background was used on the national campaign poster for the Red Cross in its fundraising efforts. (Courtesy of John Russell.)

IMAGES
of America

THE 1958 COLFAX TORNADO

Troy and Michelle Knutson

ARCADIA
PUBLISHING

ISBN 978-1-4671-0347-3

Published by Arcadia Publishing
Charleston, South Carolina

Printed in the United States of America

Library of Congress Control Number: 2018966769

For all general information, please contact Arcadia Publishing:
Telephone 843-853-2070
Fax 843-853-0044
E-mail sales@arcadiapublishing.com
For customer service and orders:
Toll-Free 1-888-313-2665

Visit us on the Internet at www.arcadiapublishing.com

To the memory of those lost and in honor of those who survived the Colfax tornado on June 4, 1958.

Contents

Acknowledgments

The preservation of Colfax history has been my goal since I was introduced to the subject as a sophomore in high school. This book is dedicated to the memory of those lost in the June 4, 1958, tornado and in honor of those who survived it. It is my hope that publishing this account of the tornado will keep the memory alive of what makes our community unique and strong for generations to come.

A special thank-you goes to John Russell, Ron Blakely, LeAnn Ralph, and Juul Noer, in addition to the numerous people who have shared photographs and stories with me. Resources that have been especially helpful in understanding the scope of this tornado have been the *Colfax Messenger*, the *Eau Claire Leader Telegram*, *Dunn County News*, Colfax Public Library, and the *1964 Colfax Centennial Souvenir Program*.

This book in no way is a complete story of the tornado and its effects, but it is a starting point. If anyone has any additional information, memories, or photographs of the Colfax tornado, I would greatly appreciate it if you would contact me.

Introduction

The morning of Wednesday, June 4, 1958, dawned sunny, hot, and humid. People described the day as being unusual. In early June in west central Wisconsin, the weather tends to be quite pleasant—not as oppressive and ominous as anything you might encounter in July or August, they said.

Residents of Colfax continued about their day, trying to find a bit of relief from the heat and humidity. Older folks sweated and toiled and used their handkerchiefs to pat the perspiration off their faces. Children rode their bikes to the river to go swimming. None of them—not for a moment—suspected the tragedy that would befall them at 7:00 that evening.

In those days, there was no weather radar. There were no warning sirens. There were no weather radios.

Dave and Mike Henderson, ages 16 and 14, were milking cows in the barn on their farm on the south side of Colfax. The static electricity in the air was like nothing they had ever experienced. They knew a storm was brewing. They could see it approaching from the southwest. Suddenly, a black cloud traveling along the ground was nearly upon them. The boys ran out into the barnyard and threw themselves down in the mud. A few seconds later, Dave Henderson believed it was imperative they not stay there, and they got up and ran and threw themselves down in the mud again.

Had they stayed where they were, the silo would have landed on top of them.

A minute or two later, the storm was past. The boys got up out of the mud, and all around them was devastation. Everything that had been there minutes earlier was now gone. Covered with mud and cow manure, the boys set out walking to another nearby farm where their parents had been milking. They were sure their mom and dad were dead. But there, in the distance, they saw two people walking toward them. Just as surely as Dave and Mike Henderson were certain their parents, Frank and Arlene, were dead, Frank and Arlene were certain their boys were dead. Meanwhile, the tornado continued across the south side of Colfax and then went on to the north side.

Lucerne Neumann, who lived on the west side of Colfax, said she stood on her porch and watched the windows snap in and out, in and out, as if the house were breathing. And she knew something very bad was happening.

On the north side of Colfax, Juel and Donna Stalson and their friend Erling Braaten were about to drive through town. Juel turned the car around and tried to outrun the storm. He attempted to hold the car steady with the brake, but the tornado pitched it end over end.

Ron Husby, driving a potato chip delivery truck, had just driven into Colfax not far from the Stalson car. Husby said the last thing he remembered before waking up by Eighteen Mile Creek with his truck nowhere in sight, was being sucked out the window and hanging onto the steering wheel for dear life.

When Donna Stalson came to, all around her looked like a scene "from hell." She started searching for her husband and their friend, and out of the destruction walked her husband, his face looking like a road map of cuts, cradling a broken arm. Erling, as it turned out, was alive too.

The Colfax tornado began as a series of thunderstorms in Minnesota. What came to be known as the Colfax tornado started near Baldwin and ended near Thorp.

All together, 12 people were killed in Colfax, and countless others were injured. Another 16 people died along the path of the storm. Those who lost their lives in Colfax included Lanny Fjelstad, age 16, and his uncle Spencer Fjelstad, 38; Nora Gerber, 66; Mildred (Gerber) Slaga, 39; Erling Lunn, 28, and his son Leon, 4; Vernon Meindell, 40; Richard Presnell, 27; Petter George Nilson, 70; Arthur Quevillon, 52; William Wagner, 50; and Thelma Woolsey Lunn, 21.

After the ominous and oppressive heat of June 4 and the fury of the tornado, Delores Jahr reported that a couple nights later, "there was frost, but it didn't hurt anything."

In the days following the tornado, Colfax was filled with the sound of chainsaws cutting up the downed trees, and the air was blue with smoke from debris piles being burned.

The Colfax Lutheran Church, which somehow escaped damage, was a beehive of activity. Women worked many long, hard hours preparing meals for those who had nowhere to prepare their own food. In the end, they served thousands of meals.

And then came the funerals. Colfax residents stopped their clean-up activities long enough to attend the funerals and pay their respects to those who had died.

After that, armies of volunteers arrived to help where they could. Many of them combed the farm fields around Colfax, picking up the nails that had once held houses together. One farmer said he had never had so many flat tires in his life. He said he could not drive any kind of equipment out in his fields without getting flats.

When the sound of chainsaws died down and the wind carried off the last wisp of smoke from the bonfires, Colfax rang with the sound of saws and hammers as people started to rebuild their destroyed houses or fix the damaged ones. There was a certain urgency to rebuild and repair. Even though the tornado struck in June, people knew winter would come eventually, and they did not have that much time.

Some people moved away from Colfax. They preferred to start over again somewhere new, someplace that did not hold the awful, terrible, tragic memories—and who could blame them? Most people stayed, though.

As time went on, the injured were healed, and by winter, through hard work and perseverance, the houses and barns were rebuilt and repaired. Many people, however, for the rest of their lives, could never shake a sense of fear and anxiety when the skies darkened, the lightning flashed, and the thunder rumbled.

LeAnn R. Ralph
Colfax, Wisconsin
November 2018

One

The Aftermath

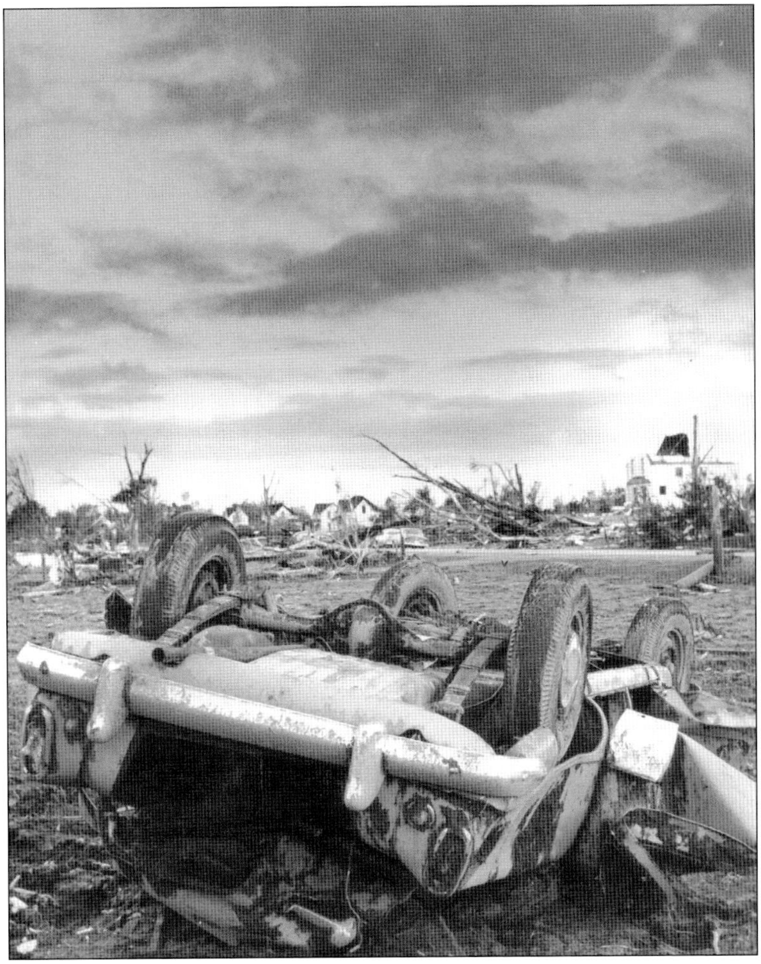

The F5 tornado left 12 people and hundreds of animals dead. Apart from the victims, it caused millions of dollars in damage and left the survivors with a very uneasy feeling during storms of any kind to this day. This iconic photograph shows some of the damage in the village of Colfax. (Courtesy of Ron Blakely.)

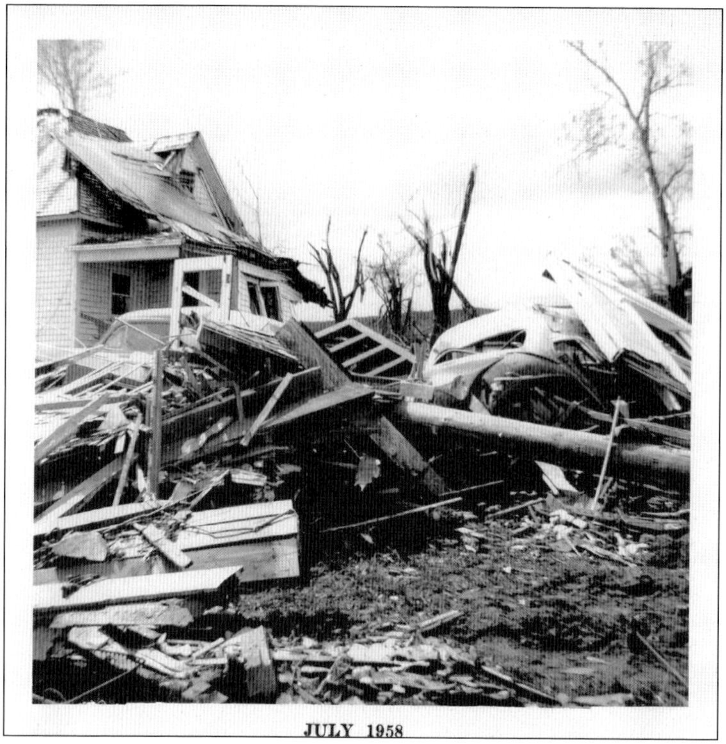

The home of Joe and Lillian Dressel suffered too much damage to be saved. It was torn down, and a new single-story home was later built on this lot. The two cars appear to have not escaped damage. (Courtesy of Thelma Mickelson Kettle.)

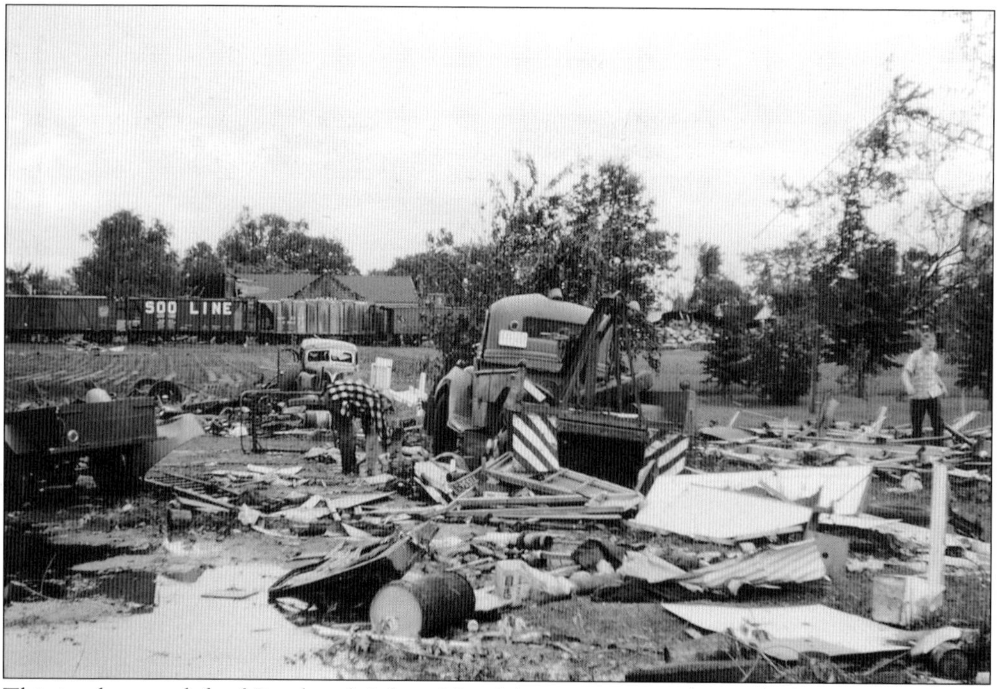

This is what was left of Savel and Arlene Haugle's maintenance shop, which really is nothing. The wrecker is surrounded by debris—everything that once was stored in the garage, which no longer exists. In the background is the train depot with damage to its roof. (Courtesy of Diane Haugle Hodgson.)

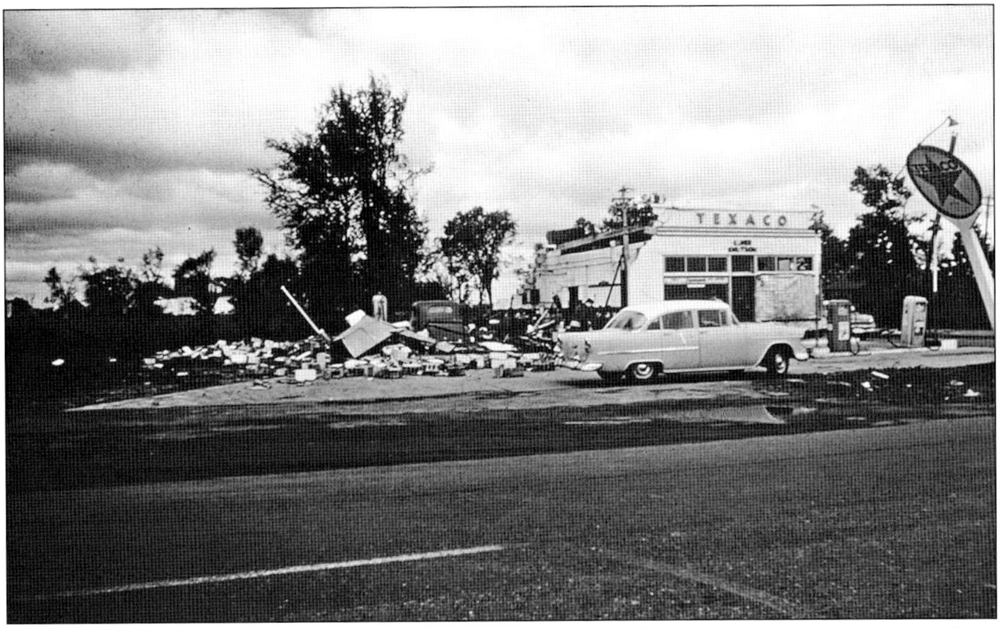

This is what was left of Elmer Knutson's Texaco gas station. Many strange stories came out of the tornado. Mary Keilholz Brenden recalls losing her family's home, but being lucky enough that the wall between her bedroom and her brother's bedroom fell in such a way that it formed a pocket that protected her yearbooks, photo albums, class ring, and other treasured items. (Courtesy of Diane Haugle Hodgson.)

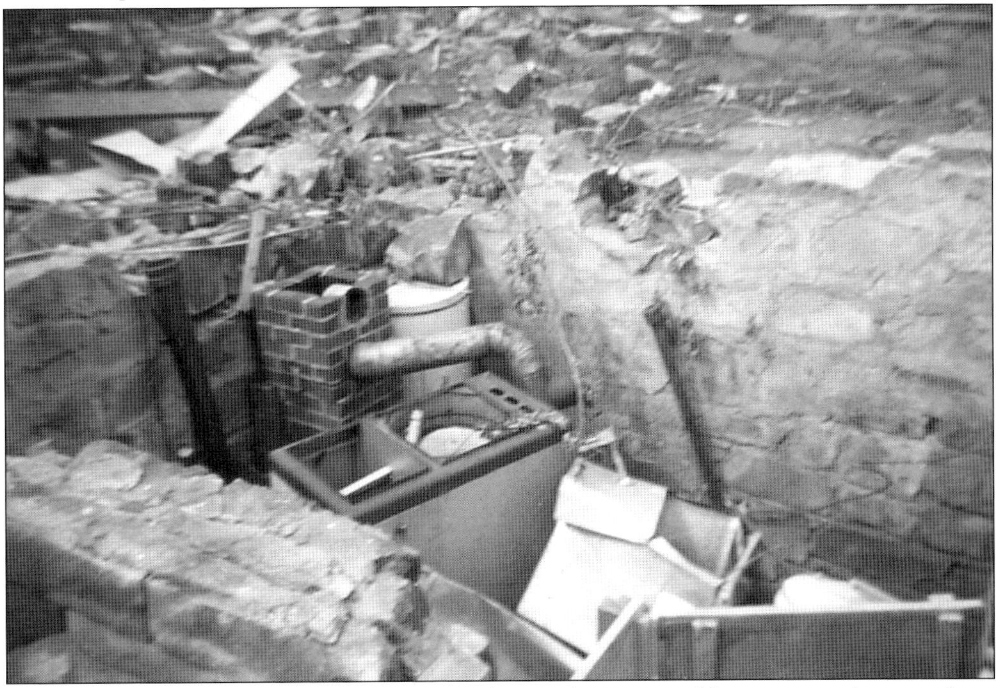

Four Puhl family members, Adele, Warren, Sylvia, and Jim, were able to survive the tornado in their cellar along with their dog Rusty. They all escaped injury. The entry door to the cellar is at lower right. (Courtesy of Jim Puhl.)

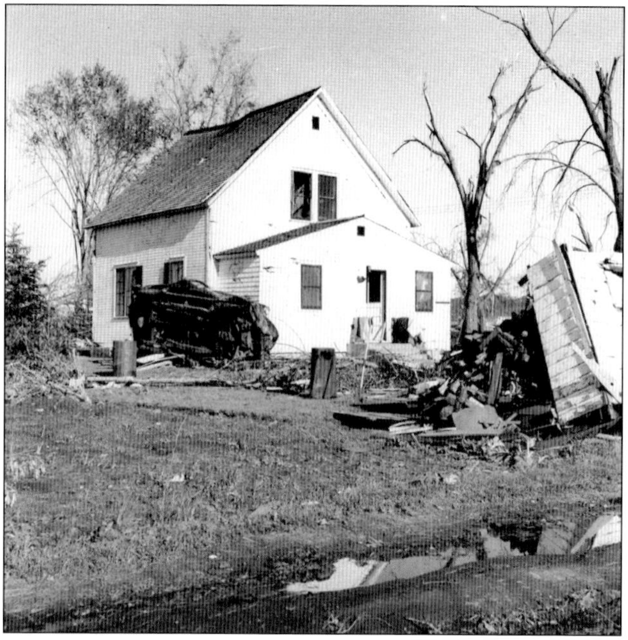

Pictured here is the home of Selmer and Aida Fjelstad on the corner of Fifth Avenue and Park Drive. Although it appears to have survived the tornado, there was much more damage than could be seen. The home had to be torn down and rebuilt. (Courtesy of John Russell.)

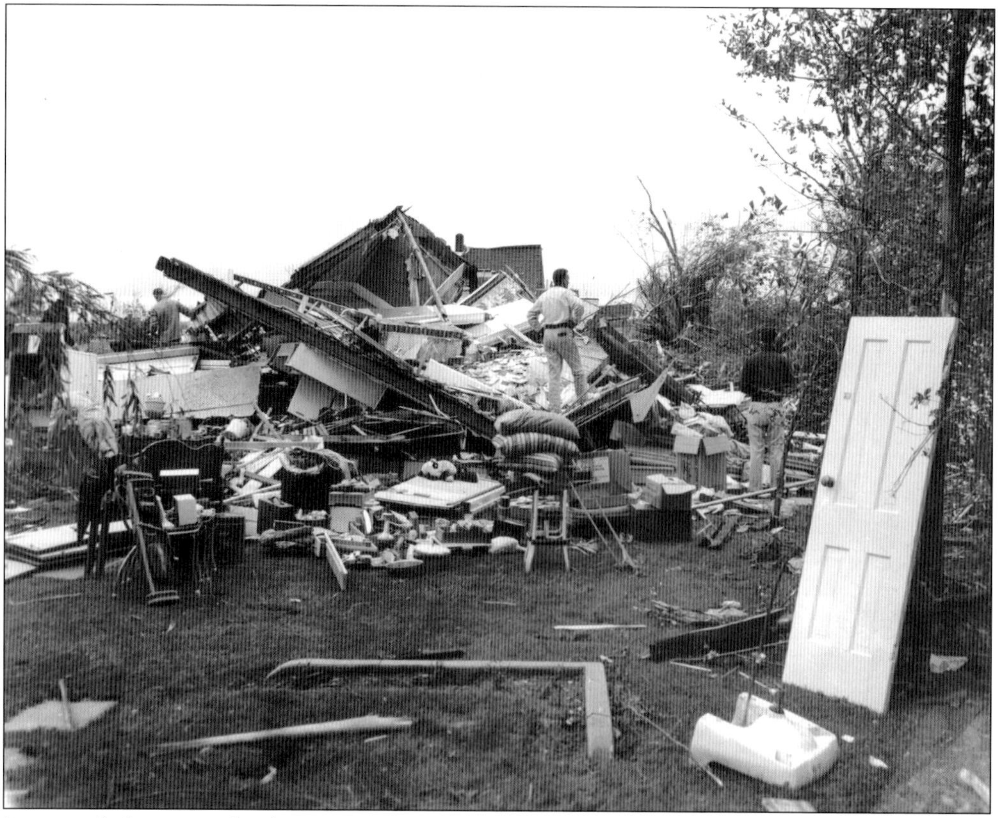

In spite of what seemed to be an insurmountable task, residents were up to the challenge. A little bit of normal could be found in a bag of golf clubs, a set of dishes, or a teddy bear recovered from what used to be the family home. (Courtesy of the Colfax Public Library.)

The front portion of Alfred Knutson's milk truck was smashed and left by his home, which had been twisted and shifted off its foundation. Marie Schindler recalls venturing outside after the storm to see the damage. Their chicken coop was completely gone, along with all but 13 of 300 chickens. (Courtesy of Ron Blakely.)

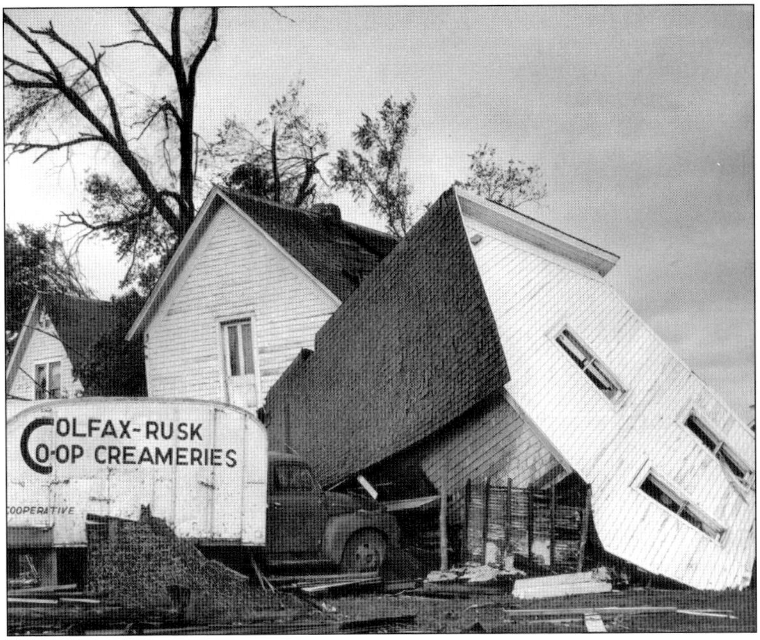

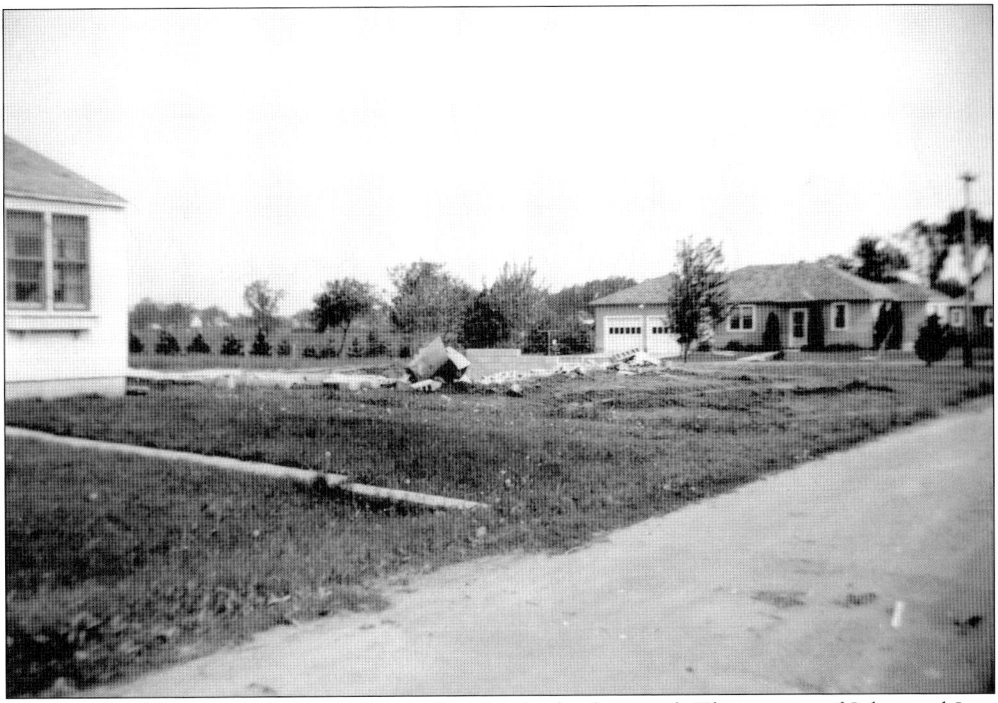

The home of Stanley Rehm is still standing in the background. The corner of John and Lou Negaard's home can be seen in the foreground. What appears to be an empty lot between the two was actually once the site of Juel and Doris Haugle's home. It home was completely demolished. (Courtesy of Marina Nichols.)

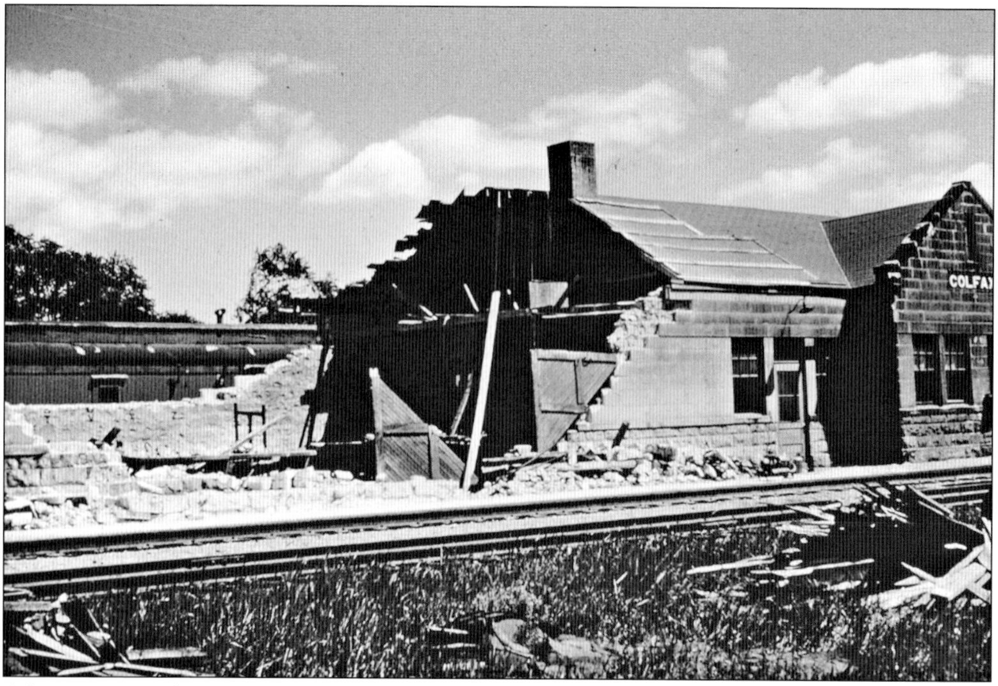

After removing the western part of the Colfax train depot, the tornado quickly moved east. Yvette Viets Flaten recalls being able to get through the police cordons the next day. When reaching her grandfather Ralph Viets's barbershop, she found it was completely gone except the front steps and his old Junger's stove. (Courtesy of Diane Haugle Hodgson.)

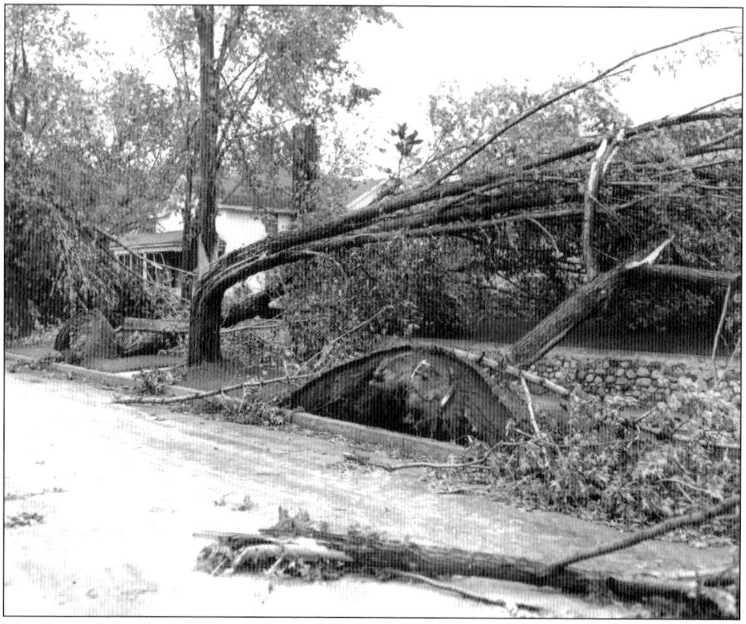
This picture was taken looking northeast on Balsam Street with the Freestone home in the background. The Frank and Dora Neumann home cannot be seen because it was completely covered by fallen trees. The boulevard, which had been lined with mature trees, would never look the same. (Courtesy of the Colfax Public Library.)

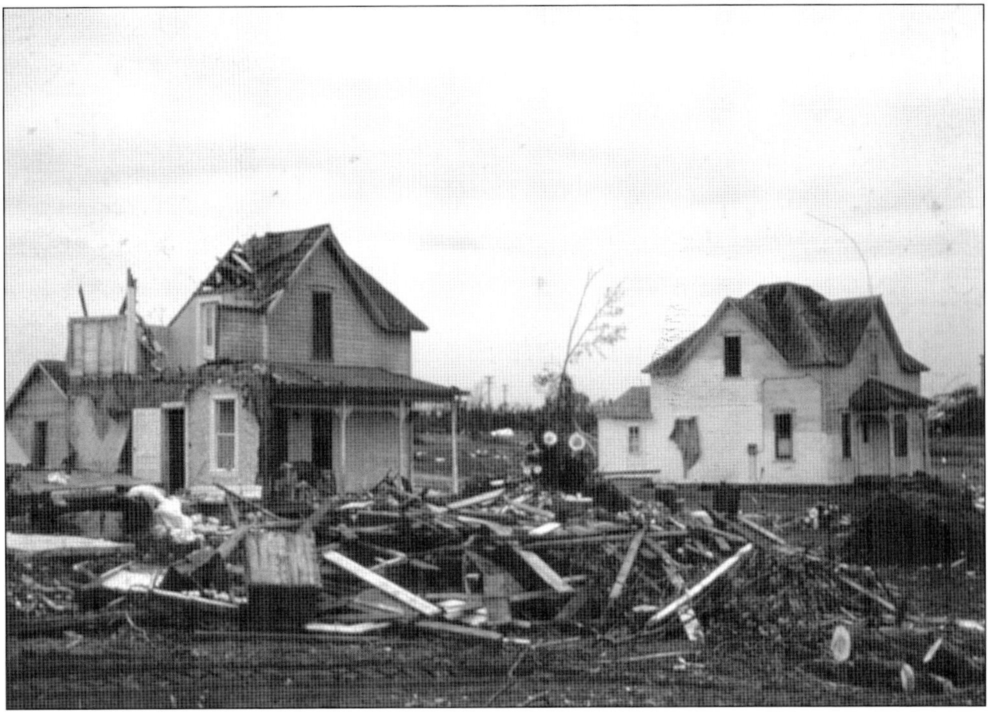

The power of the storm was unreal. A neatly folded insurance policy from Knapp, Wisconsin, was taken more than 75 miles east and deposited in a field southeast of Sheldon, Wisconsin. The engine from the local veterinarian's pickup truck was found five miles from its original location and identified by its serial number. (Author's collection.)

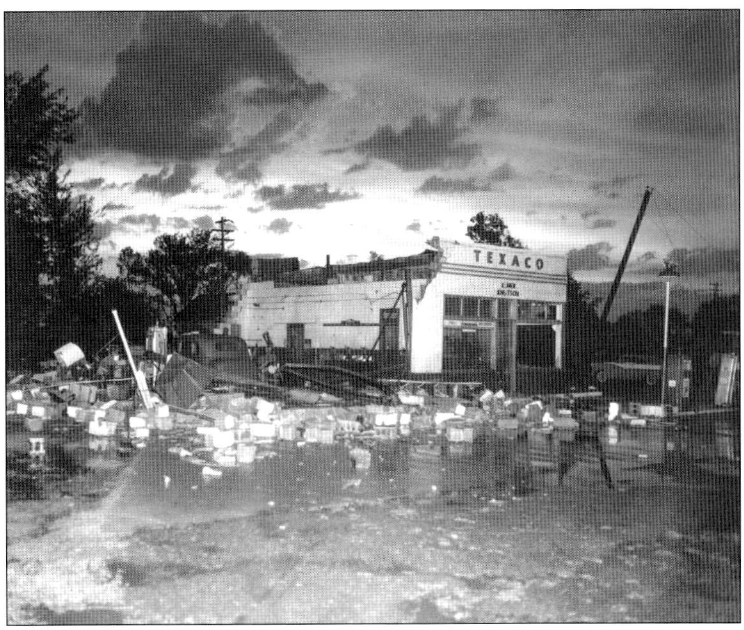

Concrete blocks were no match for the power of the tornado. Those pictured here were moved several yards from their original location—Elmer Knutson's Texaco Station. One window is blown out, while the other right next to it is still intact. (Courtesy of the Colfax Public Library.)

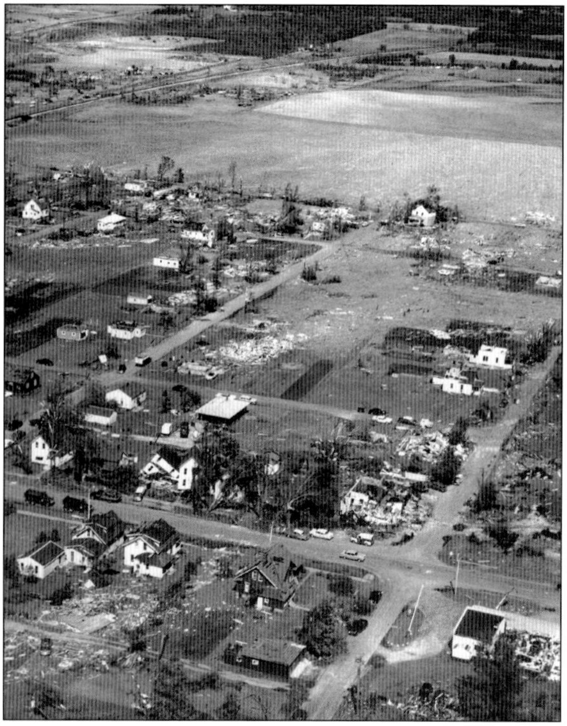

This aerial photograph shows the crippled village of Colfax after the twister blew through. It shows the main path that the tornado took. Elmer Knutson's Texaco station is at lower right. (Author's collection.)

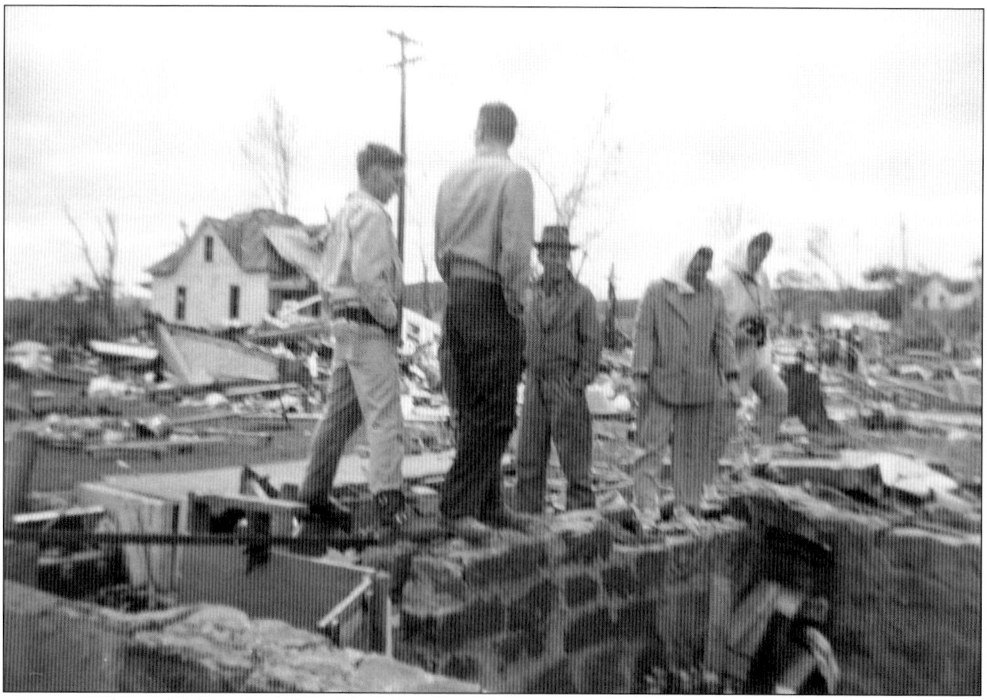

This was the Puhl family cellar following the tornado. Some of the living room furniture was in the neighbor's yard and basement, in the background. The dining room floor found its way onto their roof. It is noted on the photograph that Adele Puhl is wearing clothes donated by a local family. (Courtesy of Jim Puhl.)

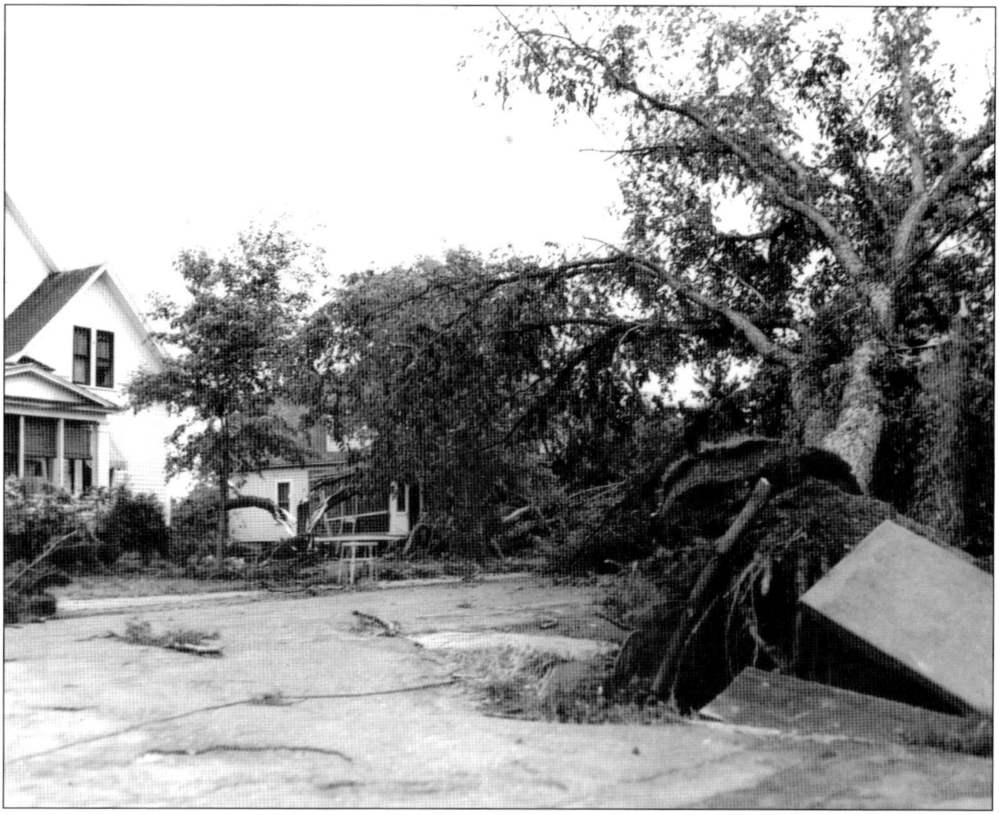

On the corner of River Road and Evergreen Street, mature trees were no match for the winds of the twister. Trees were uprooted in all directions and left the roads impassable, making it nearly impossible to get in and out of the village. (Courtesy of the Colfax Public Library.)

The Knapp Settlement School had a 4-H meeting scheduled minutes prior to the tornado. Luckily, because of the day's weather and the onset of the storm, no one was at the school for the meeting at the time. (Courtesy of the Colfax Public Library.)

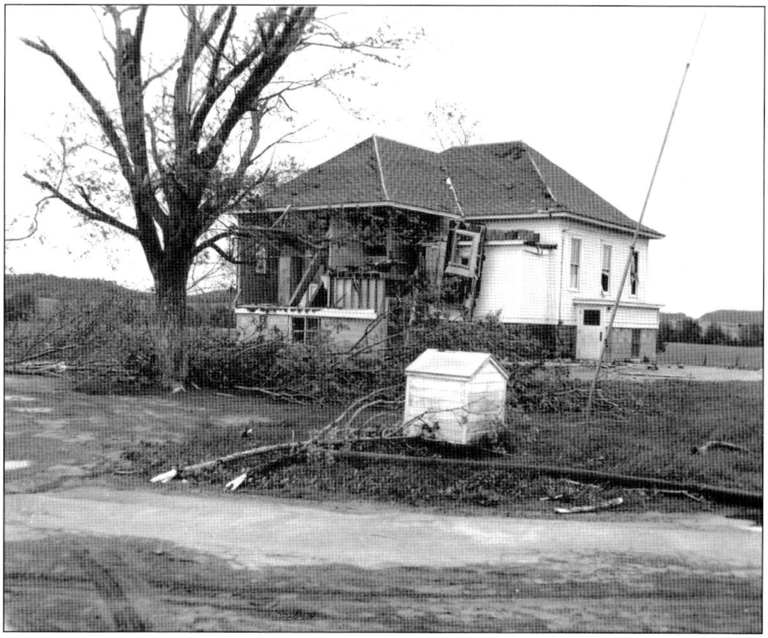

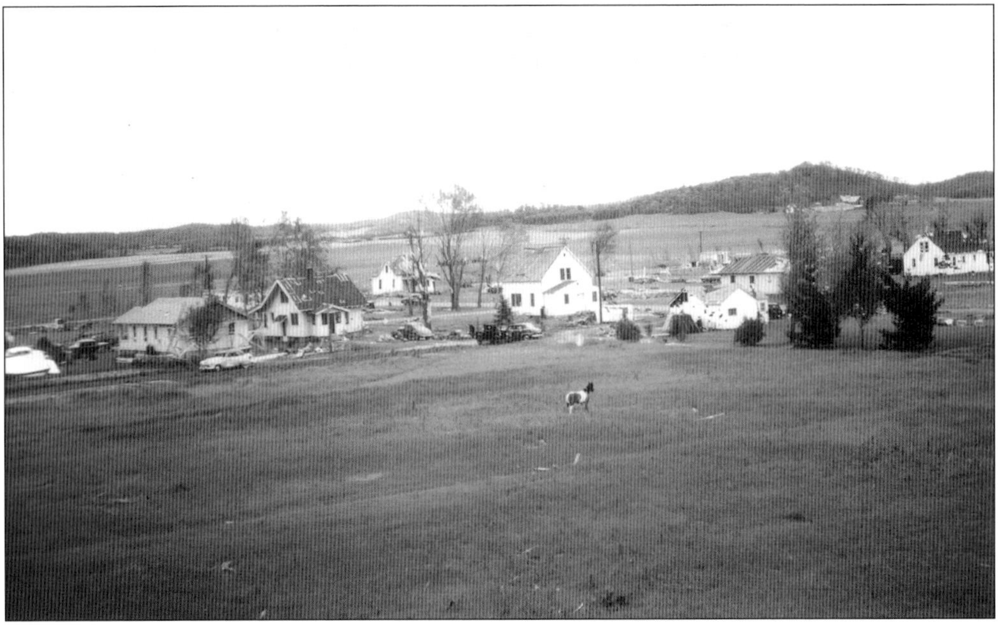

This is the south side of the village looking southeast. The remains of the two homes on the left are on Roosevelt Street, another neighborhood that was not spared from the destruction of the tornado. Unsure what has happened, a pony surveys the damage. (Courtesy of Alfred Almquist.)

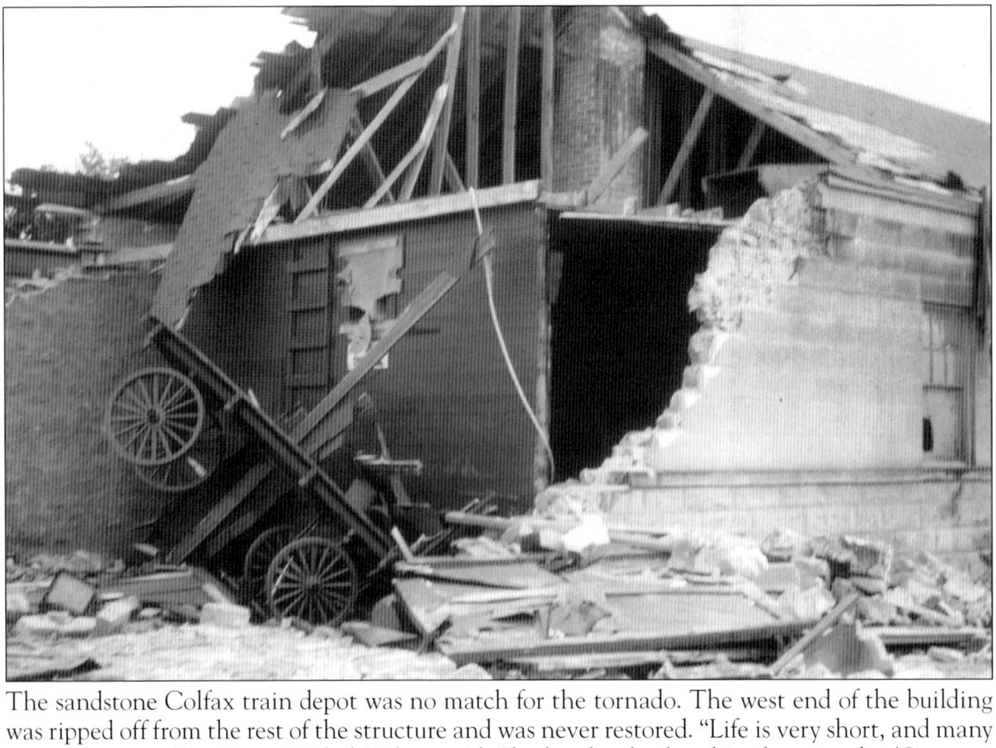

The sandstone Colfax train depot was no match for the tornado. The west end of the building was ripped off from the rest of the structure and was never restored. "Life is very short, and many memories are still with me," Ethel Nelson said. She lost her husband in the tornado. (Courtesy of Alfred Almquist.)

Here is what used to be the inside of Elmer Knutson's Texaco station on the south side of town, where the Grapevine Senior Center is currently located. Even solidly built cement block buildings were no match for the destructive force of the tornado. (Courtesy of the Colfax Public Library.)

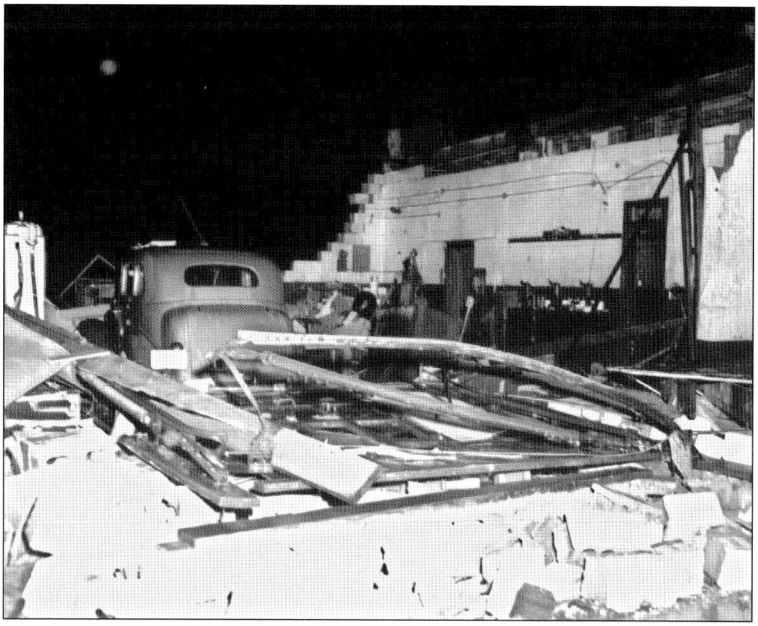

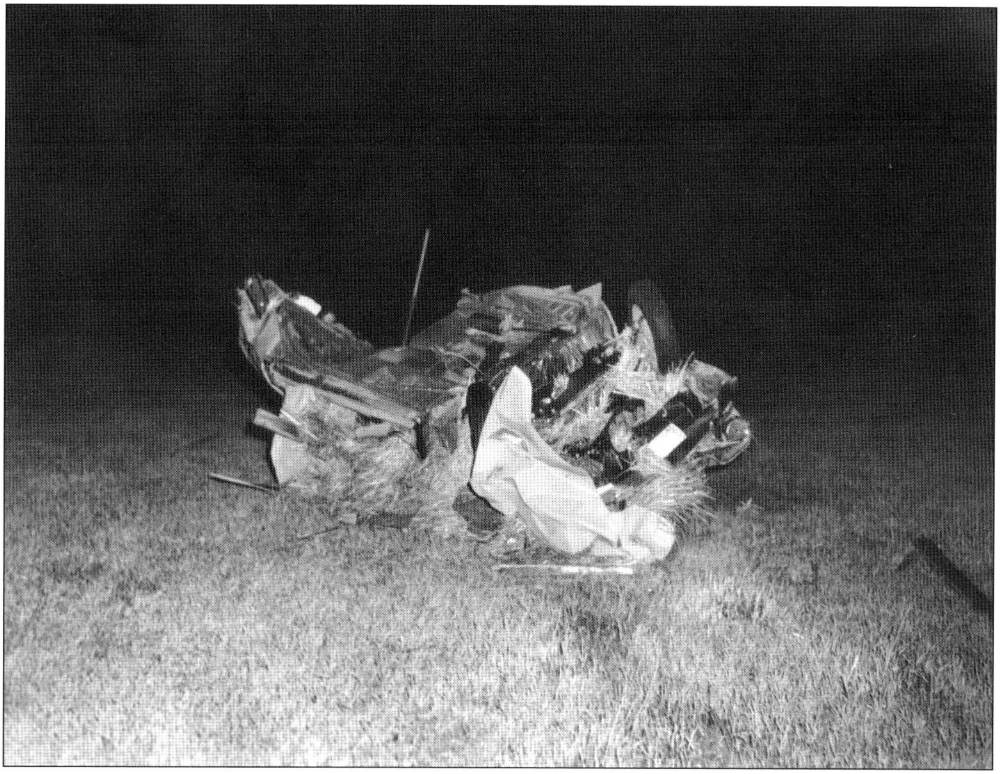

Richard Presnell and Vernon Meindell of Bloomer were traveling through the village and were surprised by the tornado. The two men were found in their car, wrapped in barbed wire. They were wrapped so tight that it was nearly impossible to remove and transport their bodies to the funeral home. (Courtesy of the Colfax Public Library.)

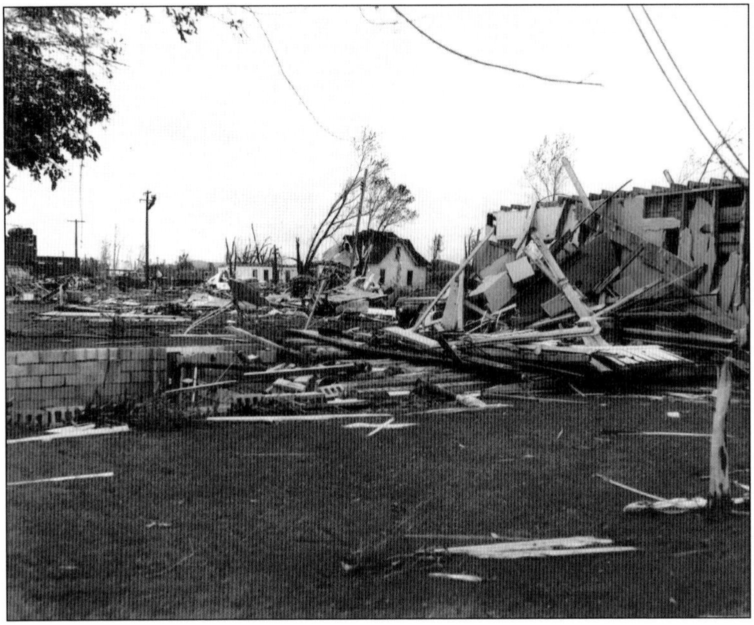

Amid the damage, people worked tirelessly to restore a sense of normal life in the aftermath of the tornado. A utility worker attempts to restore power to the community, as debris piles wait for the owners to sift through for what can be saved. (Courtesy of the Colfax Public Library.)

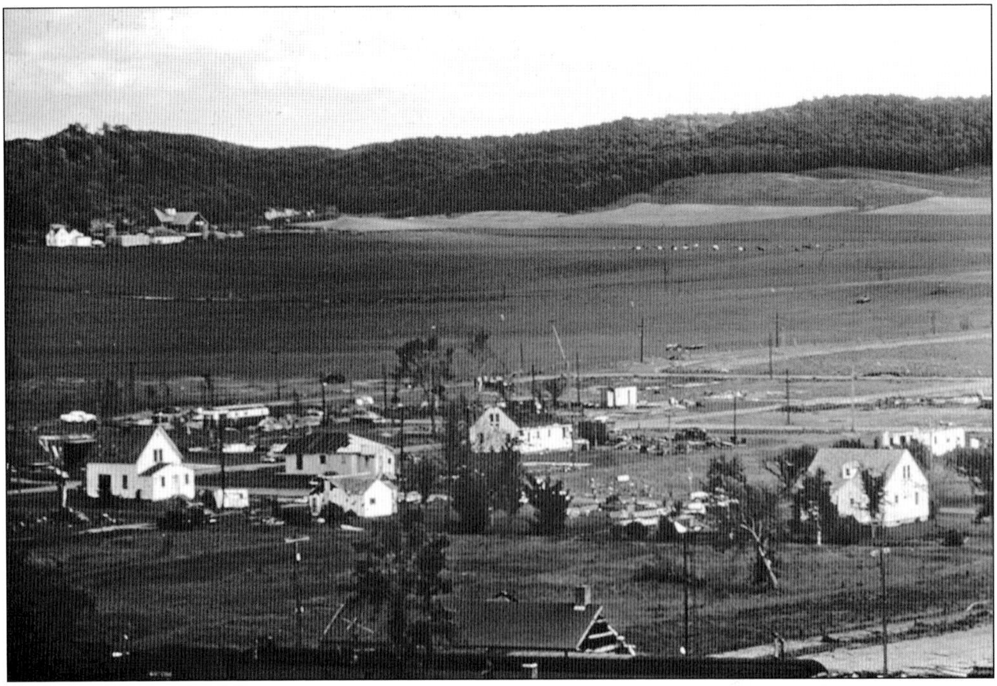

It was a devastating time for Colfax. However, the community pulled together and started over. Not everyone stayed and rebuilt after the tornado. For some, there were too many bad memories, and they wanted a new start. The population dropped from around 1,044 to the 800s. (Courtesy of Diane Haugle Hodgson.)

Debris was littered all over the village. Found in the remains of buildings and homes were items that did not belong to the homeowners. In this tree, while there are no leaves to be found, there is a water tank for the farm's animals. (Author's collection.)

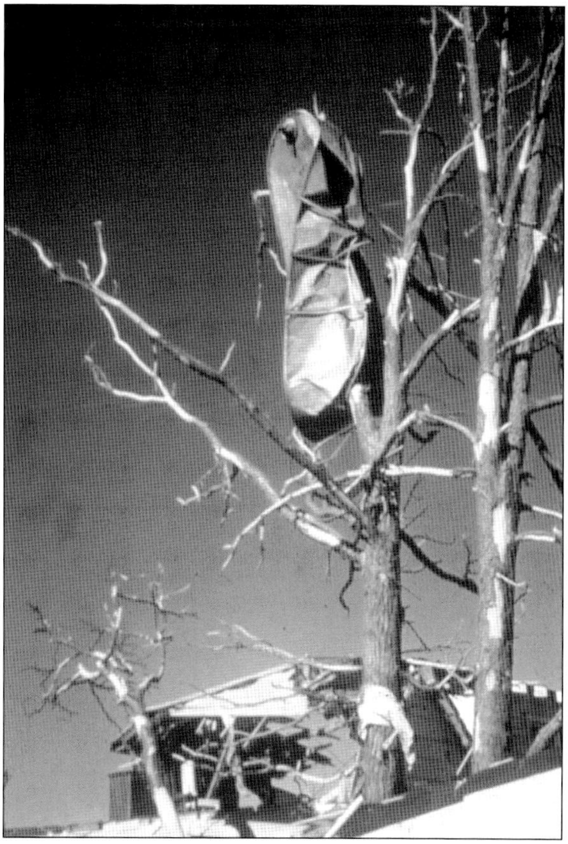

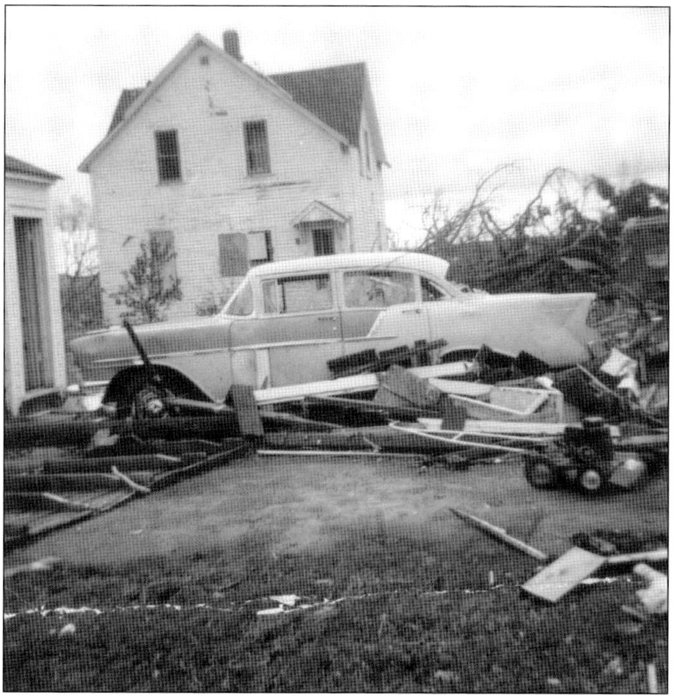

The home of Jennings and Mattie Page withstood the terrific power of the tornado. Not every home in Colfax was so lucky. At the home of Martin Olson, only part of the kitchen and a bedroom remained after the storm. During the cleanup process, Olson was sifting through the rubble. When he lifted a mattress off a bed frame, he found a pair of pants that did not belong to him or anyone in his family. (Courtesy of Sara Page Watts.)

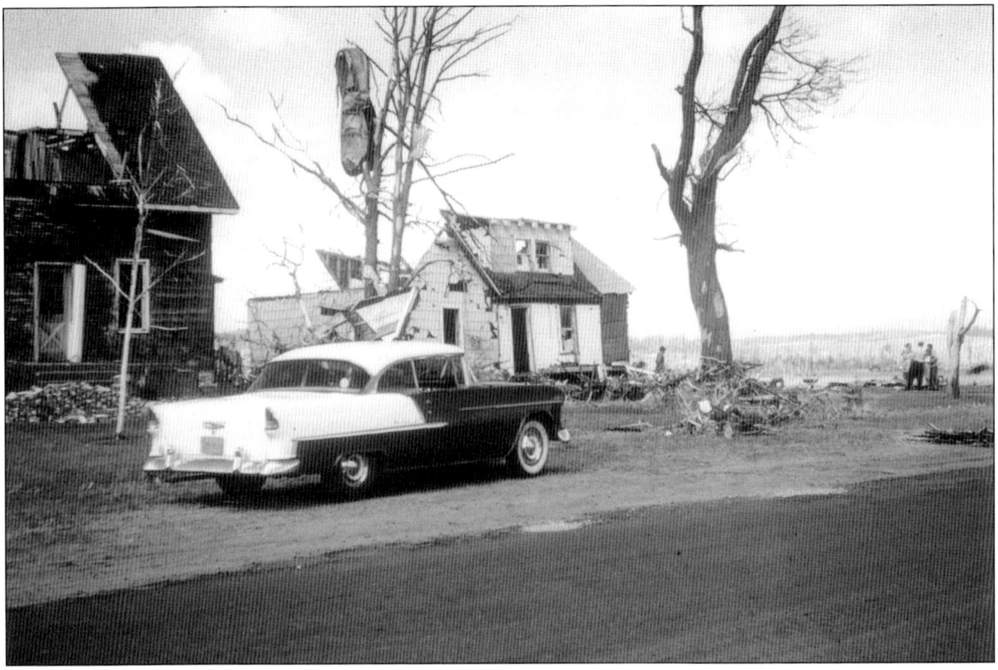

The homes of Phillip Felland and Odd Lindberg were left in pieces. Note the tangled-up water tank that was tossed up into the tree in Odd Lindberg's yard. Other trees had shingles and pieces of straw embedded in them as if someone had thrown a dart. (Courtesy of Alfred Almquist.)

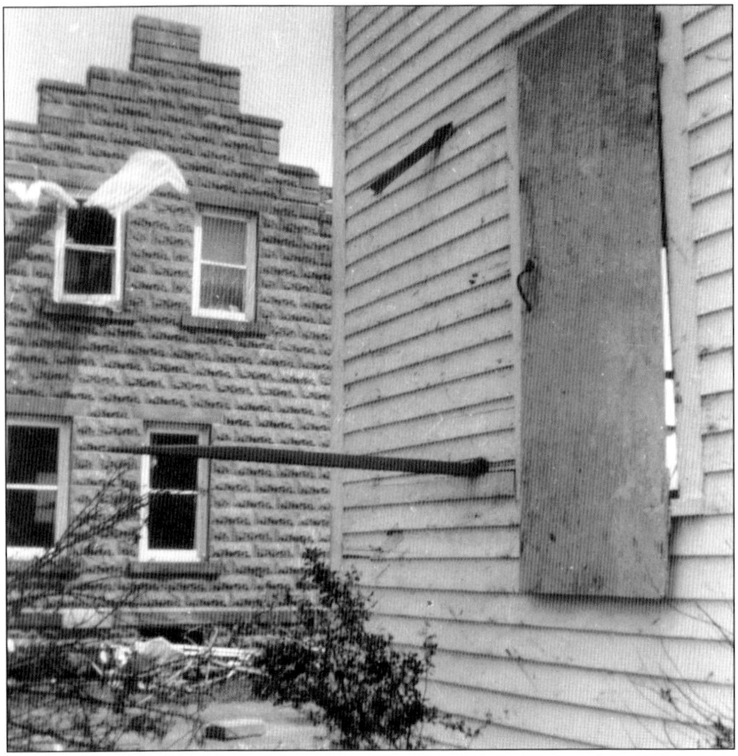

Boards pierced the walls of the Jennings and Mattie Page home. The power of the tornado was unimaginable. There are reports of pieces of straw and grass being driven into glass windows without causing the glass to crack. The home of Nora Wiseman just to the north lost its roof during the storm. (Courtesy of Sara Page Watts.)

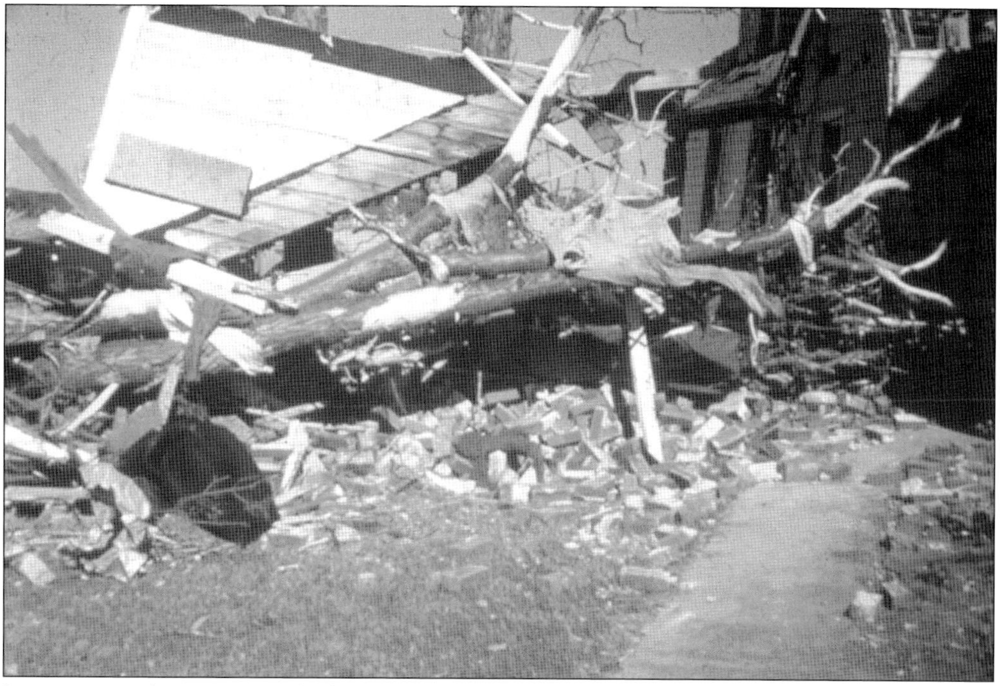

It is amazing that more people did not perish in the storm with so few warnings. Rose Jacobson, who lived on the south side, was rolled up in her living room carpet and landed outside in her back yard among the rubble and debris, a little banged up but happy to still be alive. (Author's collection.)

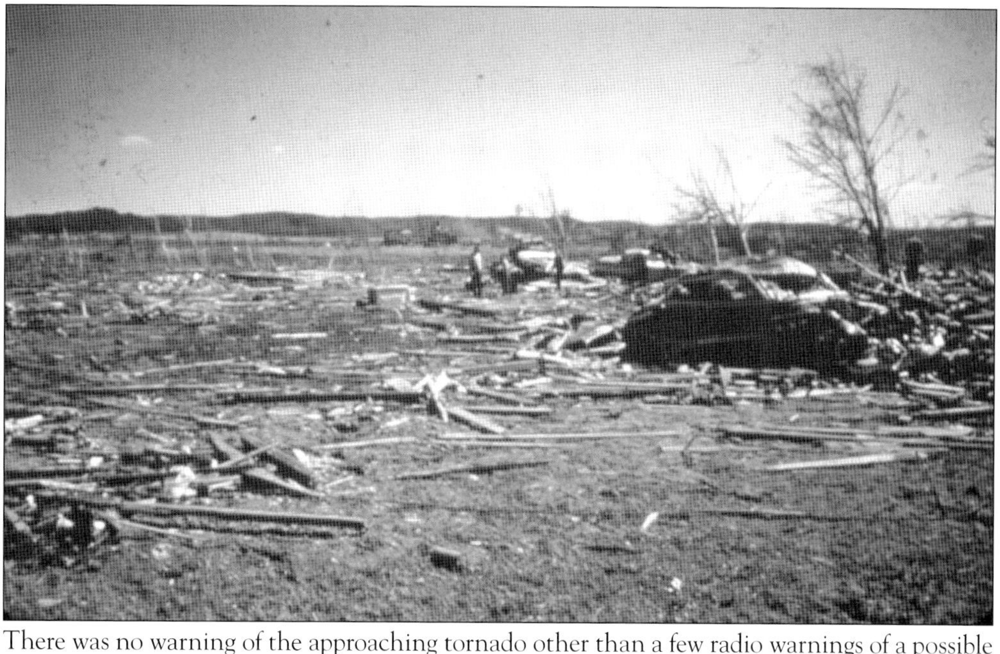

There was no warning of the approaching tornado other than a few radio warnings of a possible thunderstorm. Shirley Olson Paff had her own personal warning from her father, Melvin Olson. He had said that if there is constant lightning and thundering, it is a sign of a really bad storm. (Author's collection.)

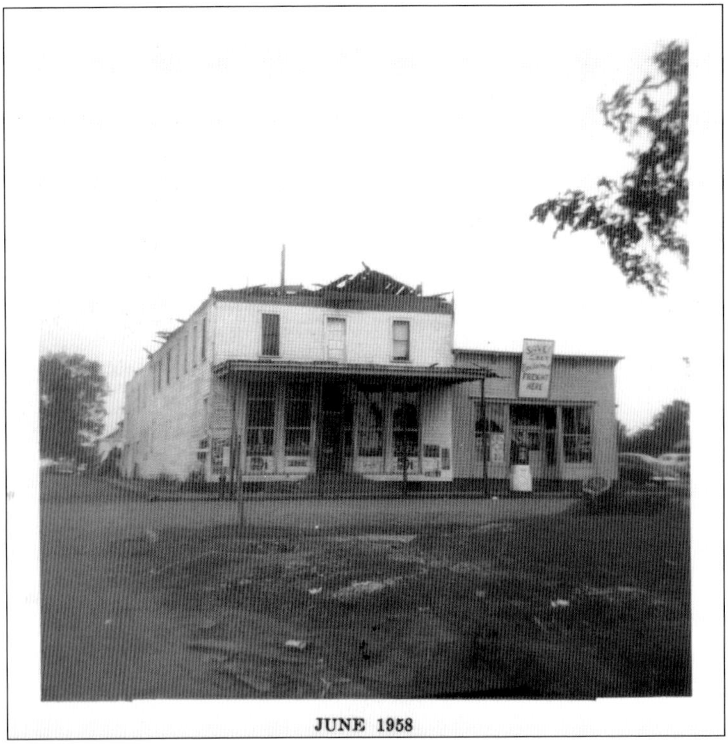

The store owned by Buck and Myrtle Gunderson had major roof damage. Children had been playing outside when the tornado arrived. In some cases, children just made it into their basements with the tornado on their heels as it destroyed the things they had just been playing with. As Jane Higbie was getting her sisters to safety, the porch that she had just been standing on was ripped from her home. (Courtesy of Joan Shong.)

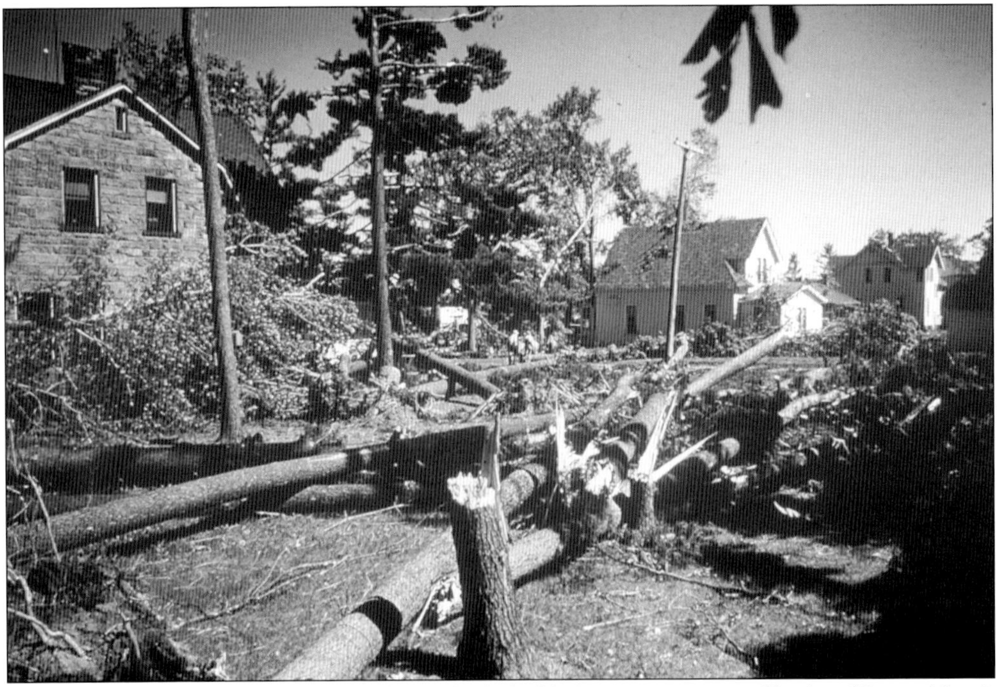

There was a lot of cleanup needed in the yard of Alvilde Saumer, just east of Juul and Penny Noer's home, after these huge pine trees were snapped off and flattened. In addition to the damage to the trees, wads of straw were stuck under staples in fence posts so tight that they could not be pulled out. (Courtesy of Lyle Christenson.)

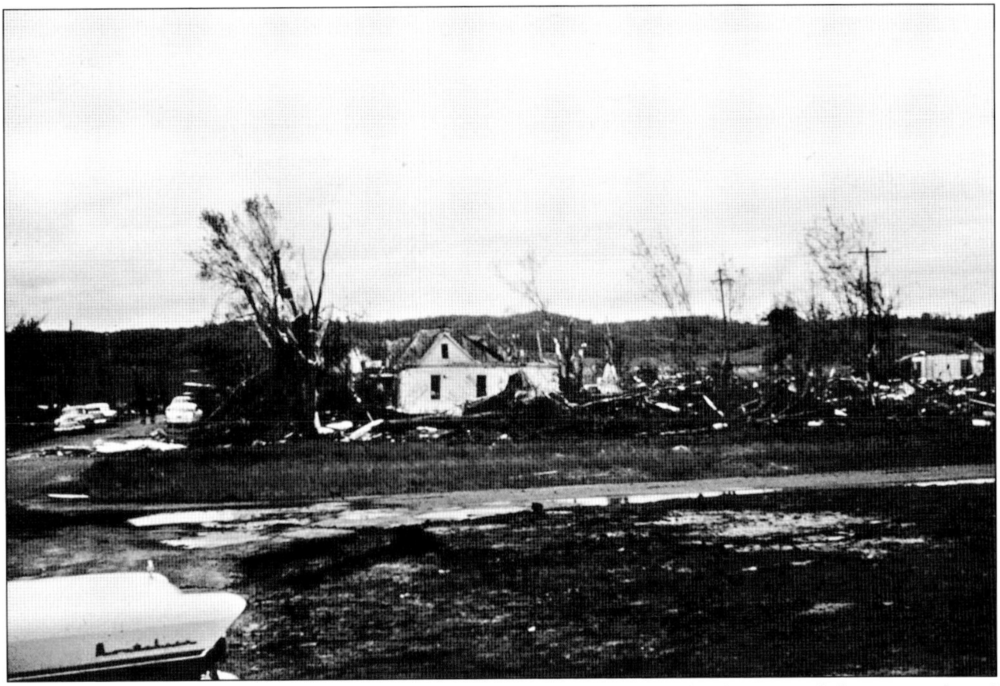

The south side of the village was severely damaged. Here are the homes of the Dressel and Rostamoe families looking southeast. The tornado leveled about 72 homes in Colfax. There was already progress being made on the rebuilding within months of the storm. (Courtesy of Diane Haugle Hodgson.)

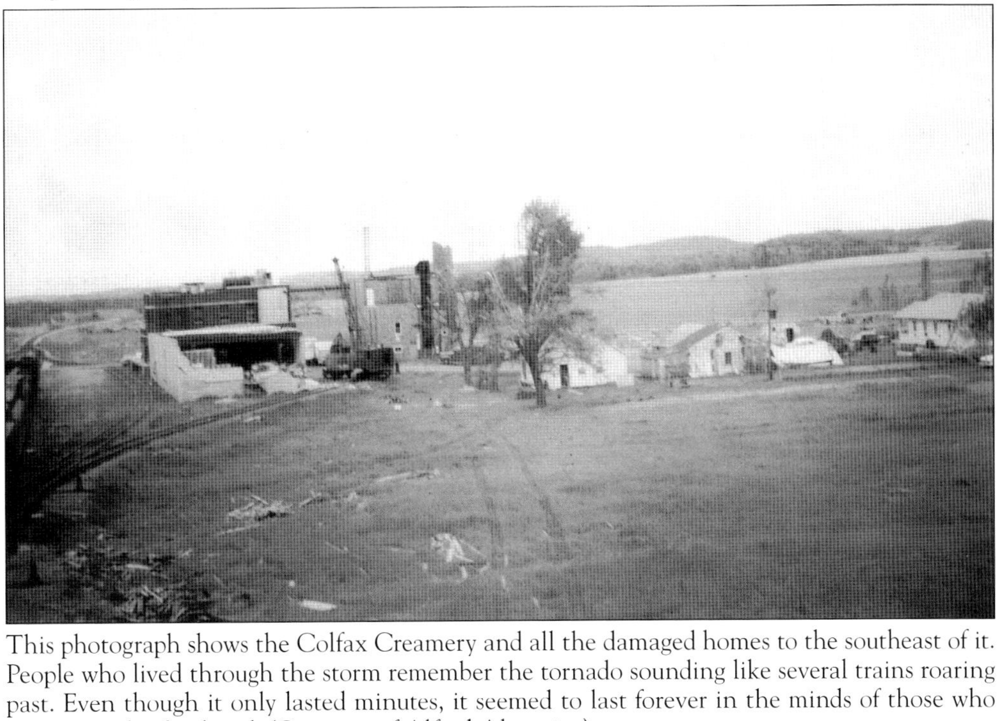

This photograph shows the Colfax Creamery and all the damaged homes to the southeast of it. People who lived through the storm remember the tornado sounding like several trains roaring past. Even though it only lasted minutes, it seemed to last forever in the minds of those who experienced it firsthand. (Courtesy of Alfred Almquist.)

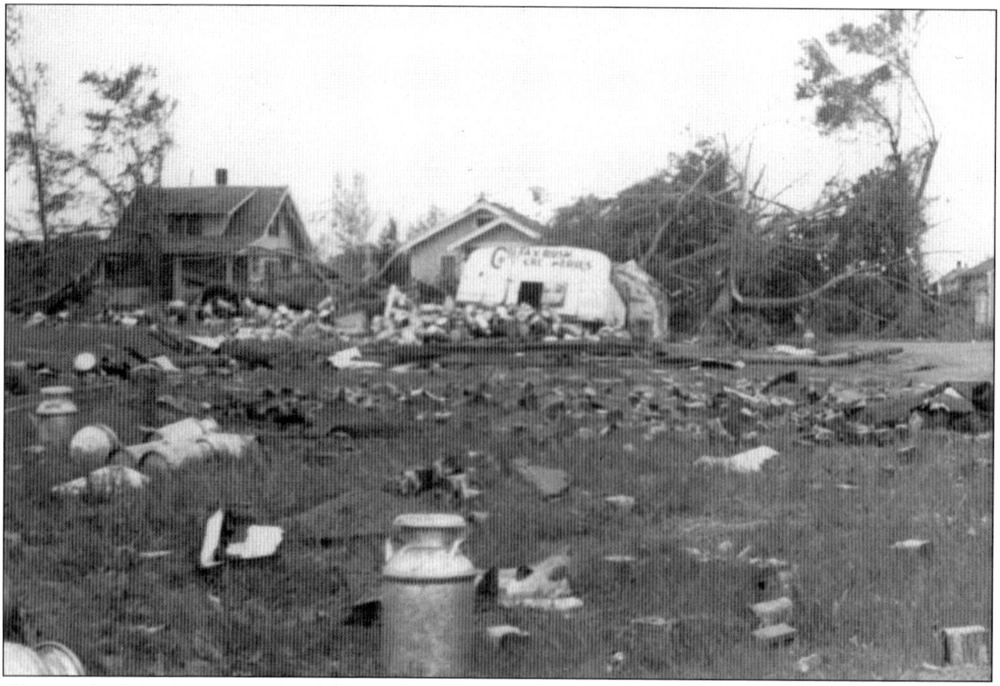

The yard of the home south of the creamery on Roosevelt Street looking west was littered with milk cans. The remains of a Colfax Creamery truck are visible among the damaged trees and homes. It looks as if they were discarded in a graveyard. Debris was widespread throughout the village. (Courtesy of Thelma Mickelson Kettle.)

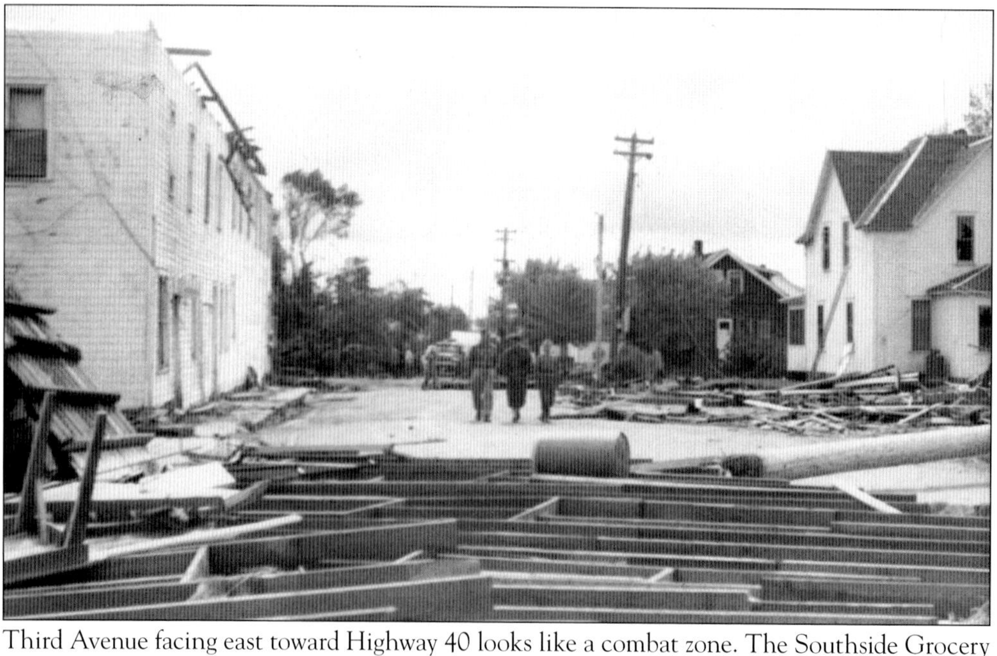

Third Avenue facing east toward Highway 40 looks like a combat zone. The Southside Grocery Store, on the left, lost its roof, and the big shed behind the store was in the middle of the street. Following the storm, the calm and quiet was surreal—no movement, no sound, and no noise. (Courtesy of Thelma Mickelson Kettle.)

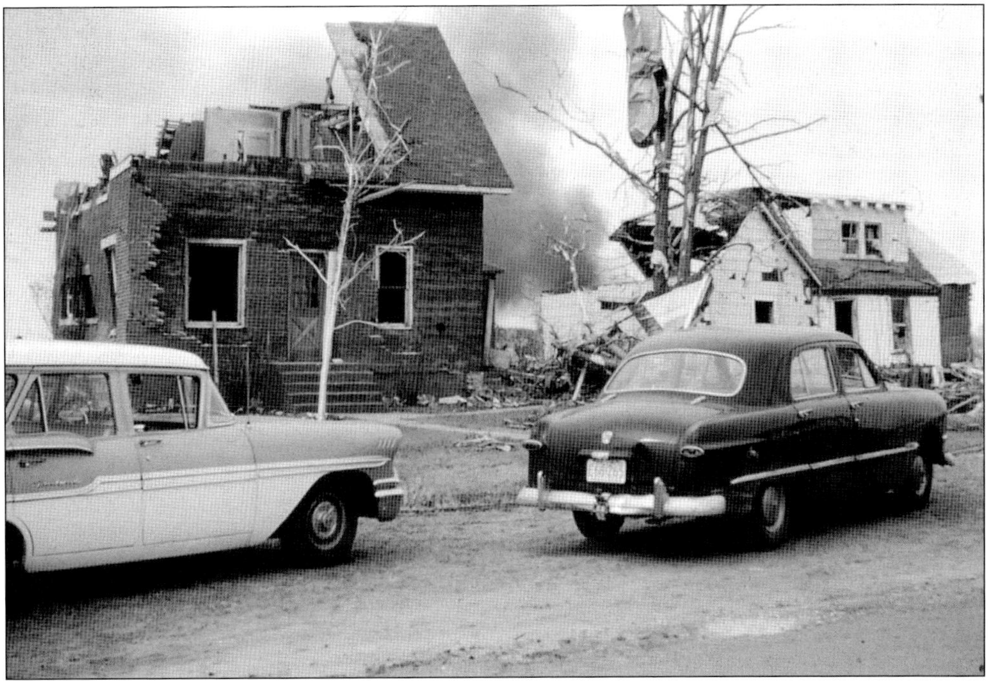

Phillip Felland's and Odd Lindberg's homes suffered major damage from the twister. The wind tore most of the brick siding off of the Felland home. Walls caved in, and oil barrels were sent to new locations in the storm, nearly injuring people yet landing in ways that protected those who otherwise would have been injured. (Courtesy of Diane Haugle Hodgson.)

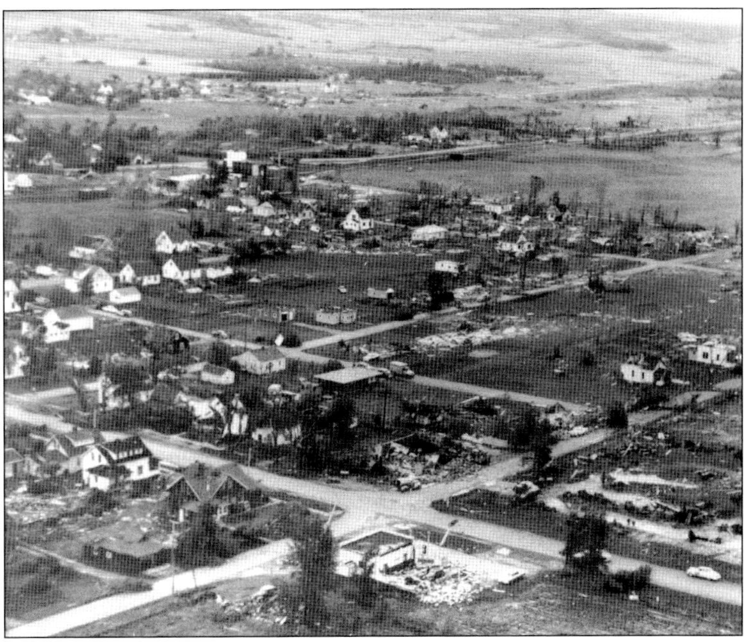

It is said that a tornado leaves a particular smell that is hard to forget, a smell of broken trees and old insulation. Many survivors were unable to have fans on afterward due to their memories of the storm. (Author's collection.)

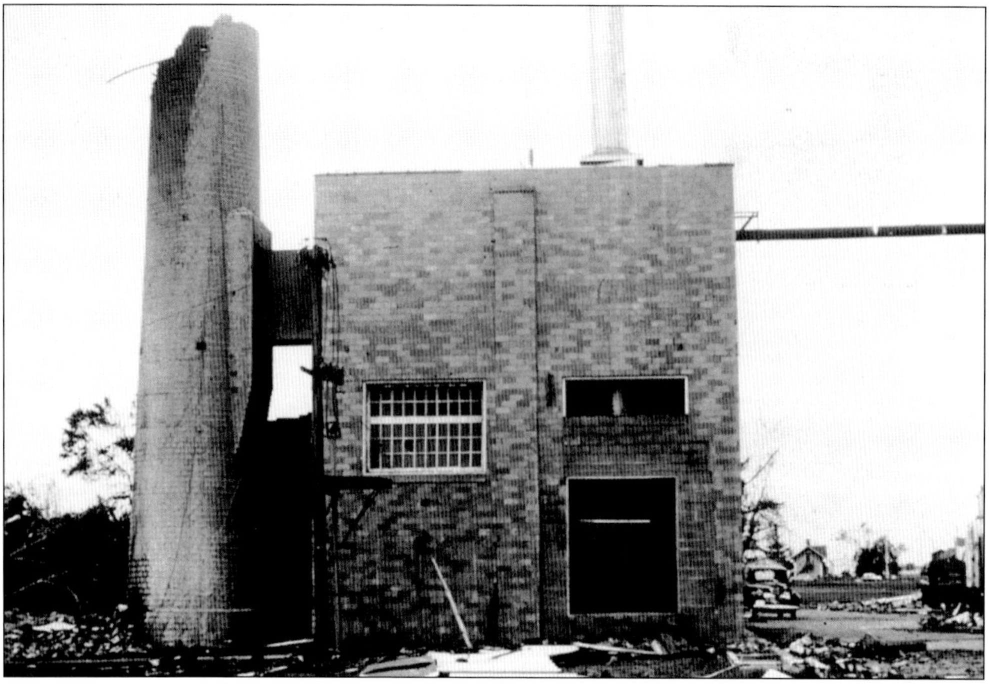

The top portion of the main smoke stack of the Colfax Creamery was blown over during the tornado. The milk cans had been loaded onto the train car, but as a result of the storm, they were set back onto the loading dock again. The employee was reprimanded for not loading the train car. (Courtesy of Diane Haugle Hodgson.)

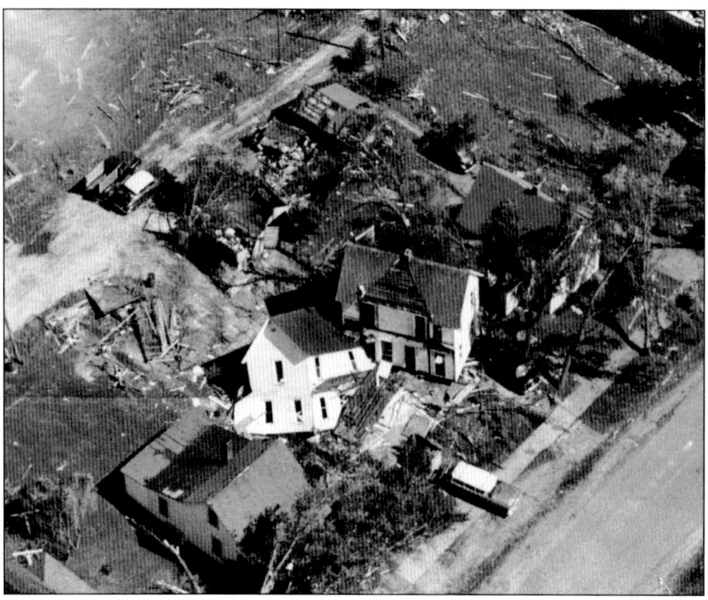

The home of Alfred and Hilda Knutson was lifted off its foundation, and part of the house was even split off from the rest. Some homes remained livable, although damaged. One had its inside stairway rip away from the wall enough to fit a cigar through, yet the family considered themselves lucky and safe. (Author's collection.)

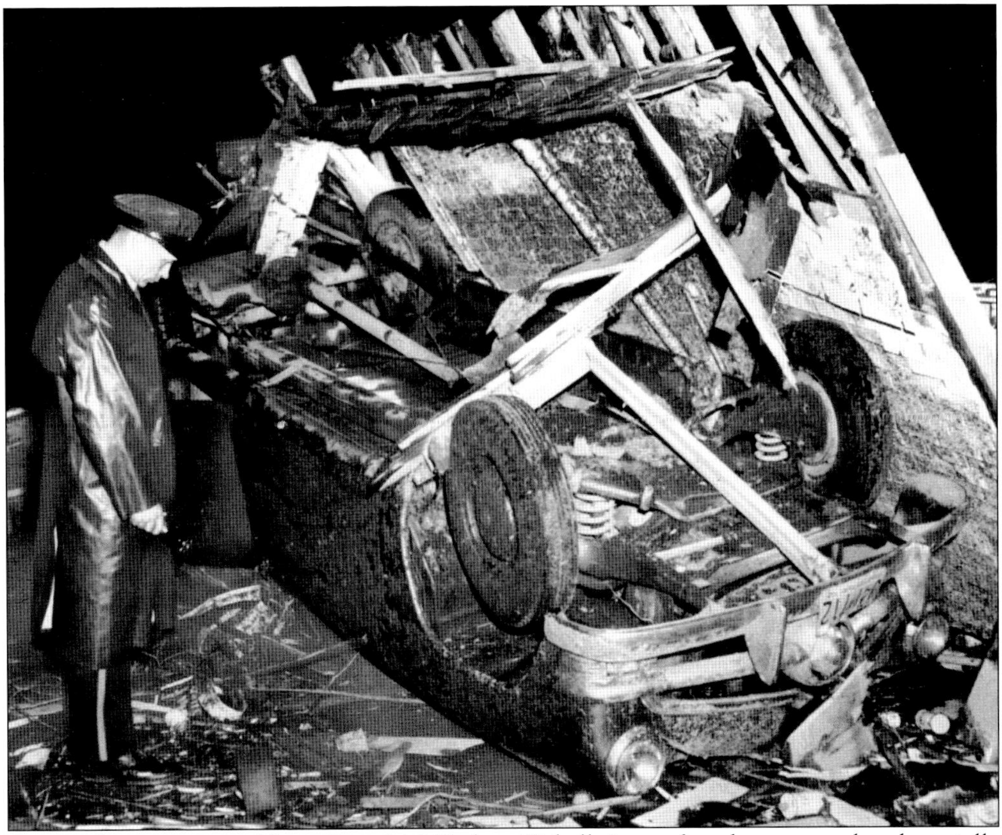

A car is being inspected by police chief Herbert Ziebell. It was found overturned and partially covered by part of a wall and roof on the south end of Colfax. The sticky, hot weather was difficult to deal with, but more difficult was trying to manage a vehicle through the destruction of the storm. (Author's collection.)

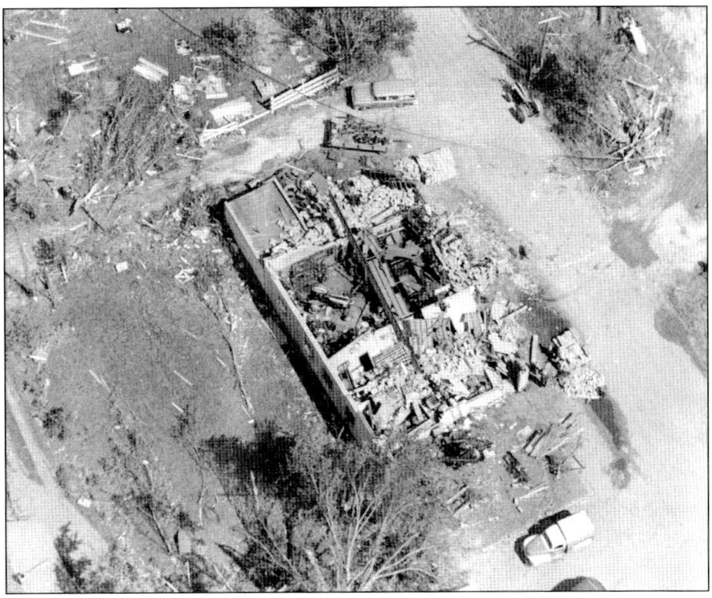

Farm machinery is seen amid the debris of the Colfax Implement Dealership on the southeast corner of Highway 40 and Fifth Avenue. Farm chores needed to be completed, even if there was no electricity, so farmers had to milk cows by hand in the wake of the storm. (Author's collection.)

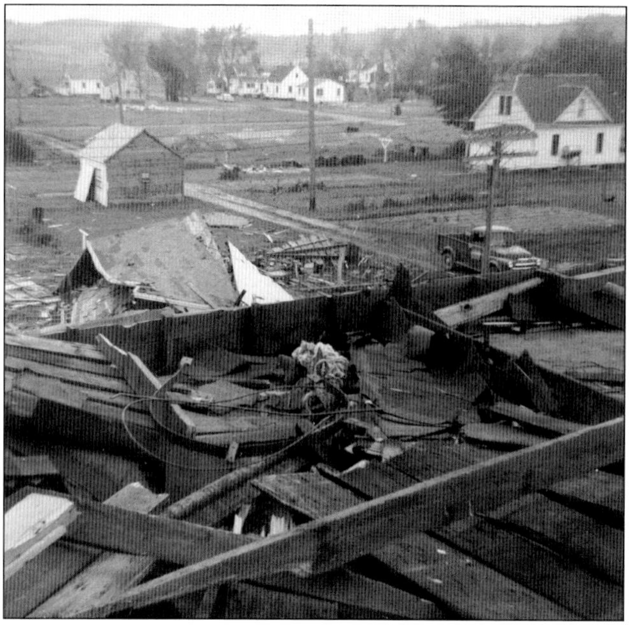

Only splinters of wood remain of the roof of the Southside Grocery Store. This photograph is looking southwest from the top of the pile of rubble. The big white house at right is 310 Cedar Street, which is the current home of the authors of this book. (Courtesy of Thelma Mickelson Kettle.)

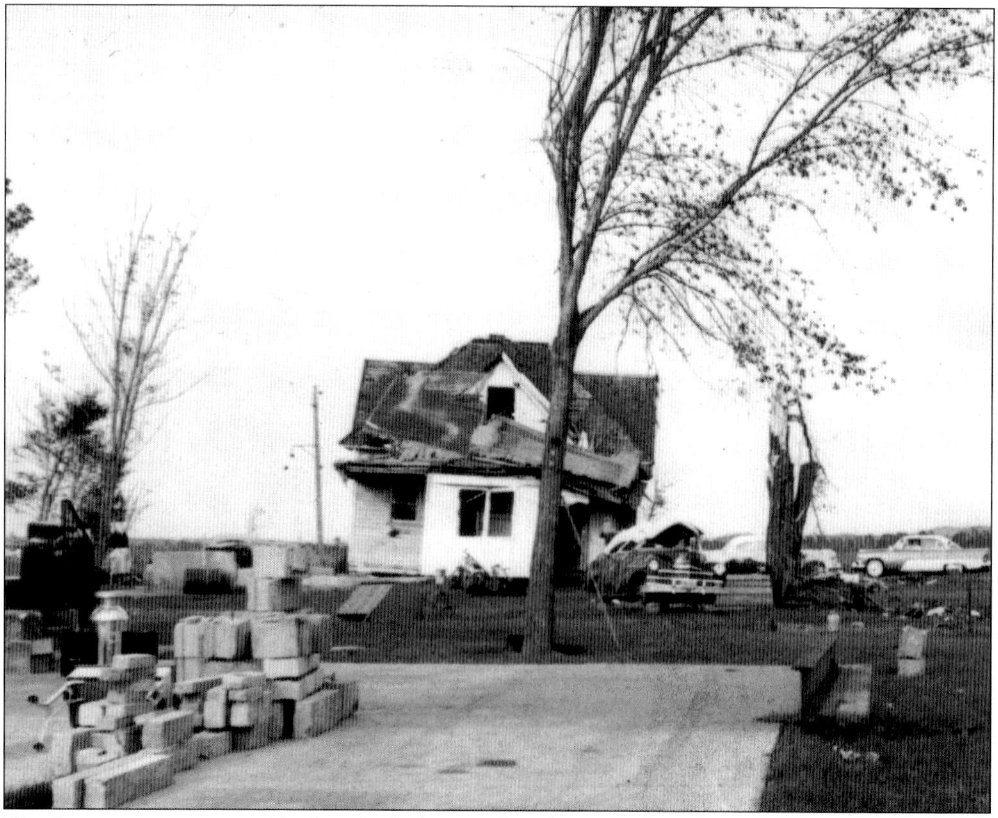

This home was just one of the hundreds damaged in the tornado. Here, a woman standing to the left looks over what was left behind in the tornado's path. (Courtesy of Joan Shong.)

The top story of the Southside Grocery Store was not able to withstand the winds and pressure of the tornado. In the middle of the pile of wreckage is a sewing machine. The debris was cleaned up, and a new roof was put back on the building. The small house in the background sat behind the store to the west. (Courtesy of Thelma Mickelson Kettle.)

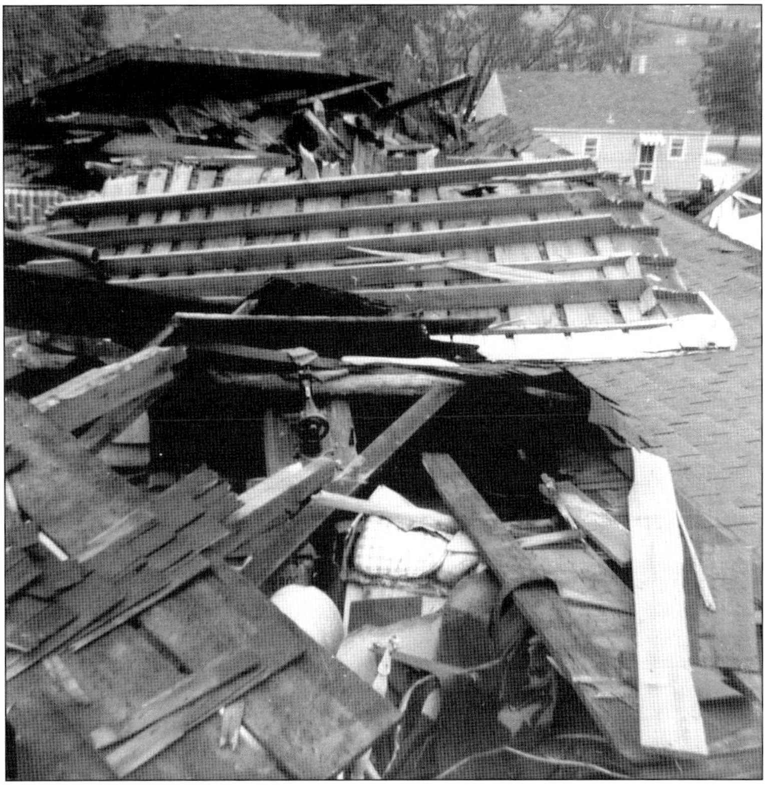

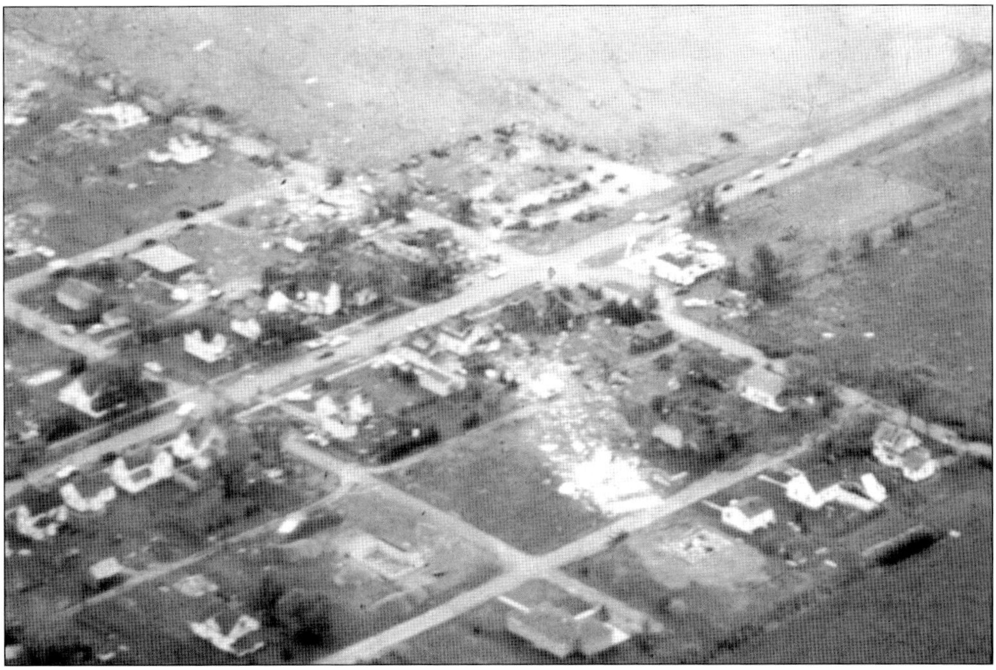

This aerial photograph of the southeast side of Colfax shows the damage there. The tornado had a lasting impact on the survivors for years. Many talked about not wanting to ride in a car in the rain ever again and being afraid of the lights going out. (Author's collection.)

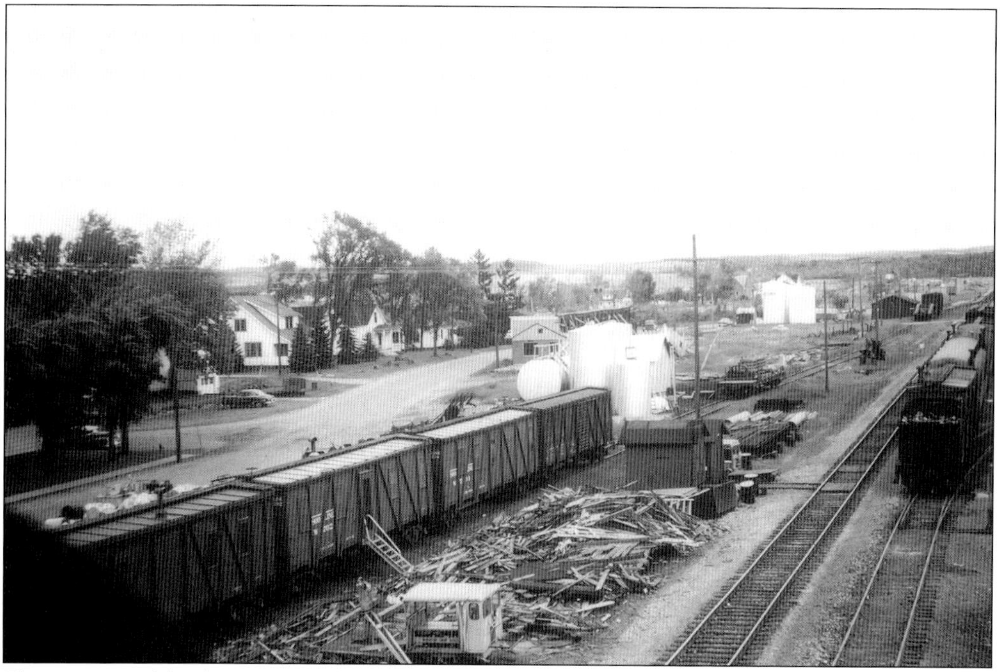

The majority of the damage in Colfax was on the south and northeast sides of the village. The people who were injured were brought to the municipal building to be treated. Many were unrecognizable due to their injuries and the mud that covered them. (Courtesy of Alfred Almquist.)

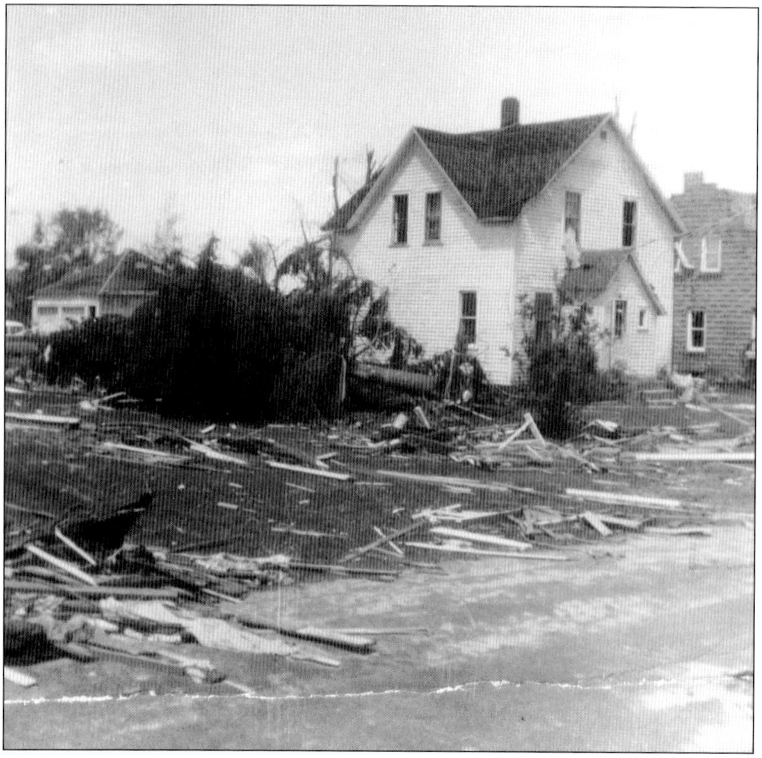

With some broken windows and other minor damage, the home of Jennings and Mattie Page was left standing after the storm. The trees in their yard were not so lucky. A big uprooted pine tree can be seen here. This part of town was one of the hardest hit. The Pages' neighbors just to the west lost their entire home. (Courtesy of Sara Page Watts.)

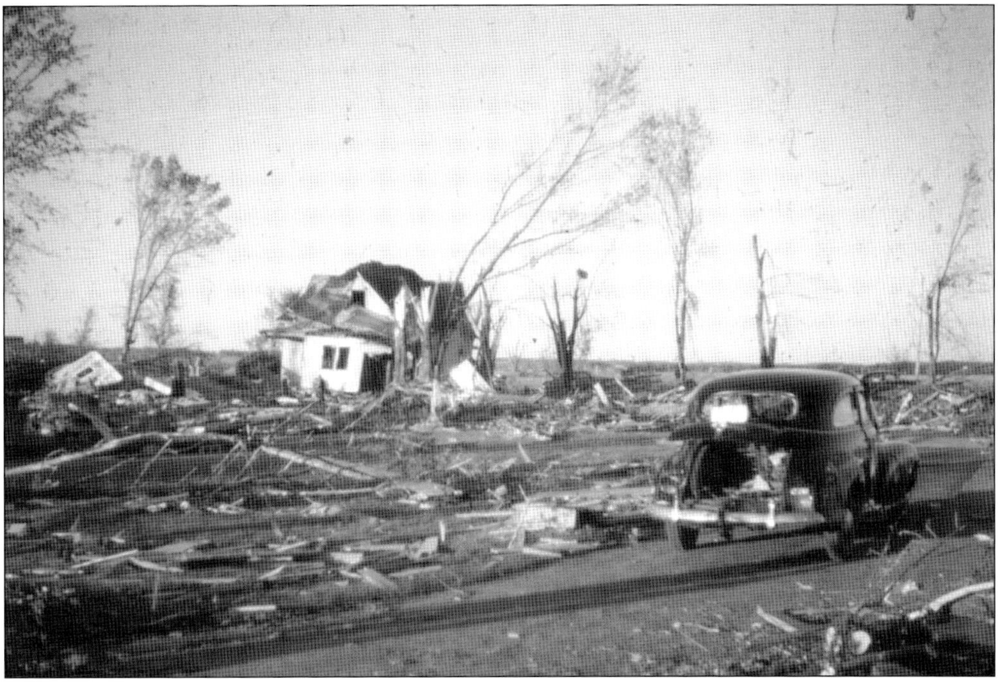

In this view of the destruction on the south side of the village, little remains of what was once a vibrant neighborhood. This home could not be salvaged, and the lives of the family that lived there were forever changed. This is a common theme among those who have survived a tornado. (Author's collection.)

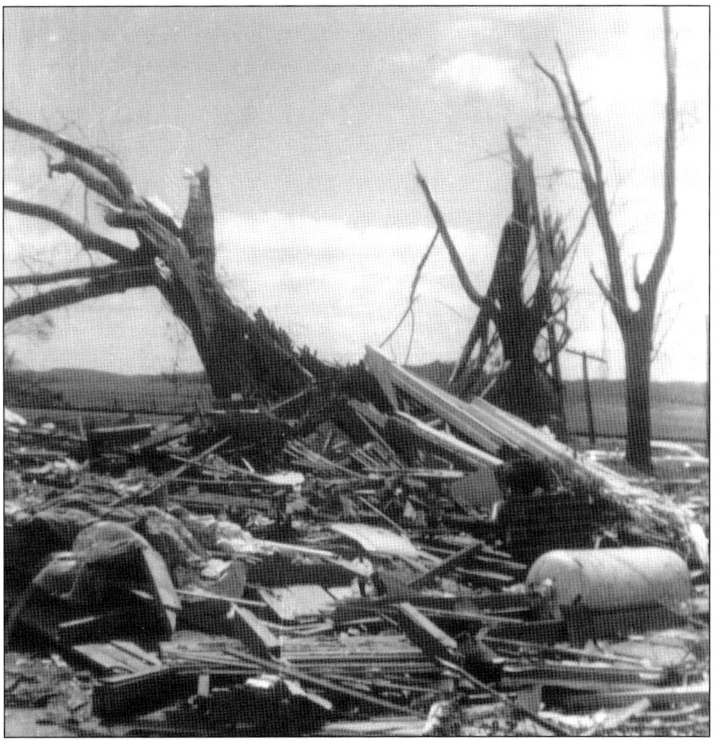

This water heater landed in a pile of rubble. The duplex directly to the west of Jennings and Mattie Pages' residence completely disappeared. After the storm, the two elderly couples who were renting there came up out of the fruit cellar and discovered that their home was gone. They went over to the Page residence and were given coats and other necessities. (Courtesy of Sara Page Watts.)

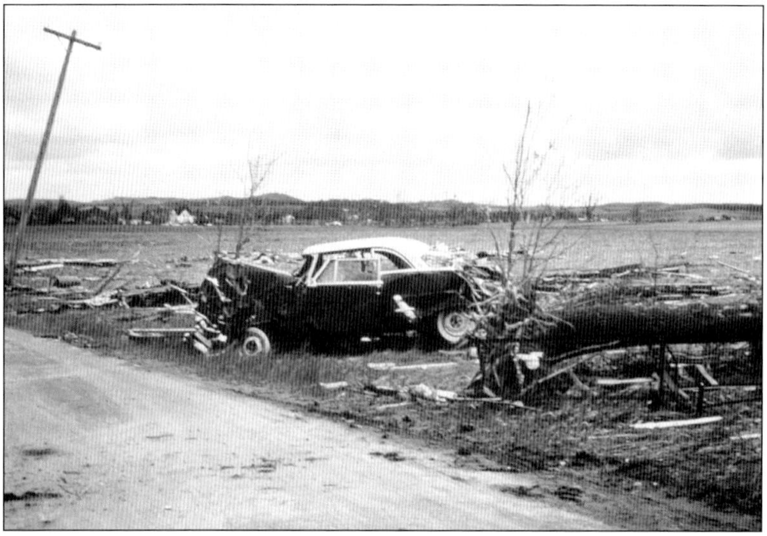

This is all that remained of Erling Lunn's car. Erling and his son Leon were both killed in the storm. "Eerie" is a word that is used over and over to describe the storm, especially in regard to the purple, black, blue, and yellow colors in the sky. (Courtesy of Lyle Christenson.)

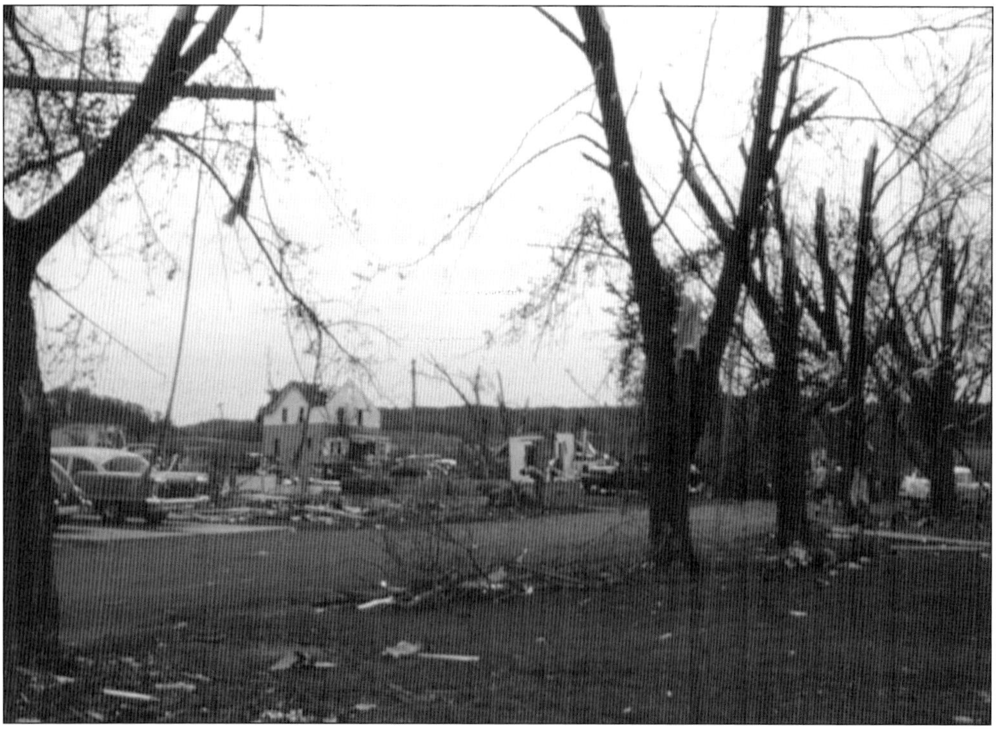

Thirteen-year-old Jim Puhl was trying to listen to the Brewers game through the static while sitting on the living room floor. As the storm grew stronger and got closer, His mom, Adele, ordered him and his siblings to the basement. The lights went out shortly after they reached the basement. The house was ripped off its foundation, and suddenly it was light again. Luckily, no one was hurt. (Author's collection.)

The home of Chuck and Gloria Billie is seen here in the foreground, and the home of Joe and Lillian Dressel is in the background. Some of the flooring from the neighboring Puhl home across the street is resting on top of the Dressel home. (Courtesy of Thelma Mickelson Kettle.)

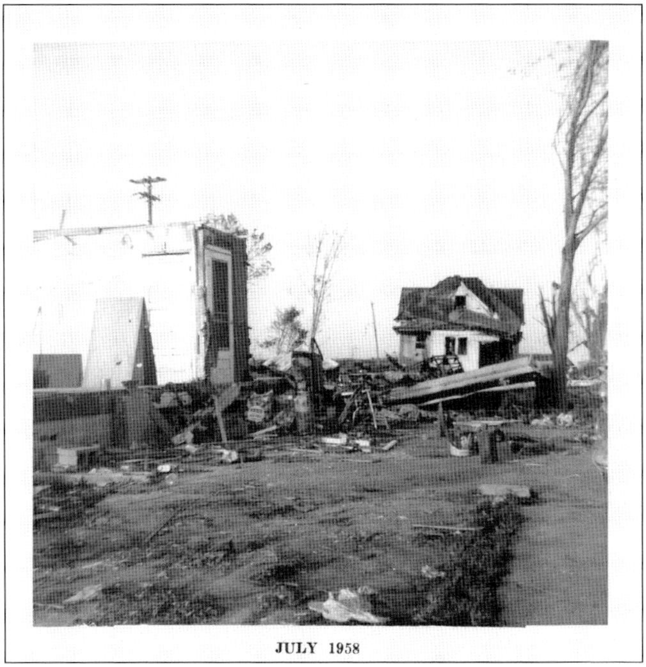

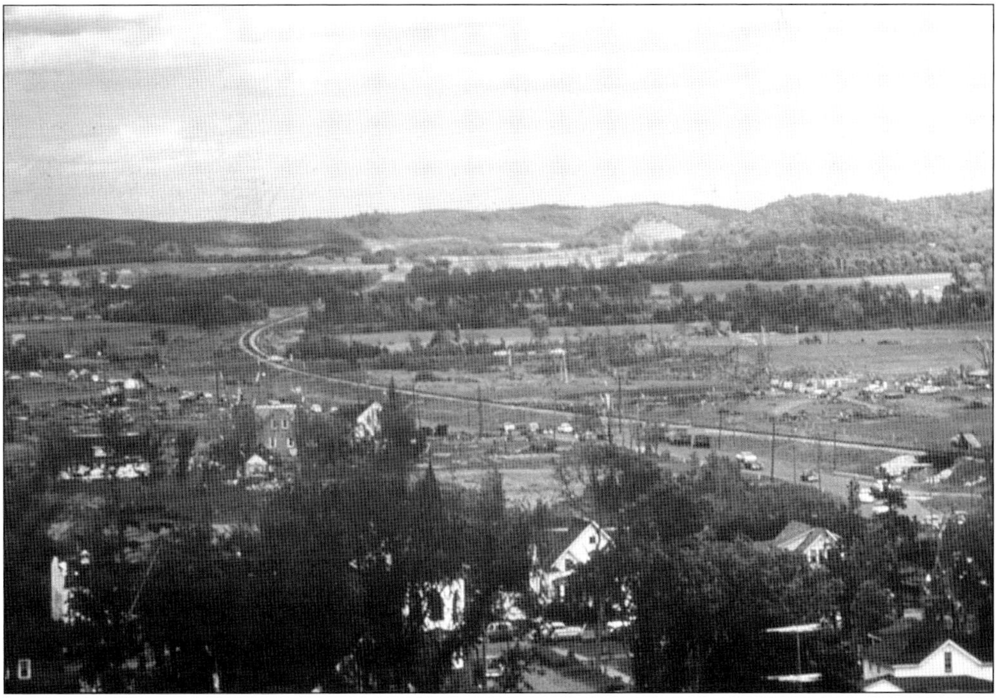

The railroad tracks shown here are heading southeast out of Colfax. The little that is left of the Jim Schindler farm is on the right. Emergency government director for New Richmond, Chuck Mehls, said that his crew did not arrive in Colfax until 10:00 p.m. on the night of the storm. They had two jeeps and six men and were worried whether all the downed power lines were still live or not. It turned out that they had been turned off. "Whoever turned the power off saved a lot of lives," Mehls remarked. (Author's collection.)

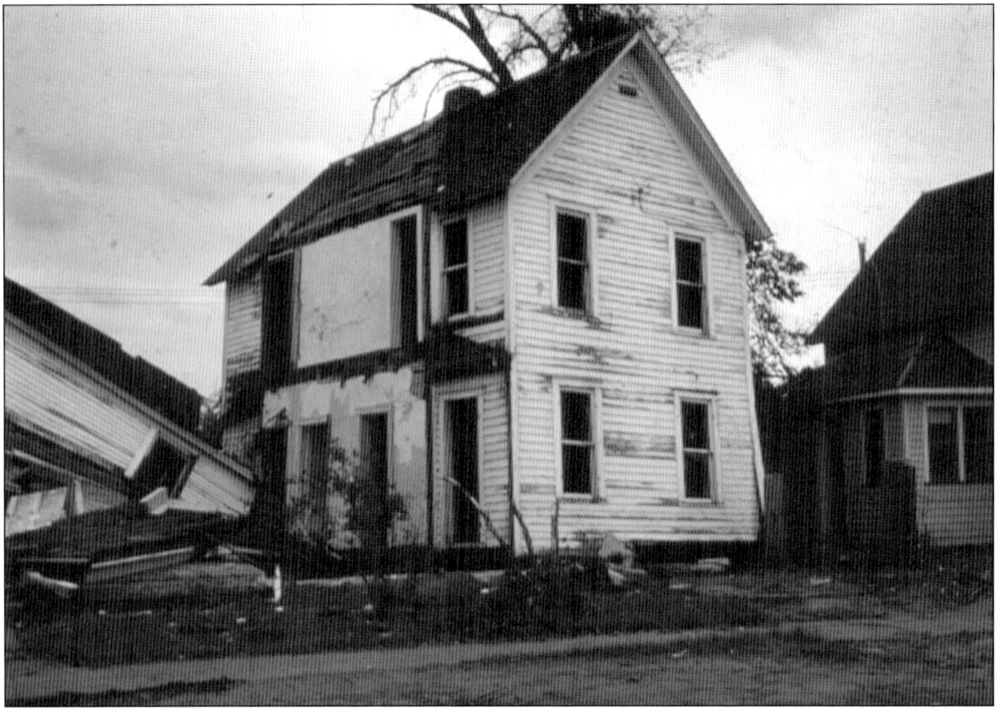

After the storm, people began to surface from their hiding spots. They all had empty eyes and were staring in shock. Gladys Tandberg remembered Odd Lindberg's milk truck looking like it had been run over by a train and cars being demolished and tossed about like cardboard boxes. (Author's collection.)

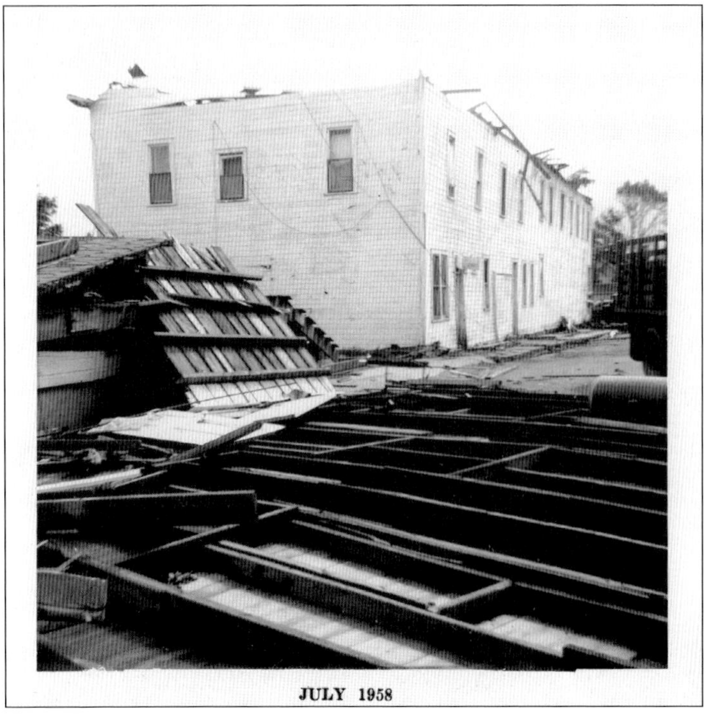

This storage shed just west of the Southside Grocery was no match for the force of the storm. The store also lost its peaked roof, which was replaced with a sloping roof after the storm. (Courtesy of Thelma Mickelson Kettle.)

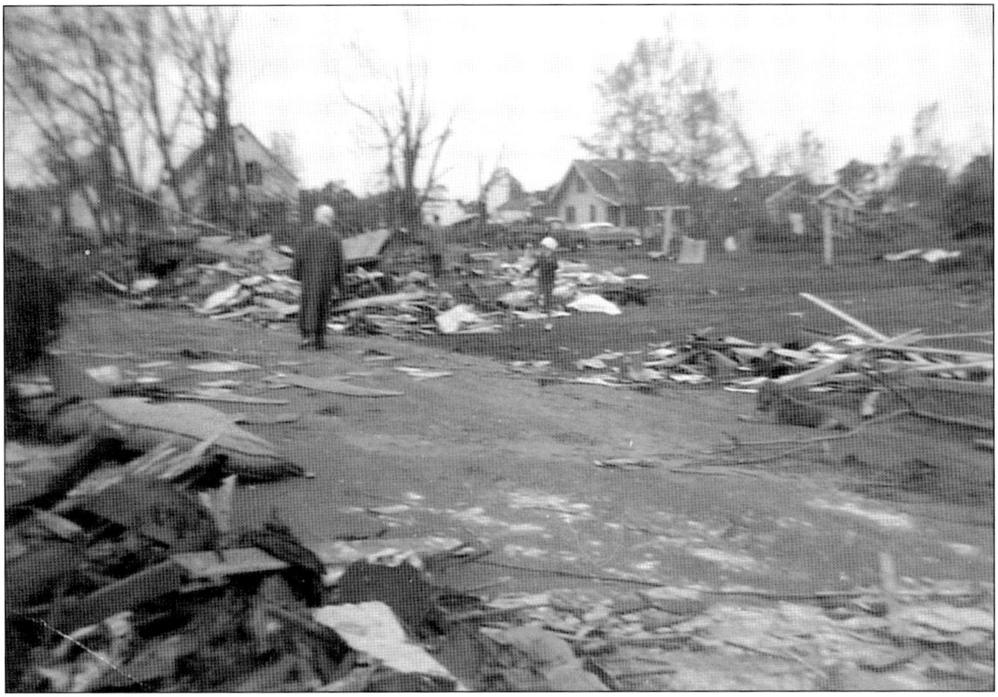

Adele Puhl and her daughter Sylvia survey the remains of their home on Roosevelt Street and East Third Avenue (on the northeast corner), which was completely leveled. The photograph was taken from the Joe Dressel property, looking to the west down East Third Avenue. (Courtesy of Jim Puhl.)

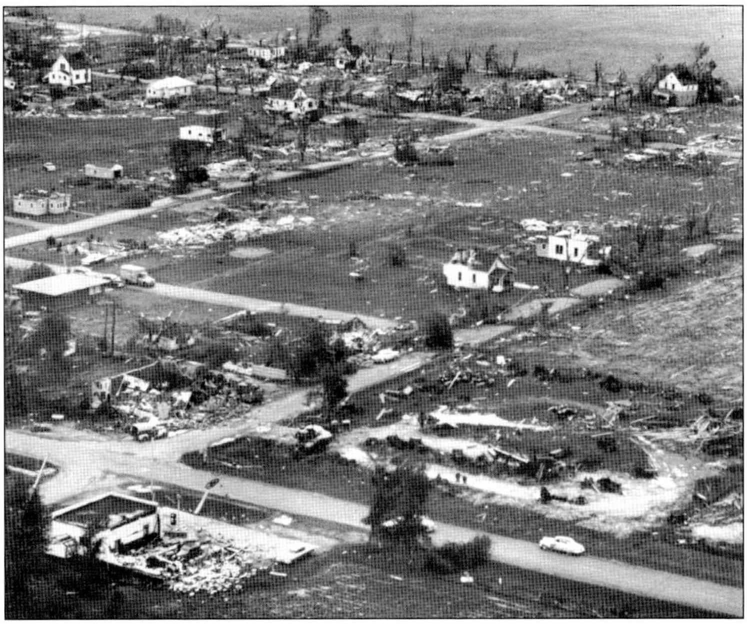

The south side of Colfax looked like a war zone after the tornado swept through. Some homes were leveled, while others next door were untouched. Trees and wires were down across the village, leaving everyone without power. (Author's collection.)

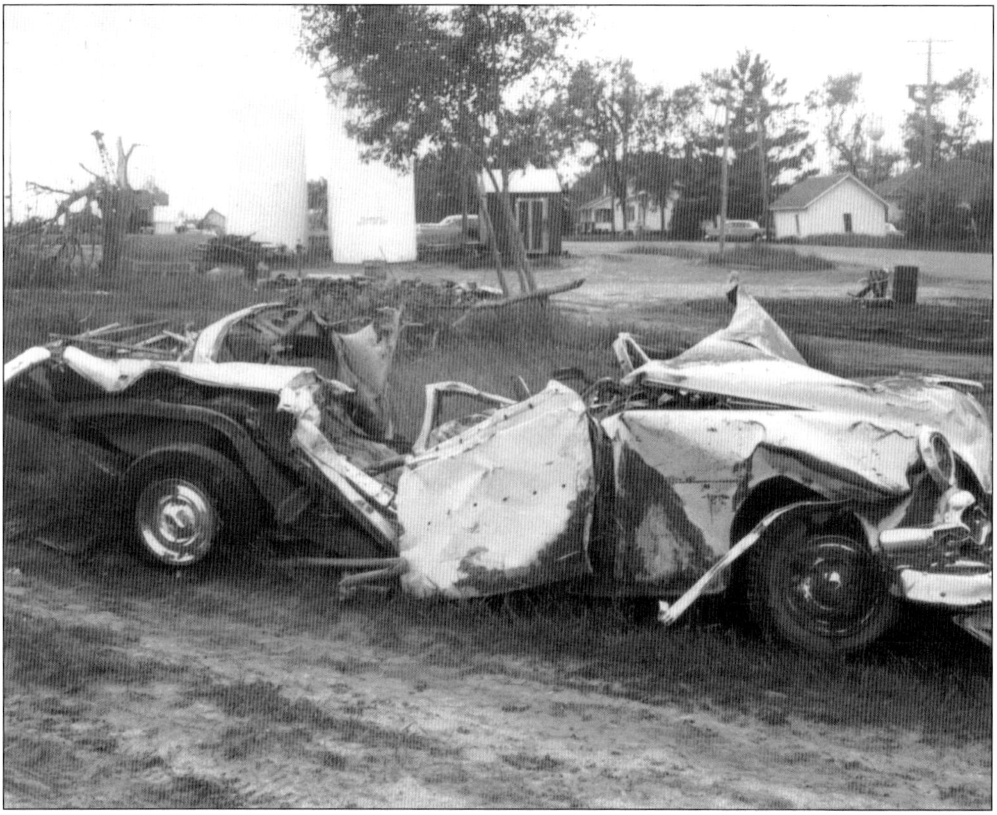

As help came into the village by the carload, victims' spirits were lifted. One group of helpers lifted up a car that needed a tire changed because the jack could not be found. Once they had the tire changed, they left to find anyone else they could assist. (Courtesy of Joan Shong.)

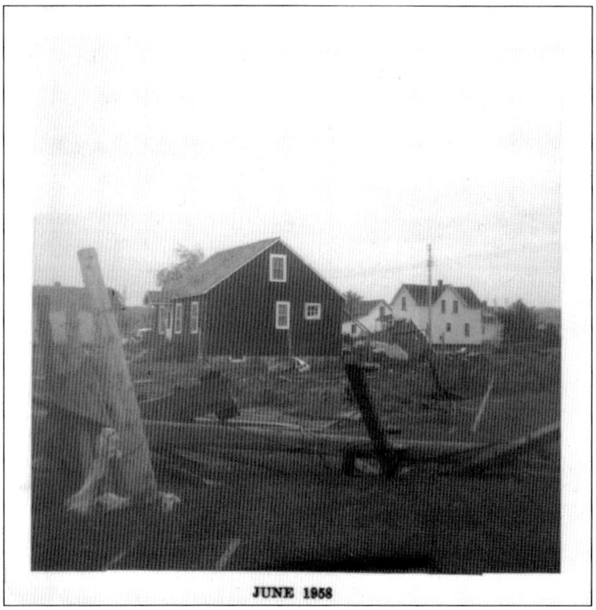

The home of Bill and Melva Ellingson appears to have little damage compared to the destruction all around them. This home is still standing on the northwest corner of Fourth Avenue and Park Drive. Many survivors remembered the horrendous sound of breaking glass, as well as nails and bolts being pulled from boards and homes torn away from their foundations. (Courtesy of Joan Shong.)

The home of Joe and Lillian Dressel is still standing, while across the street, the home of Harold and Adele Puhl was completely destroyed. Somewhere in this photograph are some of the 5,672 marbles that 13-year-old Jim Puhl had been collecting. He ended up losing just about his entire collection, salvaging only about 100 marbles. (Courtesy of Thelma Mickelson Kettle.)

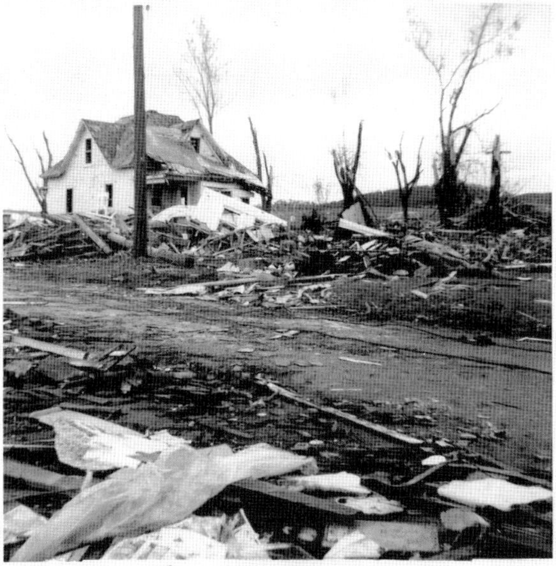

JULY 1958

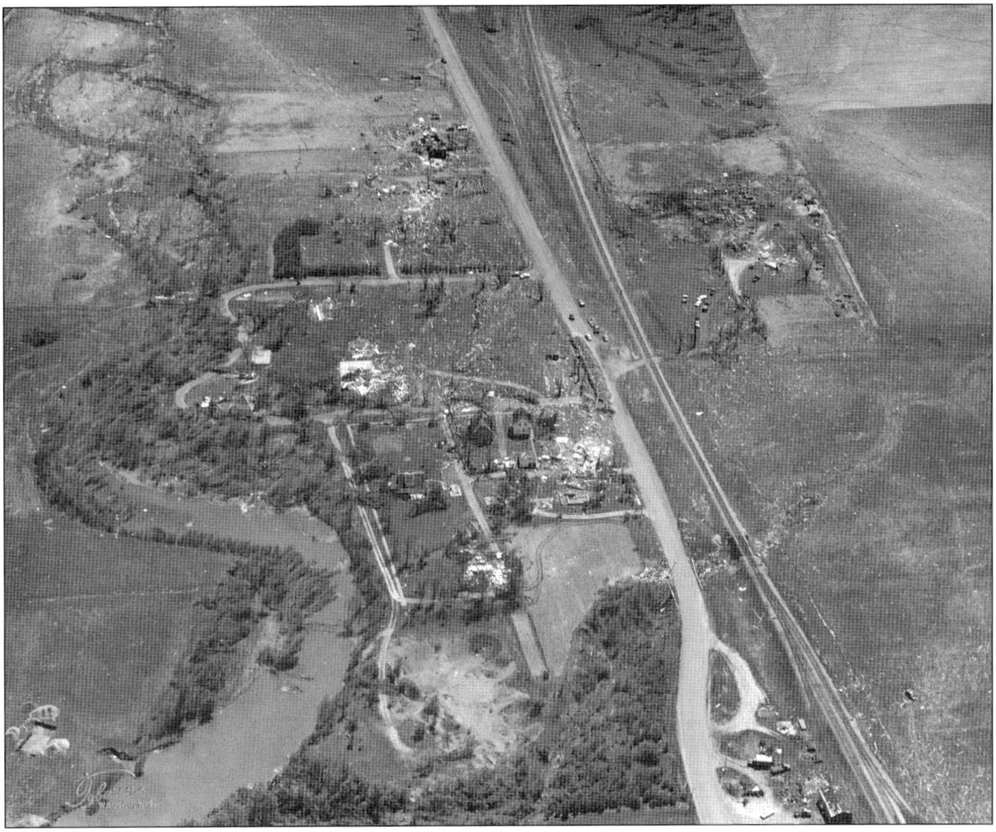

Only a few trees are left standing in the center of this photograph where the Colfax Fairgrounds once stood. What is left of the Schindler farm is just to the right of the fairgrounds. Homes were moved off of their foundations, as much as two inches in some cases. (Author's collection.)

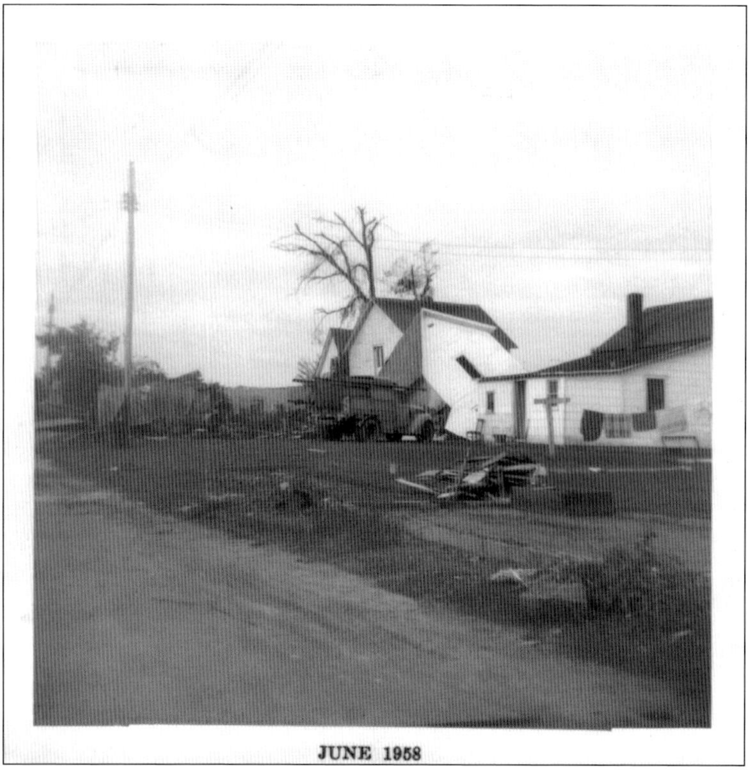

The home of Alfred Knutson (left) was severely damaged, but the home of Charlie Burling (right) does not appear to have much damage at all. Some survivors called for help from their closets where they were safe but trapped. The closet, in some cases, was the only part of the home left standing. (Courtesy of Joan Shong.)

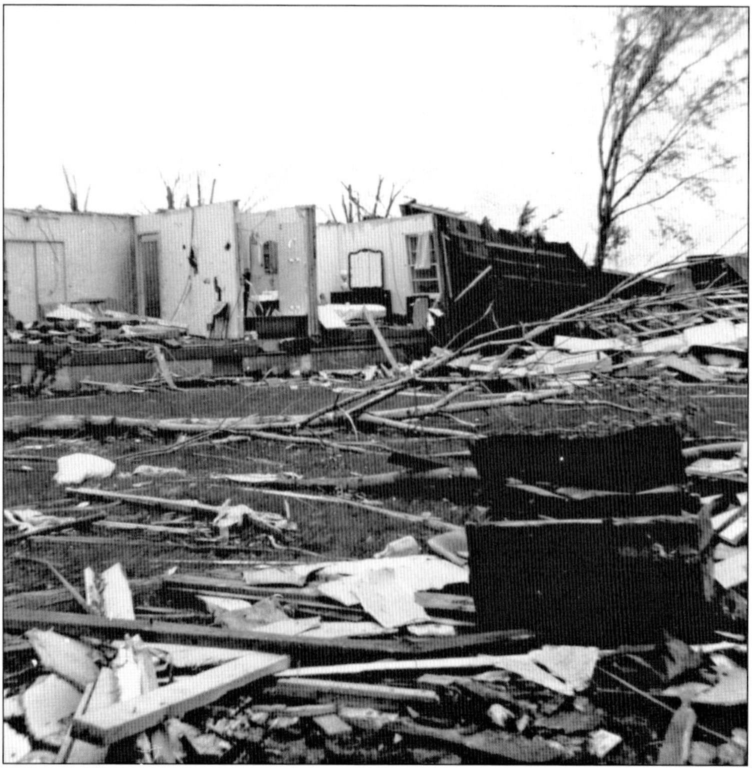

Only a shell is left of the Chuck and Gloria Billie home on the south side of town. Various items can be seen in the remains. There are some metal folding TV trays in the first room, and the bathroom tub and sink in the second. The third room holds the bedroom dresser, with a very nice, unbroken glass lamp on top. (Courtesy of Thelma Mickelson Kettle.)

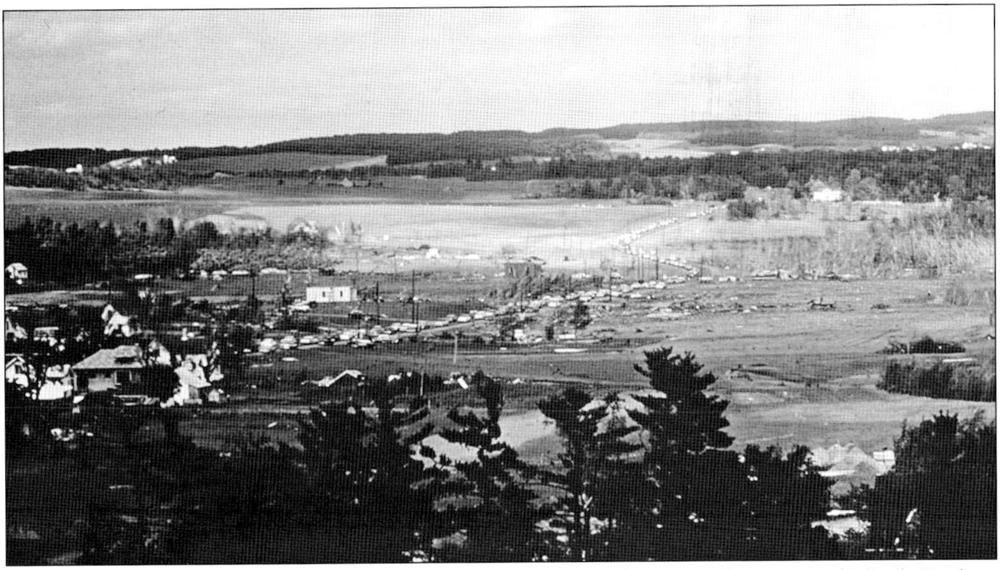

This photograph is facing east. The remains of the sandstone home of Clarence and Minda Burling can be seen at center. Also visible is the solid line of vehicles on University Avenue trying to make their way into town to check on relatives or friends and to see firsthand the damage caused by the tornado. (Courtesy of Diane Haugle Hodgson.)

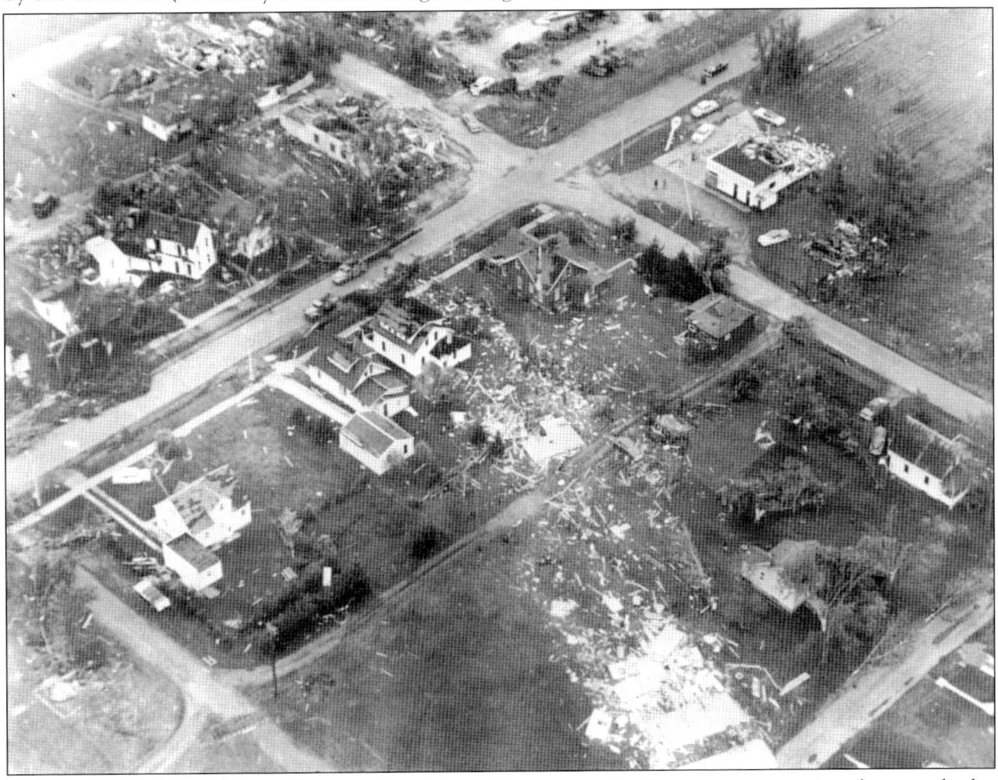

These buildings on the southwest side of the village were the first ones to receive the punch the savage tornado had to offer as it entered Colfax. What is left of the Colfax Texaco station owned by Elmer Knutson is at top right. (Author's collection.)

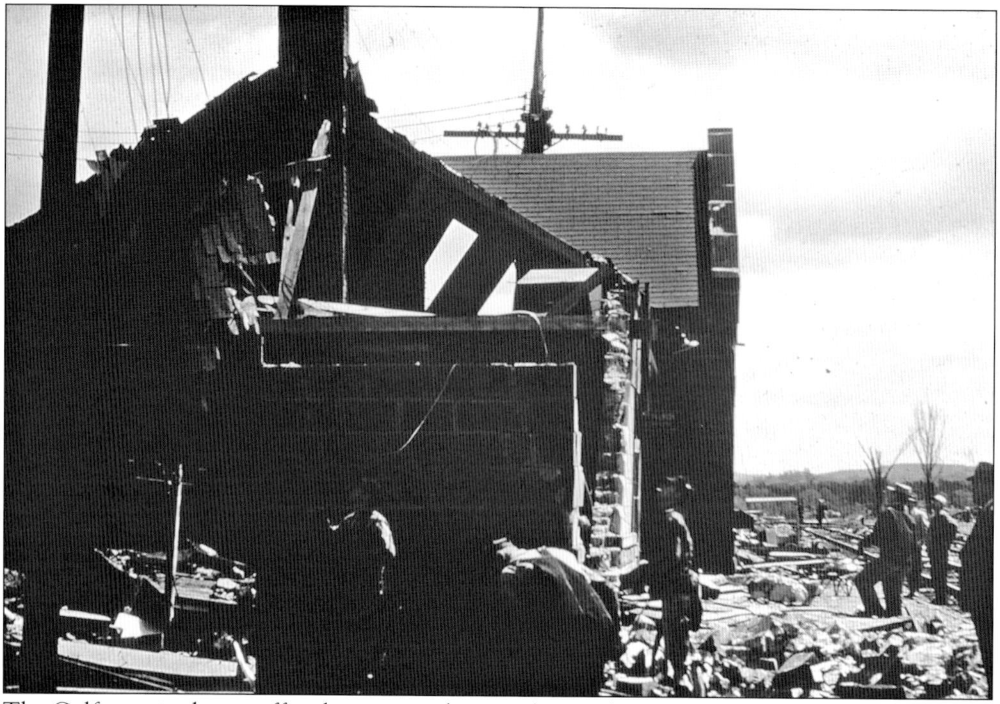

The Colfax train depot suffered extensive damage during the twister. The west end of the depot was torn off. That end of the building was once the luggage storage area. After the storm, the luggage storage area was never rebuilt. The remaining walls were taken down, and the inside was finished to become the new outside wall. (Courtesy of Diane Haugle Hodgson.)

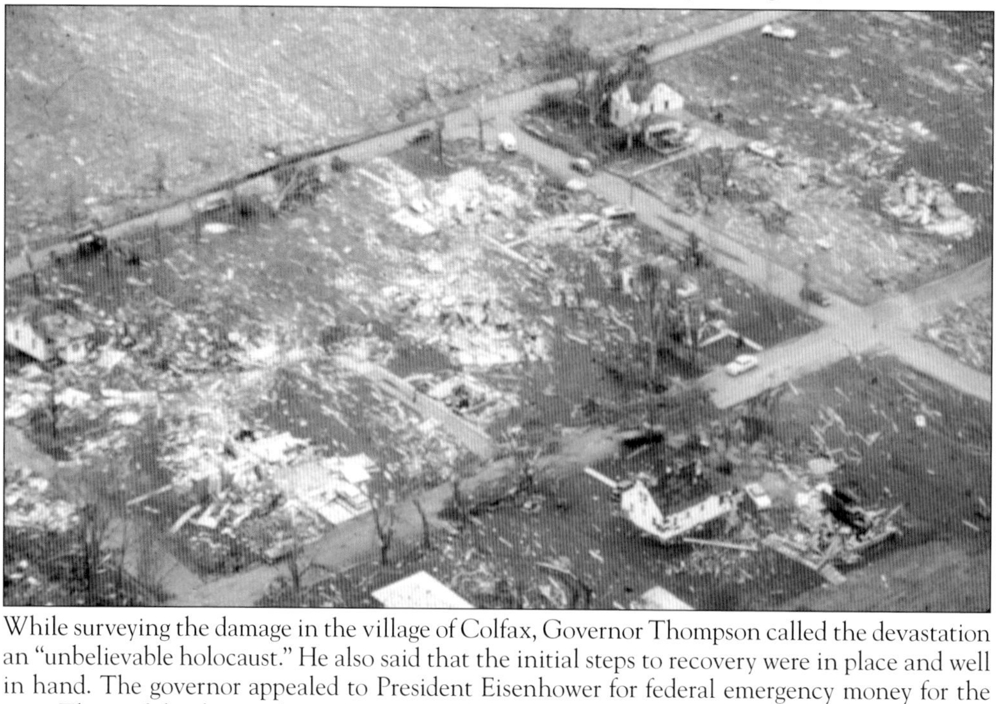

While surveying the damage in the village of Colfax, Governor Thompson called the devastation an "unbelievable holocaust." He also said that the initial steps to recovery were in place and well in hand. The governor appealed to President Eisenhower for federal emergency money for the area. Three of the damaged counties received help. (Author's collection.)

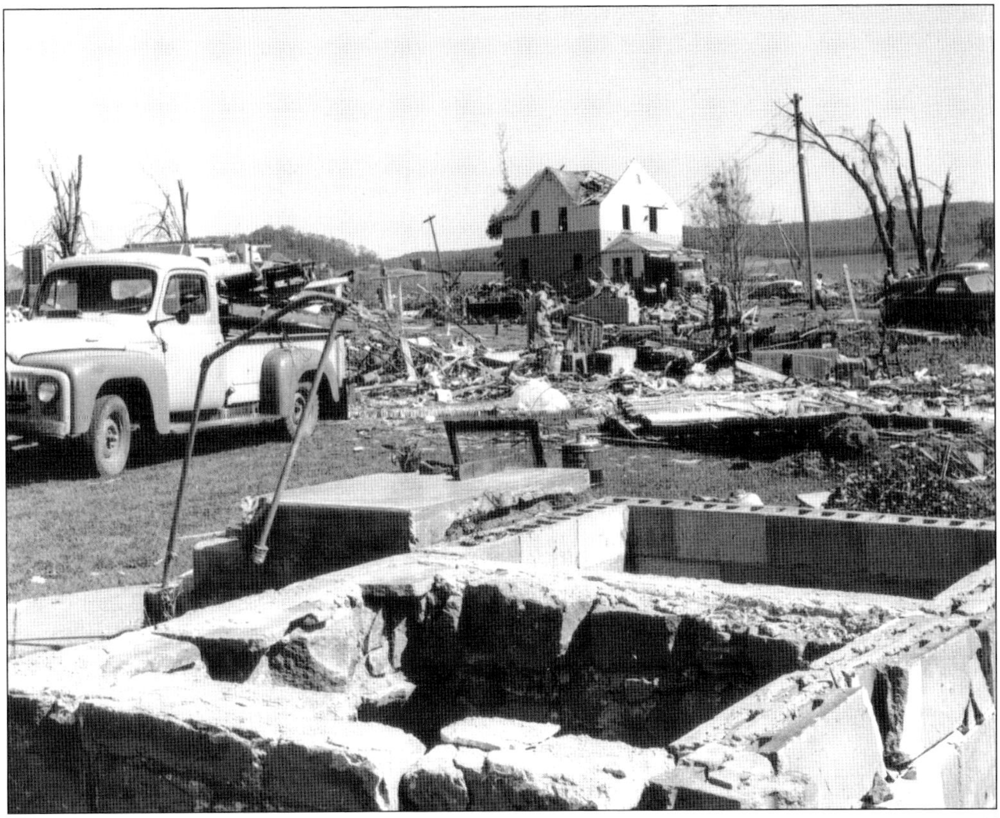

Although the south side of town was in rough shape after the tornado, friends and families all came together to help in the recovery and cleanup process. This appears to be part of the Puhl's property facing southeast toward the remains of the Dressel home. (Courtesy of Ron Blakely.)

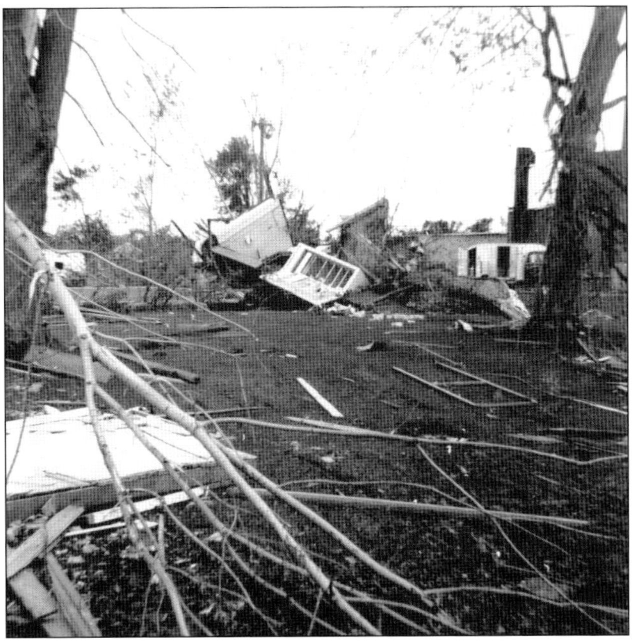

The small home and refrigerator of Lloyd Nereson were unable to withstand the brutal force of the tornado. The Nereson home was located just south of the Colfax Creamery. A milk truck and part of the smokestack of the creamery can be seen in the background. (Courtesy of Thelma Mickelson Kettle.)

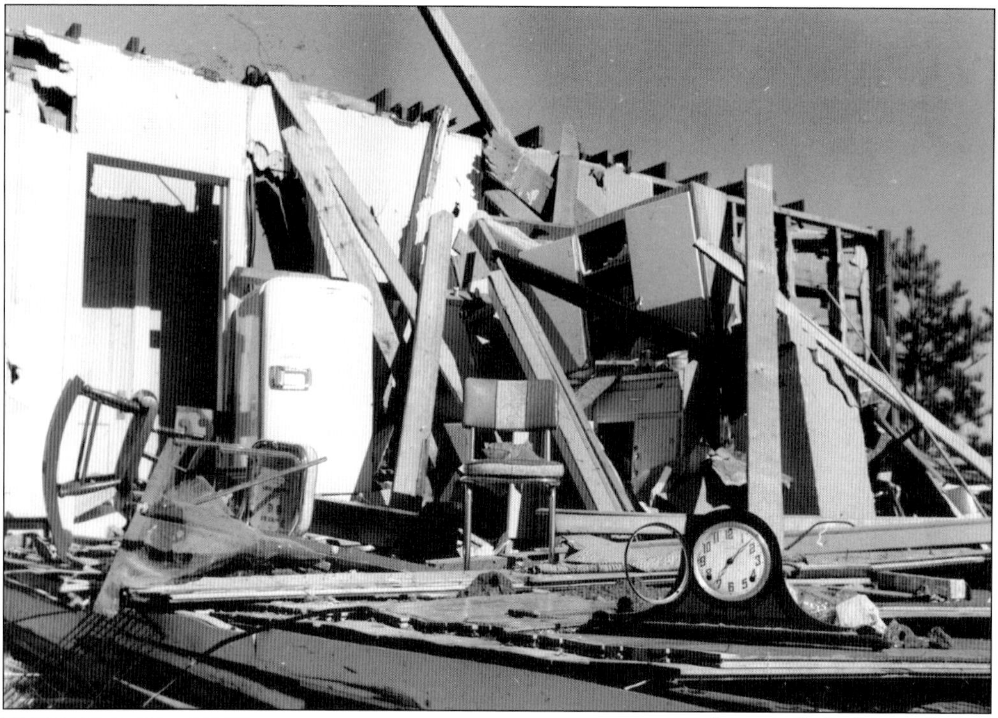

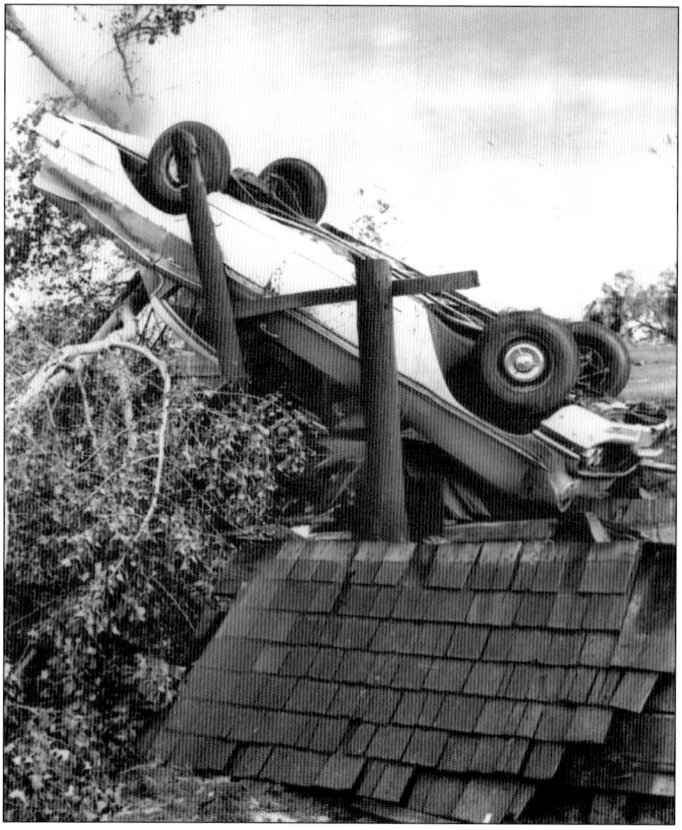

A mantel clock somehow seems unharmed after the rest of this home was completely destroyed around it. The clock landed upright and was stopped at 7:07 a.m., which was the exact time the tornado hit. (Author's collection.)

This car is overturned on top of part of a roof that has been torn off its house. The power of the tornado was unreal. A home built out of cement blocks had everything sucked out of the main level except for the table, refrigerator, and cupboards. (Courtesy of Ron Blakely.)

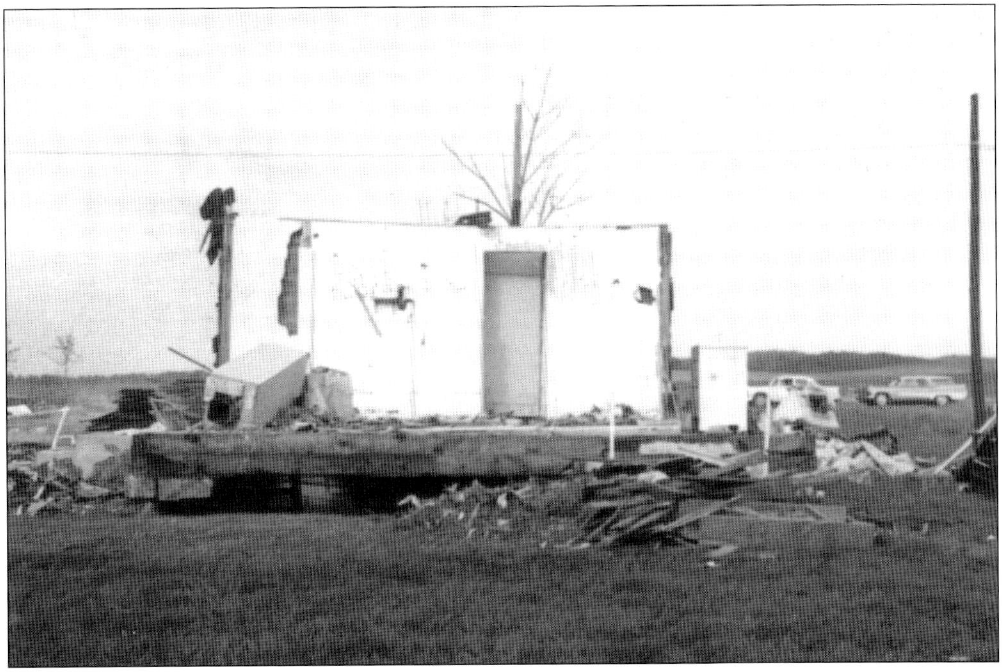

One lonely wall is left standing from this small home. The speed of the tornado left its survivors in shock. One moment everything seemed to be fine, and the next, everything that they owned was destroyed. (Courtesy of Joan Shong.)

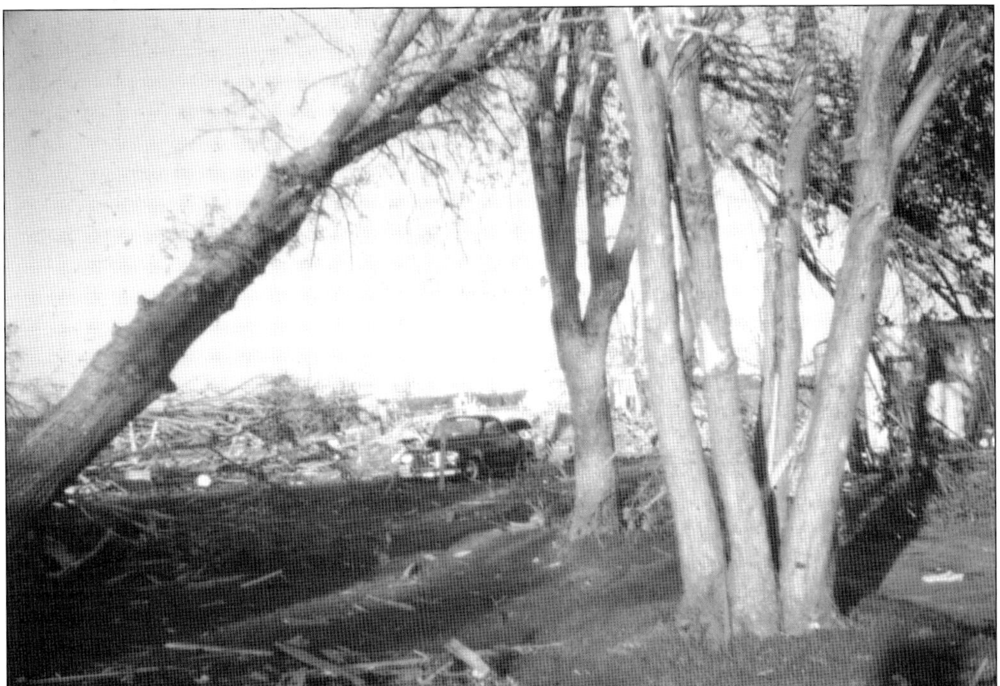

There was nothing but debris everywhere. Lawns were covered with personal belongings, clothing, boards, glass, and tin. The devastating loss of trees left the village unrecognizable and unfamiliar. The unfamiliarity was eerie for the residents who had survived the storm. (Author's collection.)

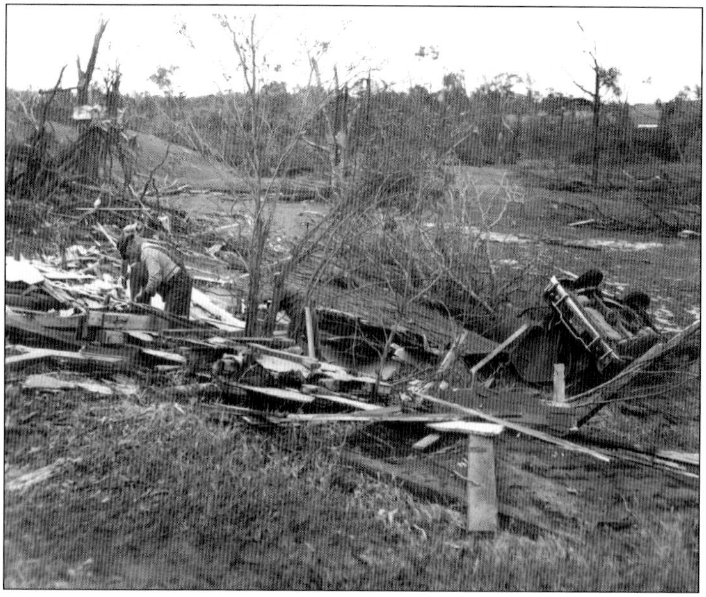

Residents were quick to get to work with the cleanup. Farmers could not wait with chores, and the resilient survivors could not wait to show the storm that they could get back to living their lives as normally as possible. (Courtesy of the Colfax Public Library.)

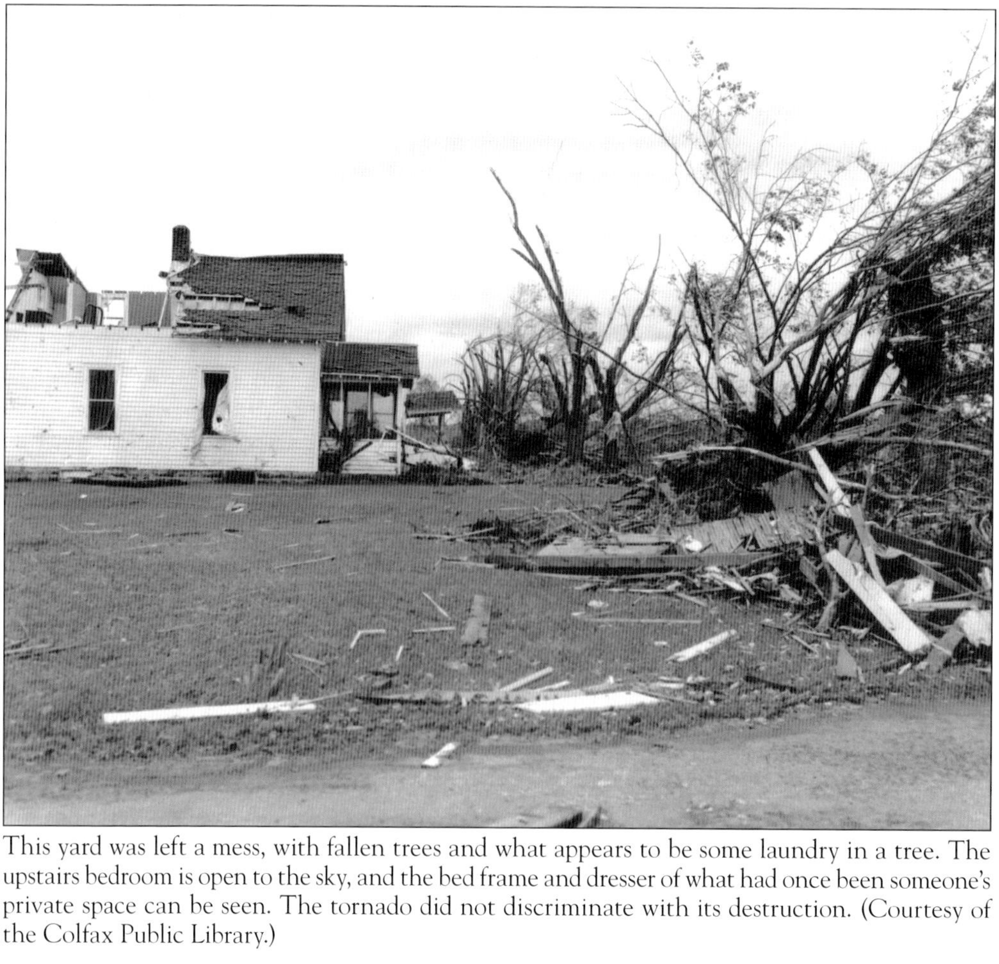

This yard was left a mess, with fallen trees and what appears to be some laundry in a tree. The upstairs bedroom is open to the sky, and the bed frame and dresser of what had once been someone's private space can be seen. The tornado did not discriminate with its destruction. (Courtesy of the Colfax Public Library.)

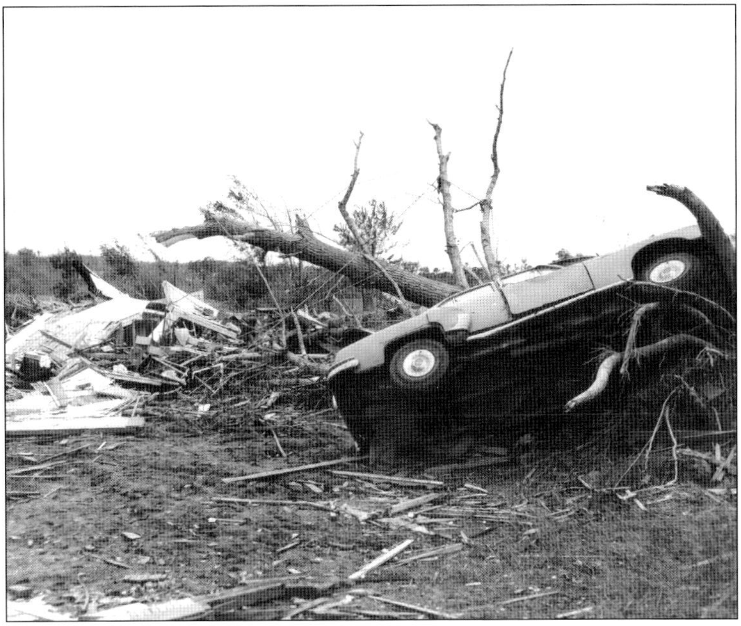

What had once been sturdy objects made of metal and wood were left in heaps and piles as if they were made of nothing but paper and glue. Automobiles flew through the air and houses came falling down around their owners. (Courtesy of the Colfax Public Library.)

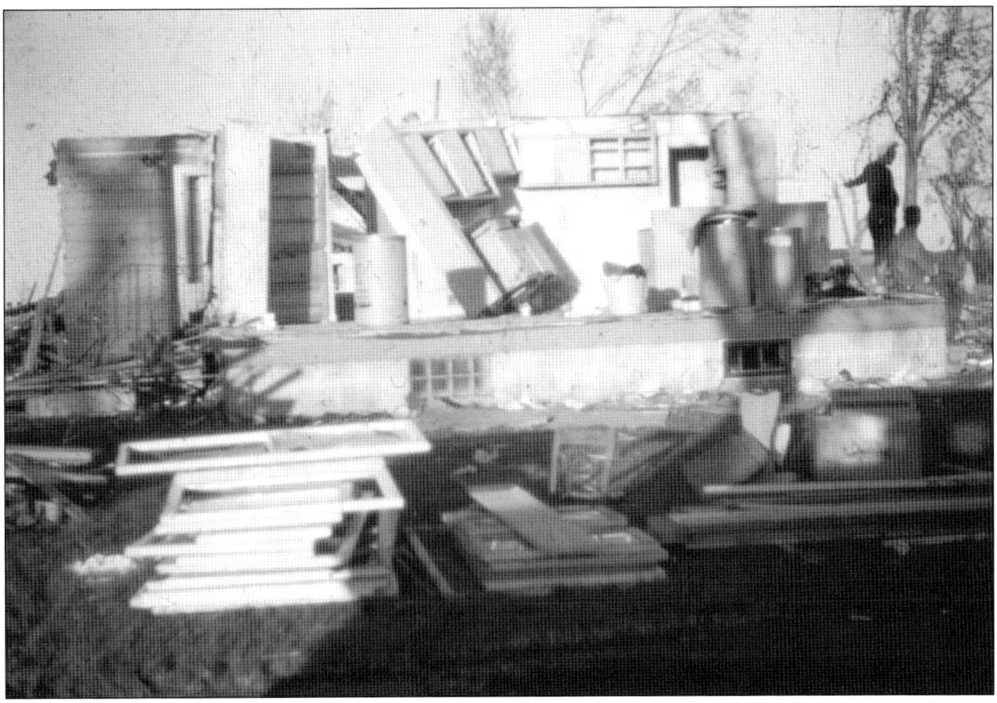

What was once the inside of a home now stands exposed to the outside. This kitchen is no longer functional, but as can be seen in the foreground, anything and everything that could be was saved and reused in the rebuilding process. (Author's collection.)

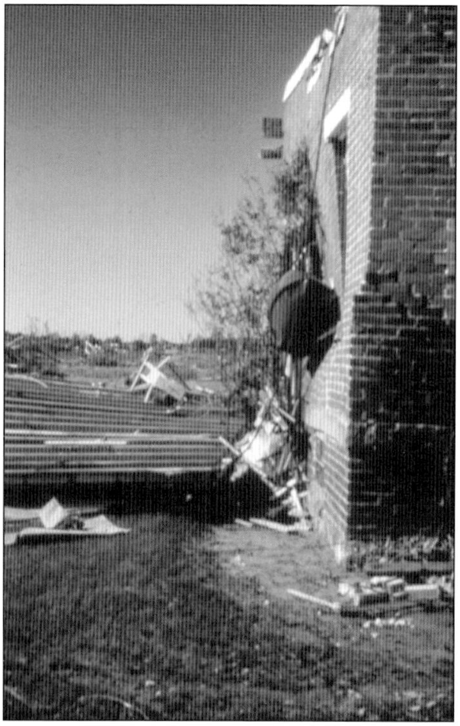

This is another image of what was once a nice family home standing in shambles. Jean Burling Alf remembers the day of the tornado very well. Her family had been going about their day as usual until the storm hit. Jean had even baked a cake that afternoon and had it sitting on the kitchen cupboard to cool. Once the family emerged from the basement to find the majority of their home gone, they were all very thankful to be alive and together. Once the shock wore off, they looked around at the damage. Jean walked into what used to be their kitchen and noticed that the only things left were the dining room table, the refrigerator, the kitchen cupboards, and the cake pan, which her cake had been in. The pan was in the same spot she had left it, but there was not a crumb on it. (Author's collection.)

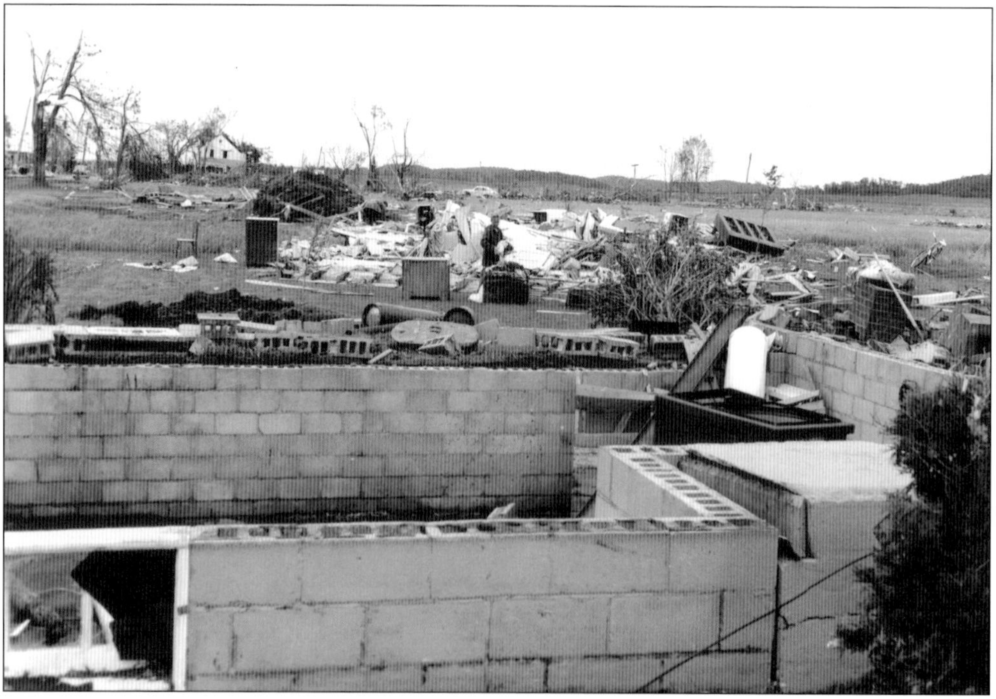

All that remains of this house is its foundation, which most likely protected and saved the family that called it home. People sorted through the remnants of their worldly possessions to see what they could salvage. Survivors would be convinced of the importance of a basement for the rest of their lives. (Courtesy of the Colfax Public Library.)

Piles of rubble are all that is left of the Art Quevillon home across the street from Evergreen Cemetery along 18 Mile Creek. Art was one of the 12 people killed as a result of the tornado when a chimney fell on him. Following the storm, there was looting, but that was quickly ended by local authorities. (Courtesy of Thelma Mickelson Kettle.)

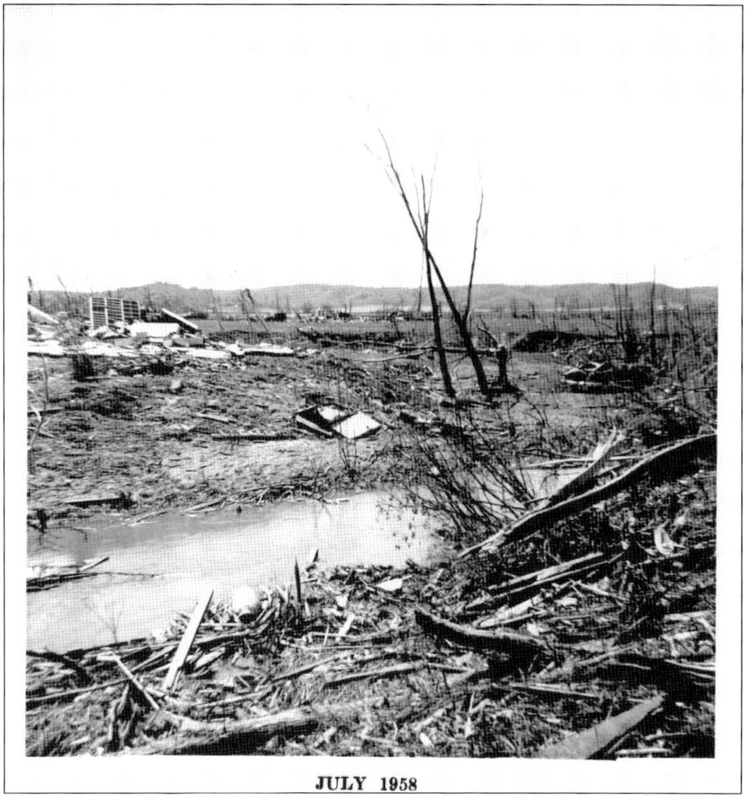

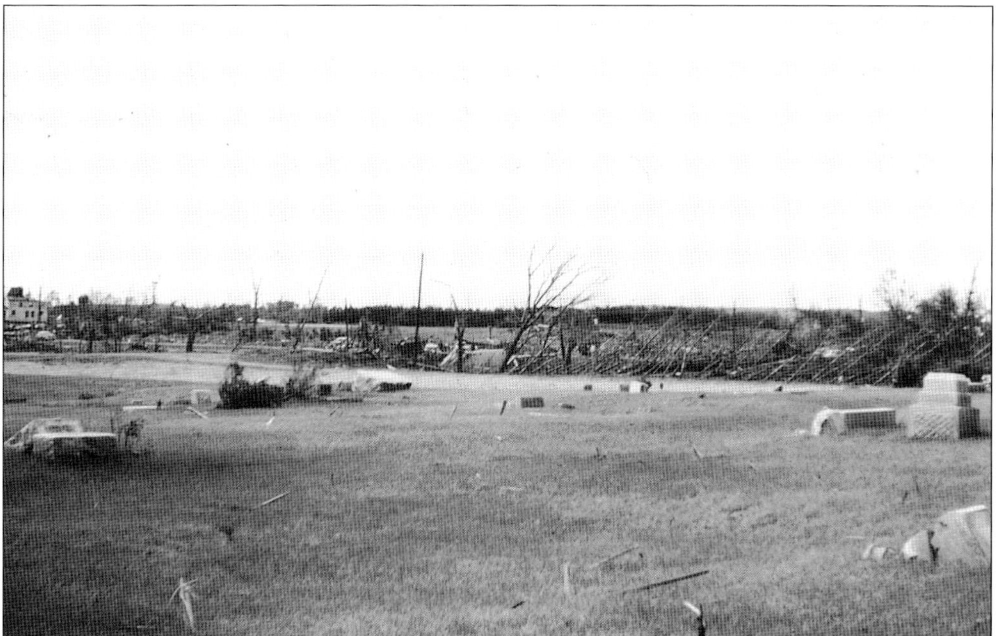

This photograph shows a view from Evergreen Cemetery looking north. Just as the trees were no match for the storm's power, the granite headstones were toppled as if they were simple building blocks. The Burling home can be seen at upper left. (Courtesy of Diane Haugle Hodgson.)

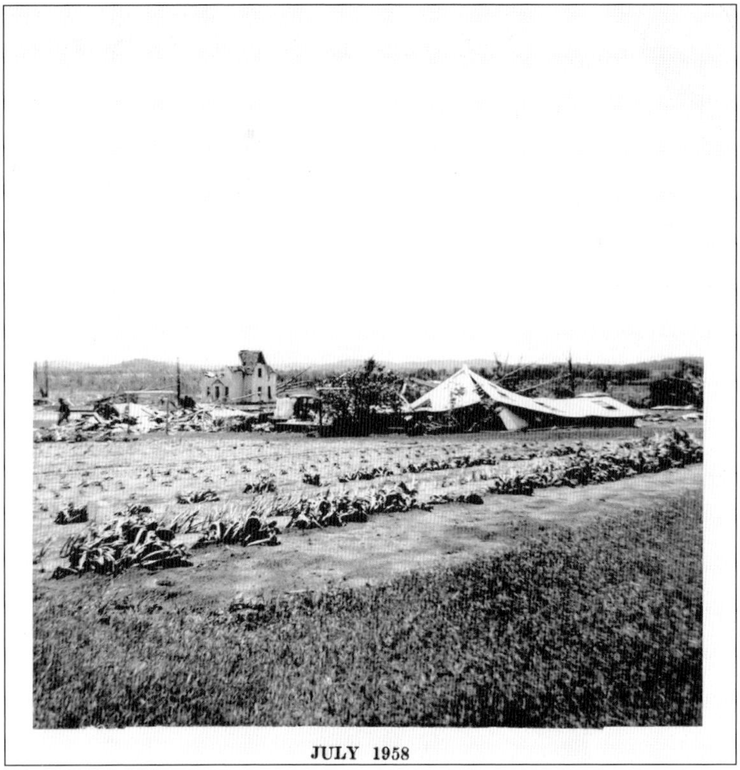

The rows of Frank Langel's vegetables seem to be beat up after going through the storm. The Clarence and Minda Burling home can be seen in the background, along with what appears to be the walls of a blown-over garage on the left. (Courtesy of Thelma Mickelson Kettle.)

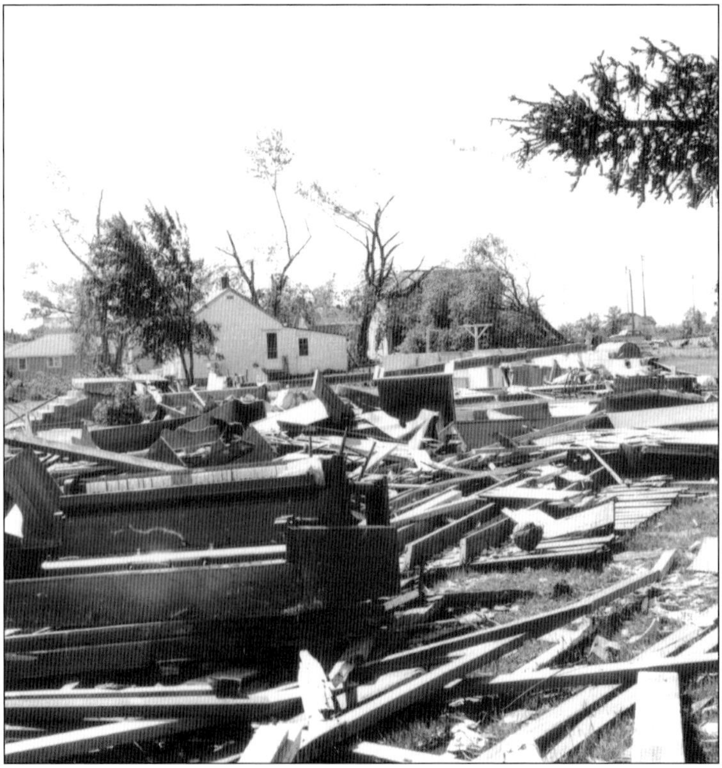

The white framed building that was once the Bethany Lutheran Church collapsed from the force of the storm. Note the smashed organ and dismantled church pews in the debris. It was amazing how one building could be completely destroyed while a house right next door was left standing, apparently unharmed. (Courtesy of John Russell.)

The intense damage to the north end of town can be seen here. If this aerial photograph of University Avenue had been taken just a little farther west, it would be possible to see the Colfax School. Many had to start over with mortgage payments because there was not enough insurance to cover the damage. (Author's collection.)

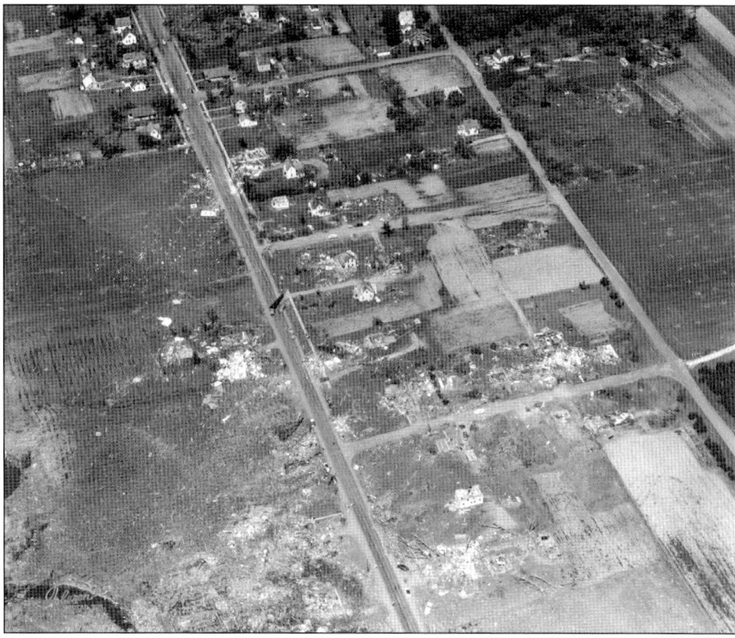

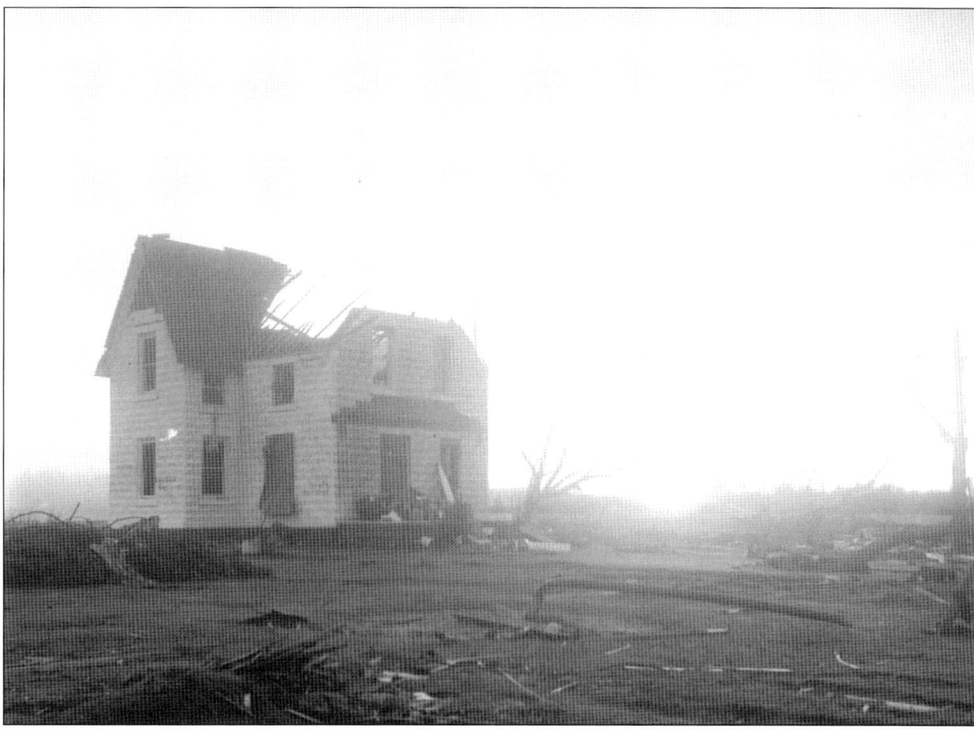

This is what was left of the Clarence and Minda Burling home. Some farmers who had been in the middle of chores recognized the seriousness of the storm and stopped to seek shelter. Fritz Larson, who was 11 years old at the time, remembers seeing the neighbor's barn explode, sending hay flying through the air. He knew he could not make it to the safety of his house, so he lay as flat on the ground as possible and watched the destruction of his family farm. (Courtesy of John Russell.)

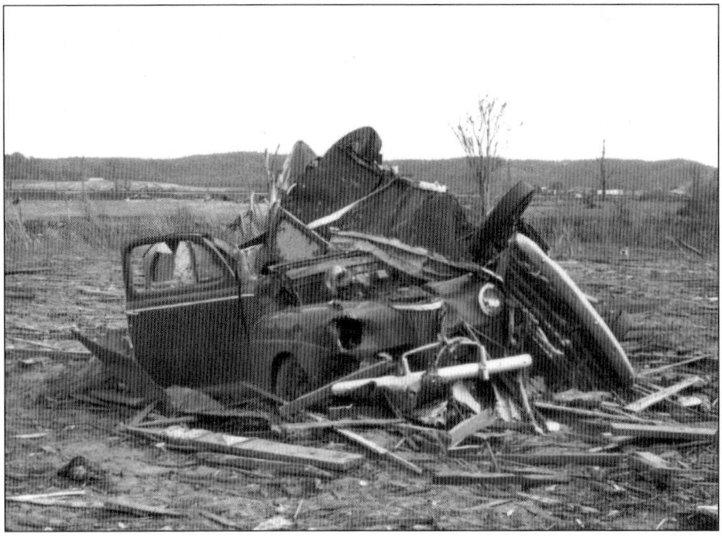

These two cars were left almost completely unrecognizable. People were willing to help in any way they could. One resident who was trying to sell their station wagon loaned it out to drive the injured to the hospital in Eau Claire. This care, concern, and generosity was evident throughout the village. (Courtesy of Joan Shong.)

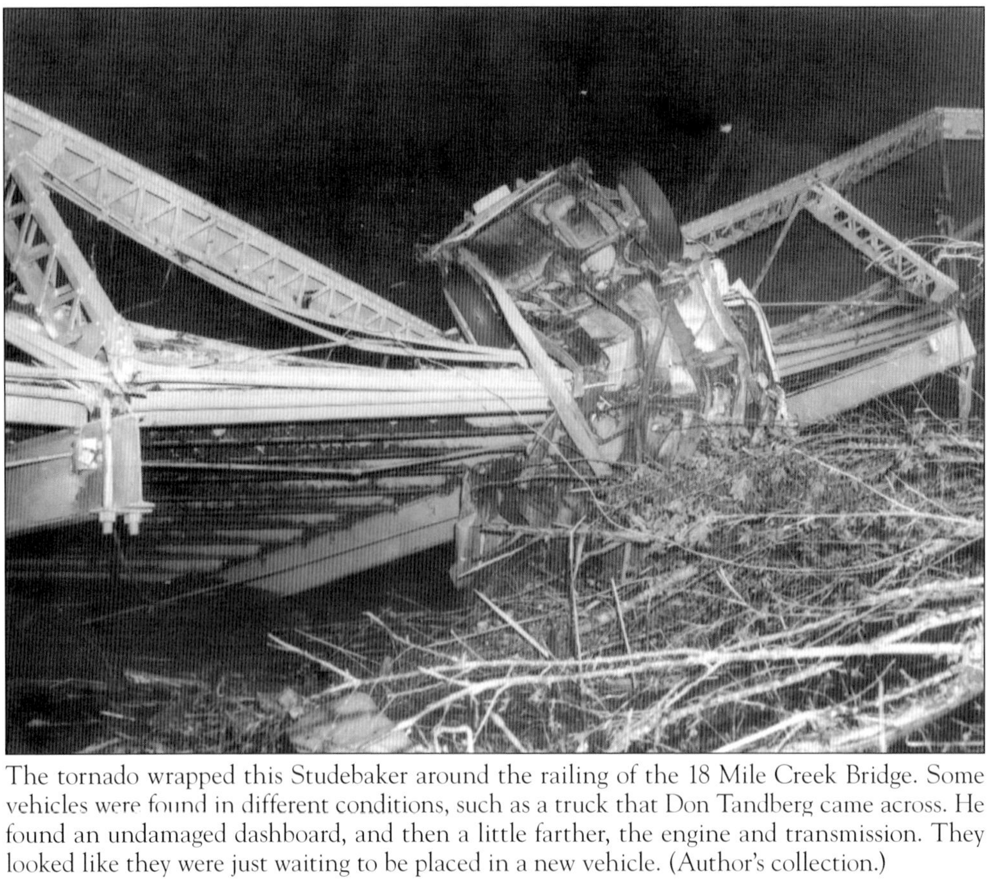

The tornado wrapped this Studebaker around the railing of the 18 Mile Creek Bridge. Some vehicles were found in different conditions, such as a truck that Don Tandberg came across. He found an undamaged dashboard, and then a little farther, the engine and transmission. They looked like they were just waiting to be placed in a new vehicle. (Author's collection.)

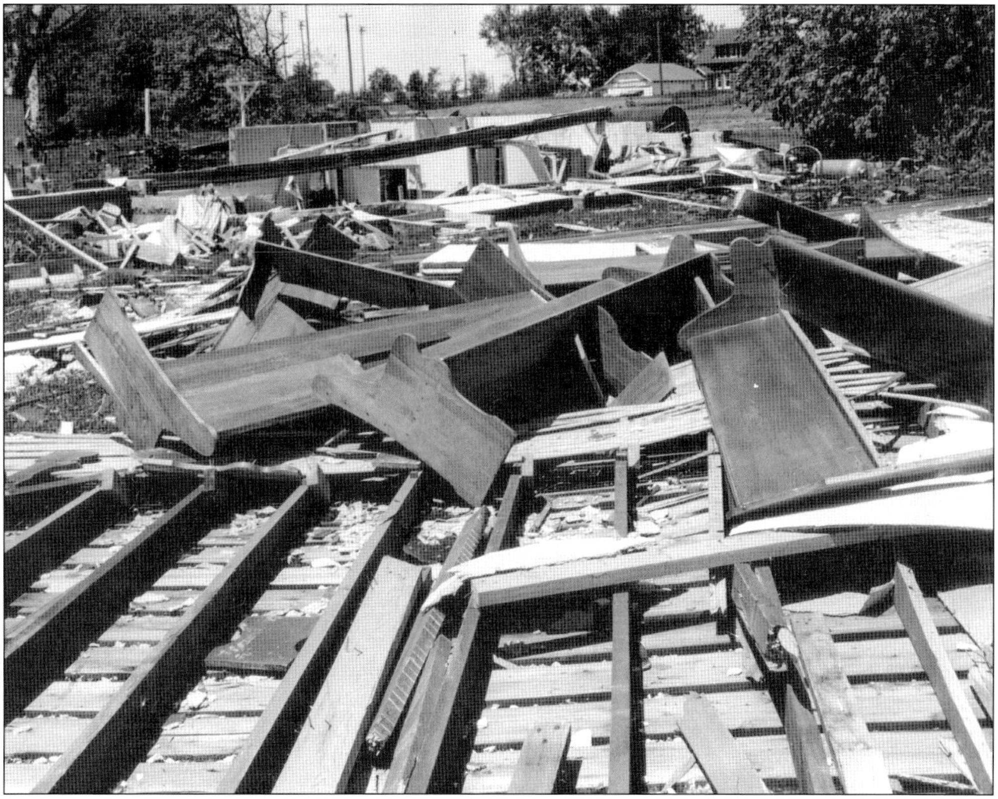

The beautiful church pews of the Bethany Lutheran Church were in shambles after the storm. The Bethany congregation did not give up, however. Church services were held in the basement of the municipal building while they rebuilt. The new church dedication took place the following summer in 1959. (Courtesy of Ron Blakely.)

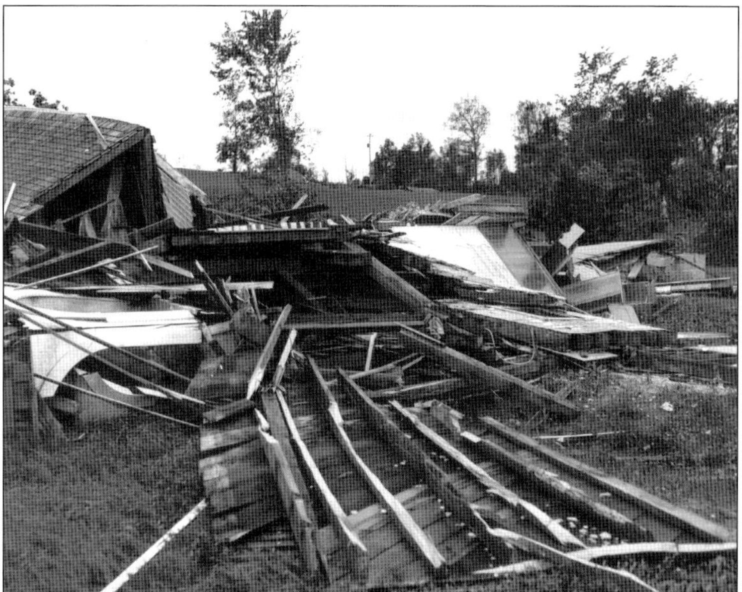

Bethany Lutheran Church was ripped apart as the tornado made its way through the village. The timbers of the walls were reduced to kindling, and the pews were stacked on top of each other. (Courtesy of the Colfax Public Library.)

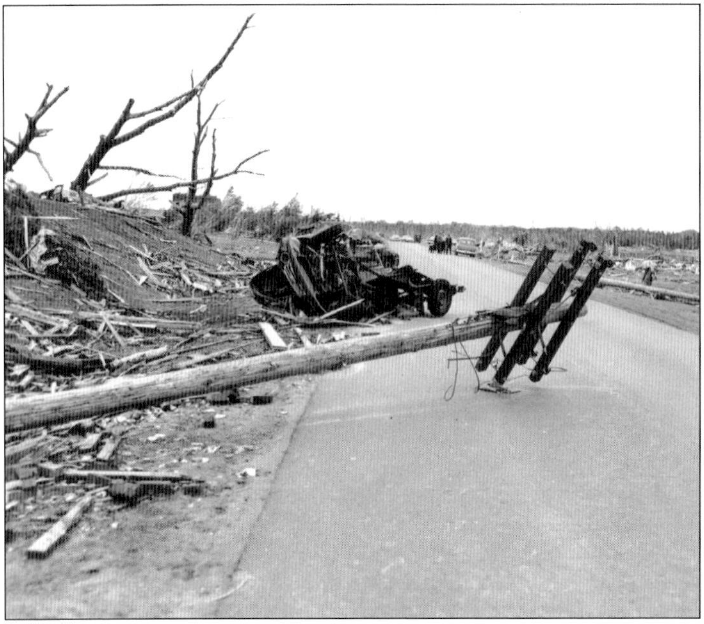

This scene on the north side shows the force of the storm, with bare trunks of trees, tangled automobiles, and downed power lines leaving the area in disarray. Even though 12 people and numerous animals lost their lives, it could have been worse. (Courtesy of the Colfax Public Library.)

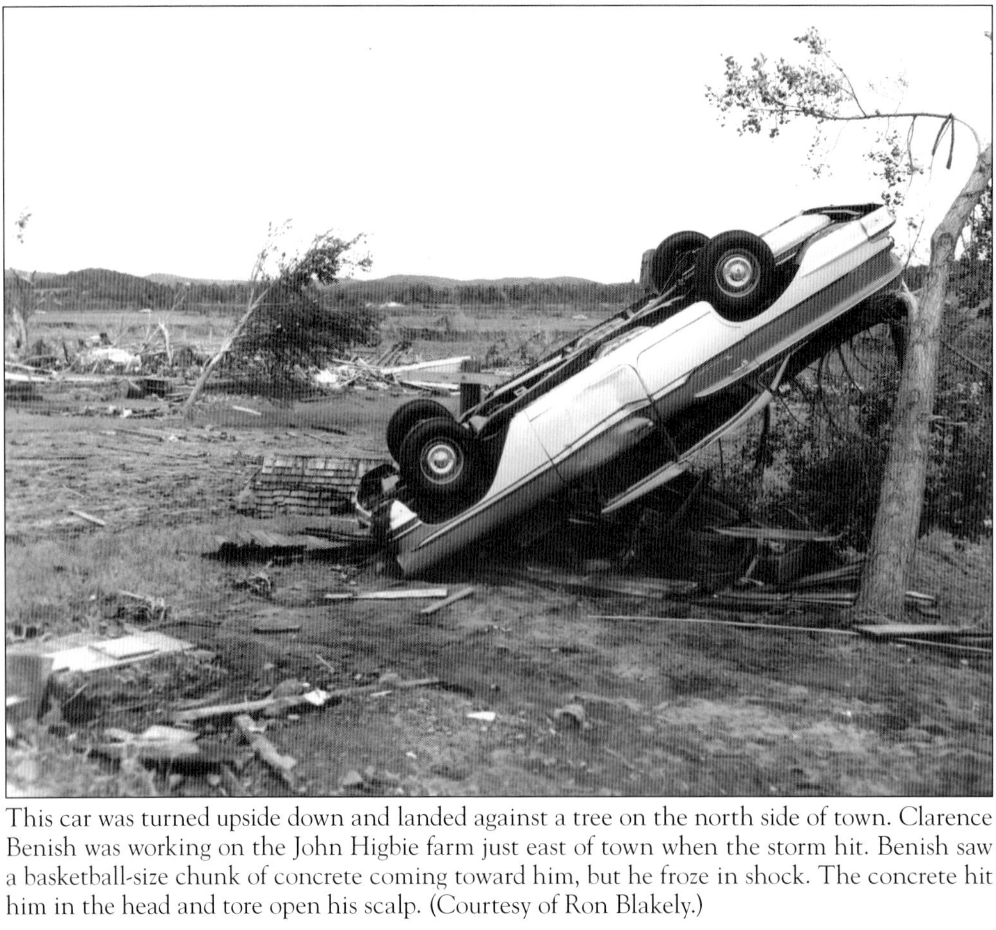

This car was turned upside down and landed against a tree on the north side of town. Clarence Benish was working on the John Higbie farm just east of town when the storm hit. Benish saw a basketball-size chunk of concrete coming toward him, but he froze in shock. The concrete hit him in the head and tore open his scalp. (Courtesy of Ron Blakely.)

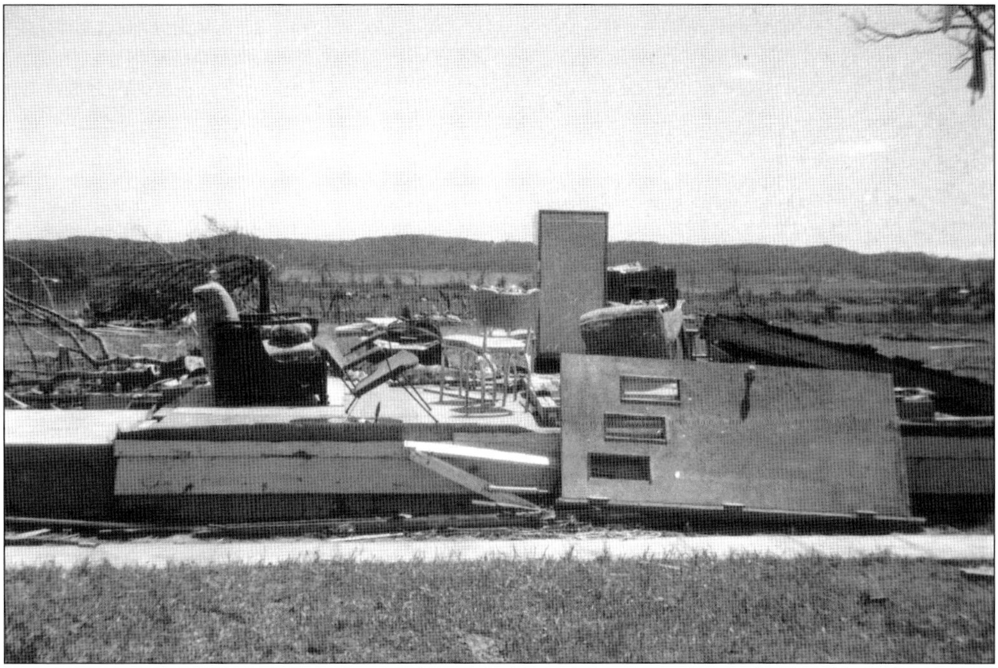

Only a few chairs remain at the home of Donald and Shirley Paff on High Street. Lila Whitted remembered looking at the west side of the Farmers Union feed mill. When the storm stripped off the white wood siding, an old ad for flour was revealed. (Courtesy of the Colfax Public Library.)

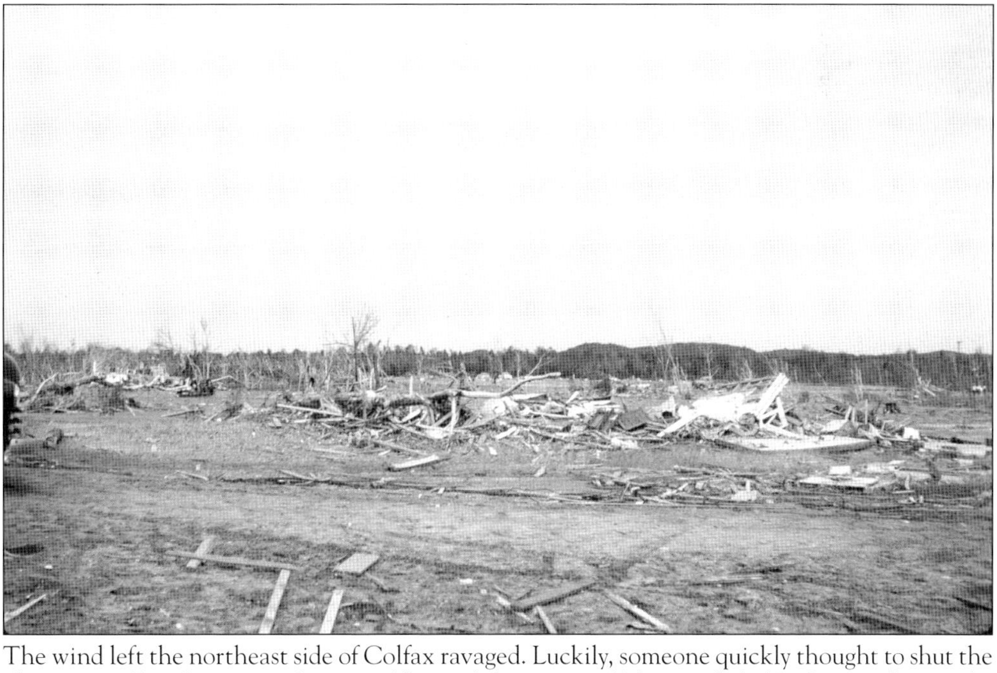

The wind left the northeast side of Colfax ravaged. Luckily, someone quickly thought to shut the electricity off at the power plant so additional damage could be avoided. (Author's collection.)

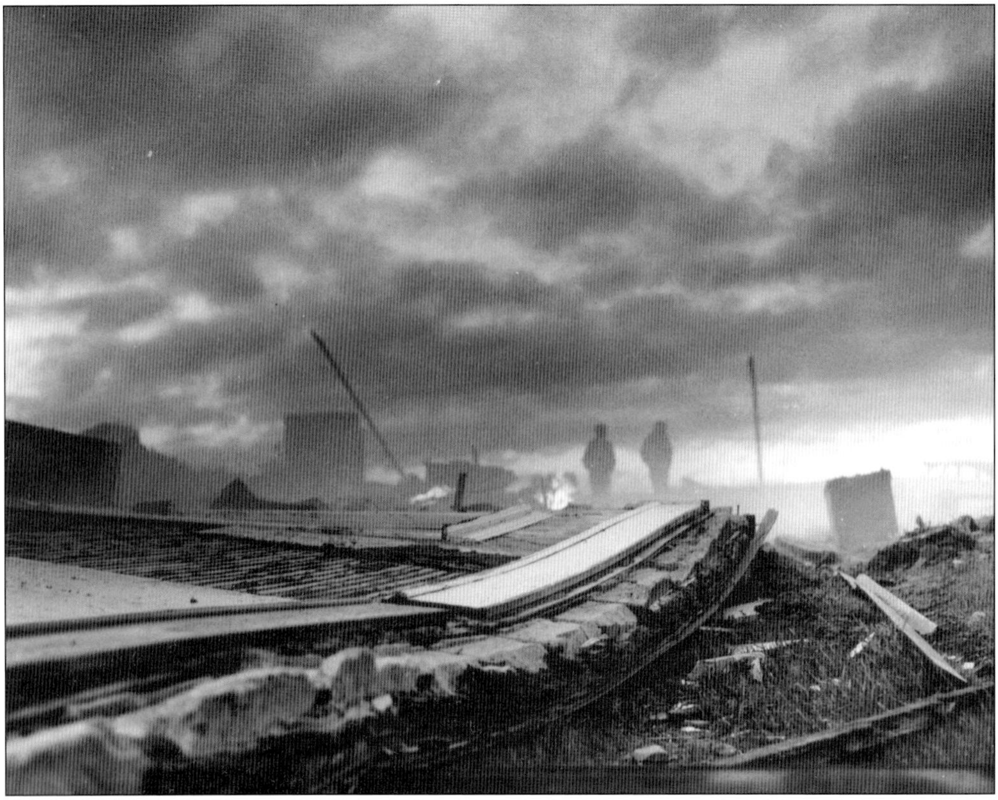

This image shows how eerie it must have been when people first came out of their hiding spots and saw the destruction. When Roger Vance and Grace Vance Larson came up out of the basement of a house they rented north of town on Highway M, they were in disbelief. Grace found one of her full-length bedroom curtains plastered on the ceiling as if it had been glued there. (Courtesy of Ron Blakely.)

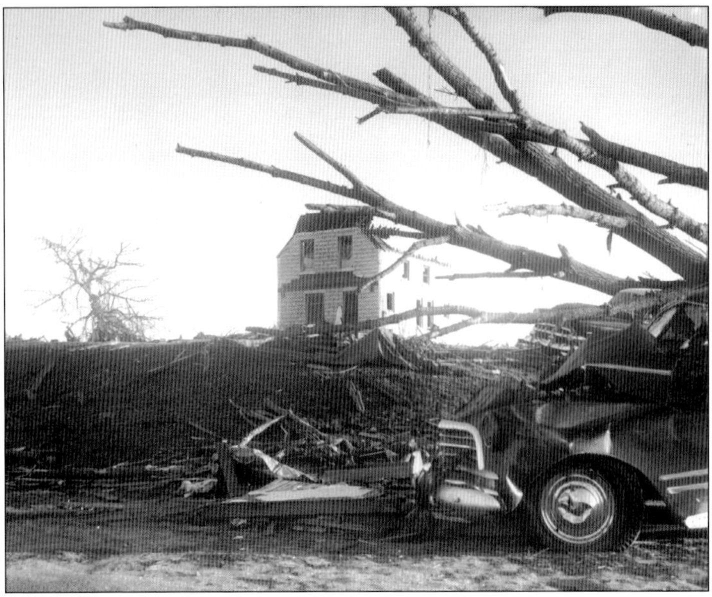

The north side of Colfax was in shambles after the tornado. Even after all the horror and tragedy, some people were looking on the bright side of things. Carl Nelson and his wife had been talking prior to the storm about removing the front porch on their home. "The tornado did it for us," he said. "We just didn't expect it to happen that way." (Courtesy of John Russell.)

Only part of the basement walls of the Melvin Hendrickson home on the northeast side of town remained after the tornado. Richard Hendrickson recalls his dad saying "into the basement, into the basement!" After the storm passed, Richard looked down and saw an 8-by-10-foot beam on the floor between his legs that used to be overhead. How it got onto the floor without falling on any of the five huddled under it is a mystery. (Courtesy of Diane Larson Heppner.)

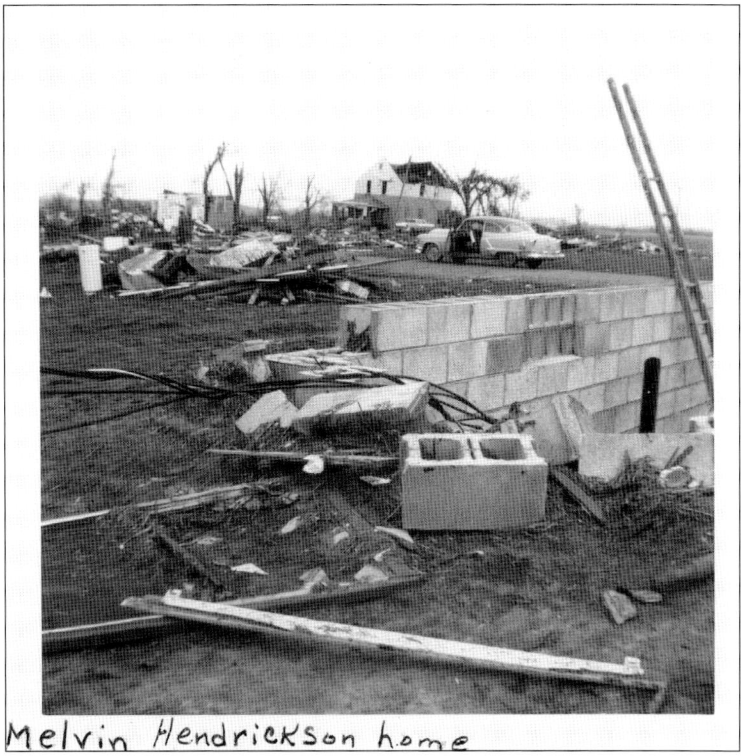

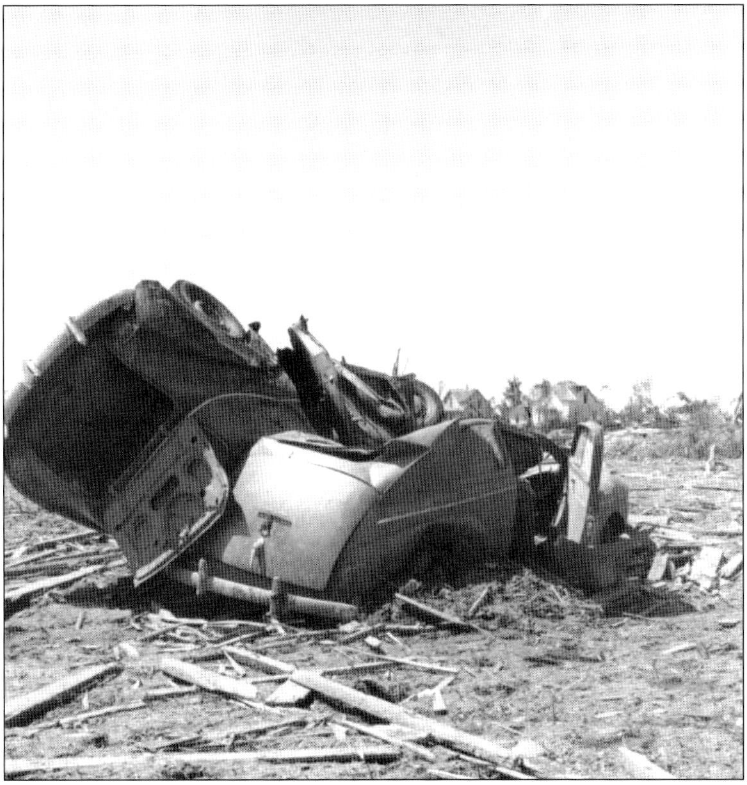

These two cars were turned into one pile of steel after being blown and tangled up together. "The noise of the tornado was unbelievable," Dave Henderson said. "I cannot describe it. It was like a freight train, but worse." Metal and machinery flew through the air as if they were feathers. (Courtesy of John Russell.)

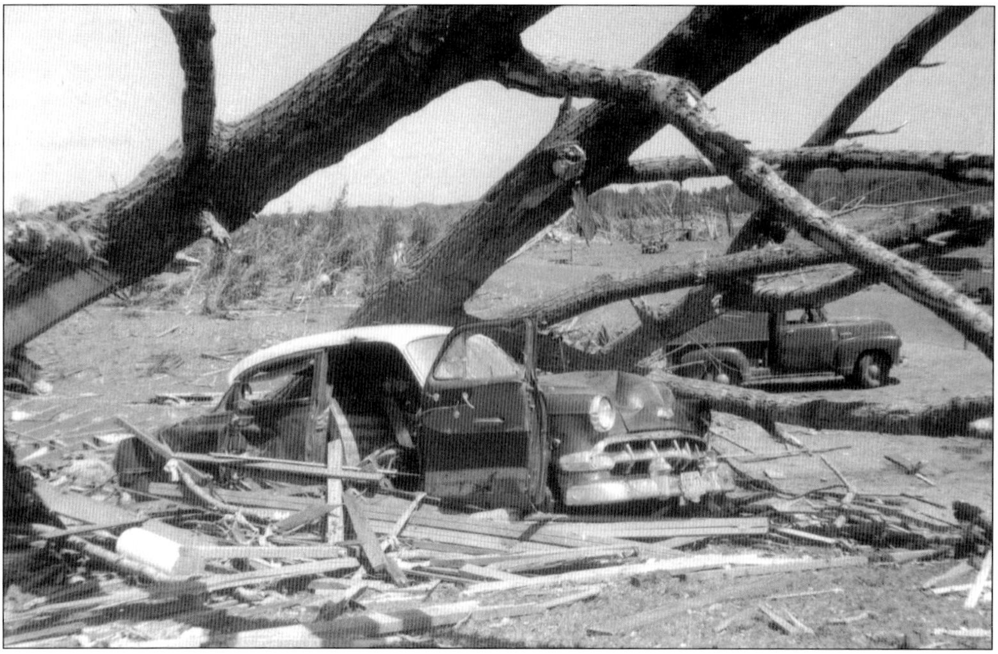

This car on the north side was likely unfixable. Bullet the dog, belonging to the Kenneth and Lois Sundby family, was unable to get into the basement with the rest of the family when the tornado hit. After the storm, he was nowhere to be found. However, two days later, he came walking home. Bullet also wanted to get in the basement during storms after that. (Courtesy of the Colfax Public Library.)

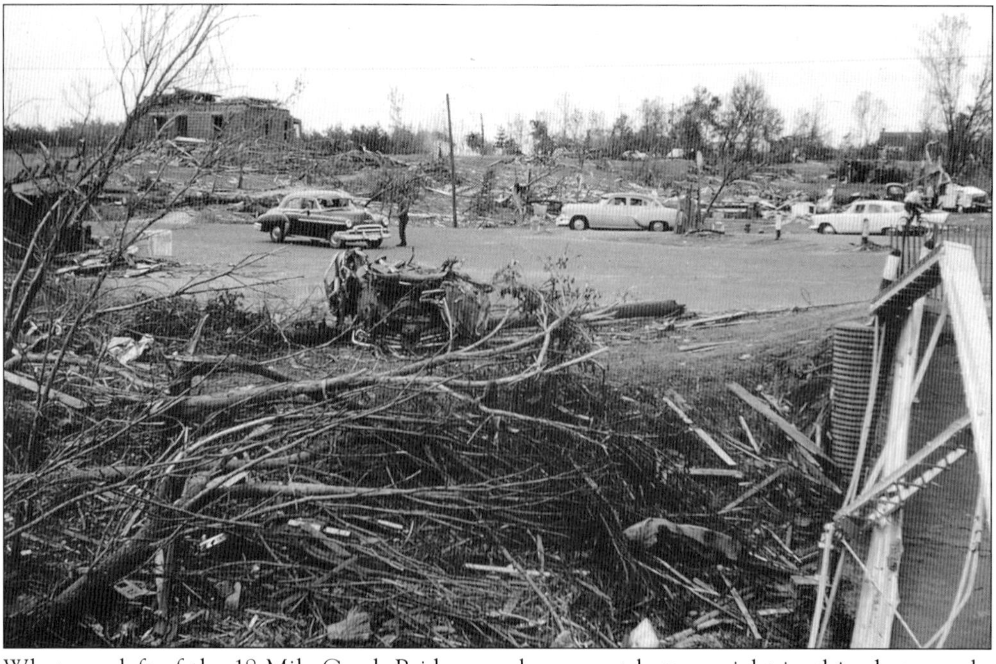

What was left of the 18 Mile Creek Bridge can be seen at bottom right in this photograph. Curious sightseers were stopped by a National Guard member to ensure the safety and security of the village and its residents. (Courtesy of Diane Haugle Hodgson.)

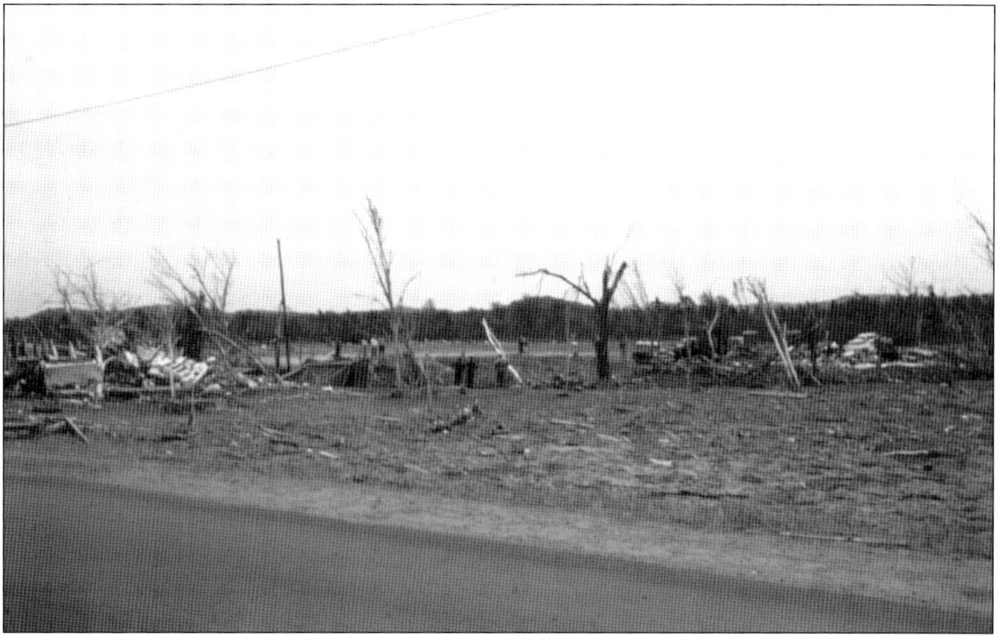

Only debris-littered basements remained on the north side of Colfax. Families found shelter in their basements, pushing each other down the stairs and getting the doors secured just in time. (Author's collection.)

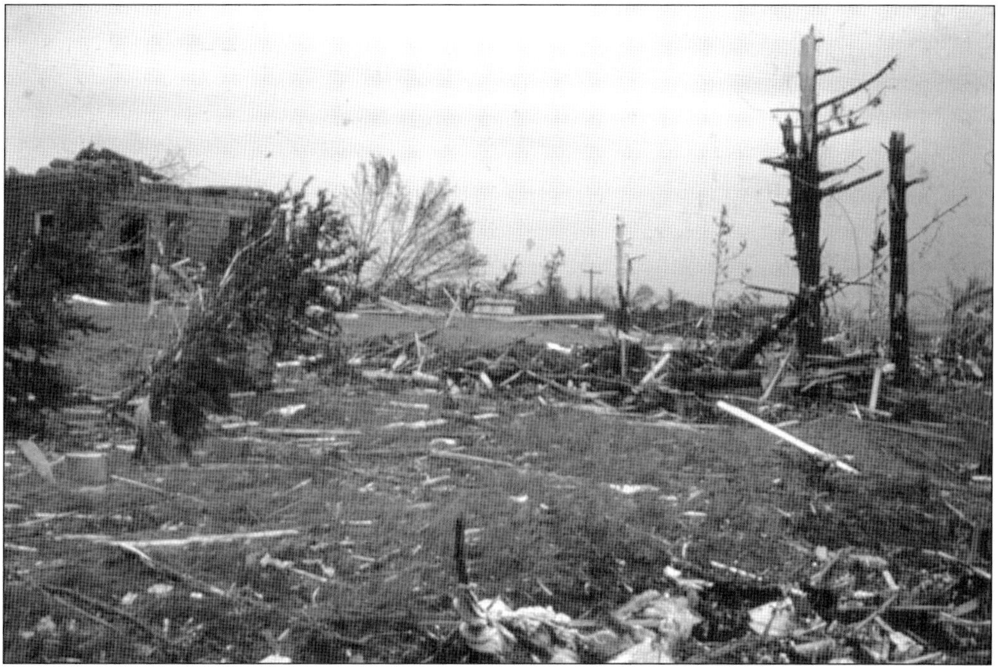

This is the north side of Colfax. Just southwest of town was the farm of Jim and Delores Huber. Delores had been at the Tainter Methodist Church at the time of the storm. Although no one in their family was badly hurt, the cleanup process was painstaking. A farm equipment dealer in Rusk by the name of Jack Bechel loaned the Hubers a 5 Star Moline tractor with a huge magnet under it to pick up nails and other metal items from their property. (Author's collection.)

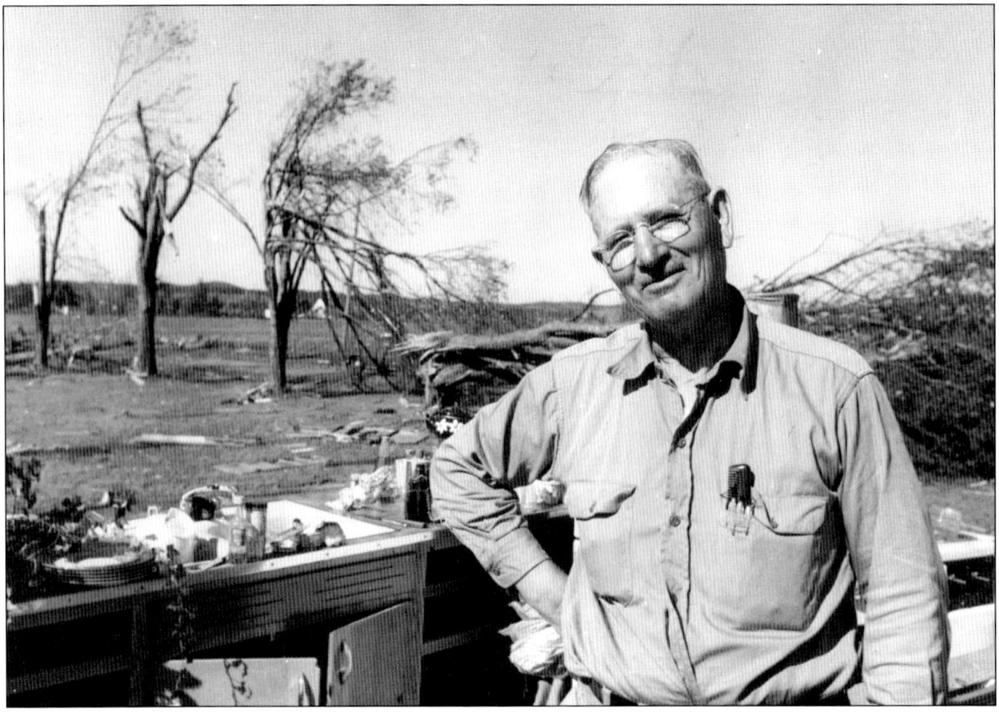

Henry Gilberts looks over what is left of his home and store, finding not much more than the kitchen sink. Ron Husby was in his second year of running his route as a truck driver for Sno-Flake Foods. Upon entering Colfax, he saw the approaching storm and thought he could beat it. The storm had a different idea. Husby was stuck in front of the Gilberts' Four Corners Store, facing the destruction head on. (Author's collection.)

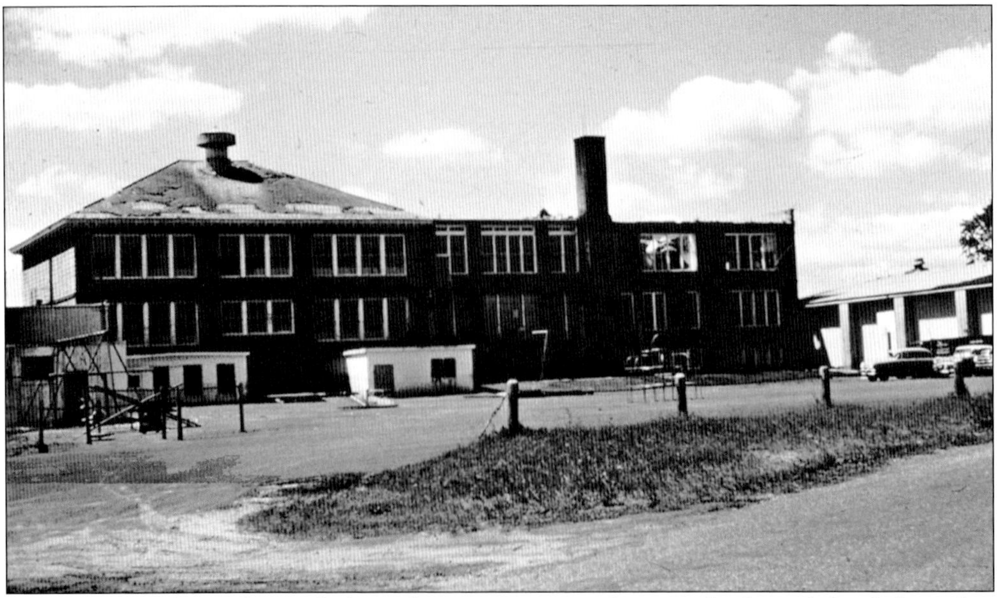

The damage to the newly installed gym floor was put to good use as a display rack for clothing that had been donated to the community for those who had few belongings left. Boxes of donations were sorted to make it easier on the survivors. (Courtesy of Diane Haugle Hodgson.)

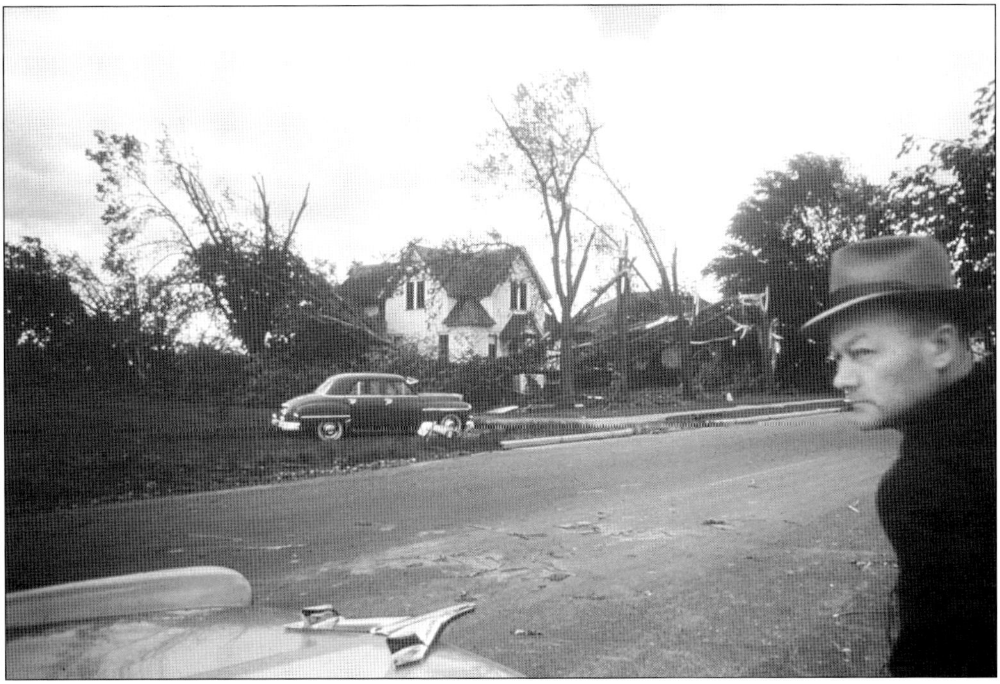

These are a few of the homes that were damaged on the northwest side of town. Most of the damage was done to the south and east sides of the Colfax School. Don Wiseman is seen here inspecting the damage. Beautiful trees and homes were destroyed block after block. (Courtesy of Lyle Christenson.)

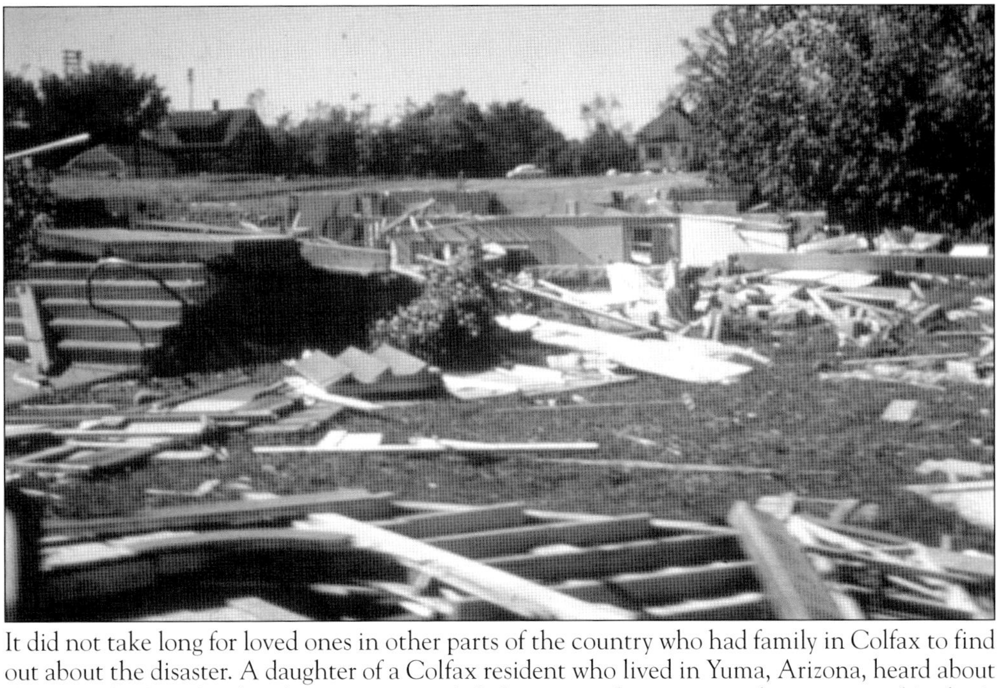

It did not take long for loved ones in other parts of the country who had family in Colfax to find out about the disaster. A daughter of a Colfax resident who lived in Yuma, Arizona, heard about the tornado from her local news station while hosting a dinner party that evening. (Author's collection.)

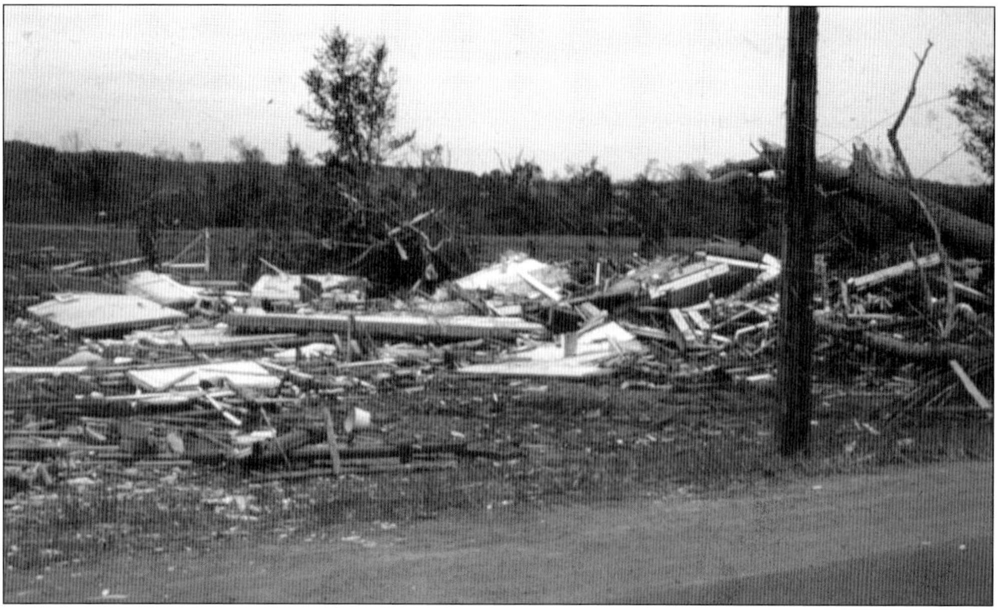

"We felt the suction," said Melvin Hendricks. The wind was twisting and blowing items in their basement, and rain was pouring in on them as they huddled together. The water heater in the middle of the basement was the only thing not moving. "I looked up, and our house was gone," Hendricks said. (Author's collection.)

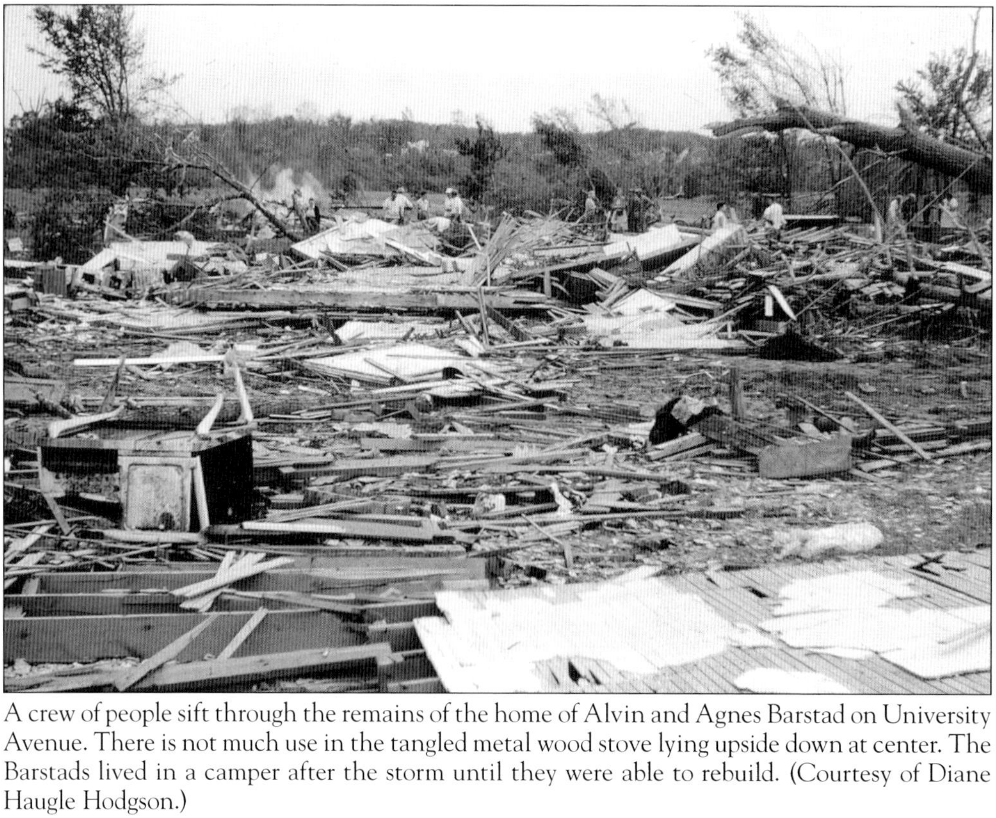

A crew of people sift through the remains of the home of Alvin and Agnes Barstad on University Avenue. There is not much use in the tangled metal wood stove lying upside down at center. The Barstads lived in a camper after the storm until they were able to rebuild. (Courtesy of Diane Haugle Hodgson.)

One of the bizarre things that occurred during the tornado concerned a rug in the upstairs hallway of the Alvin and Arlene Berge home. The rug ended up rolled up, and inside it was a dresser scarf that had been on top of the heater in the living room downstairs. (Author's collection.)

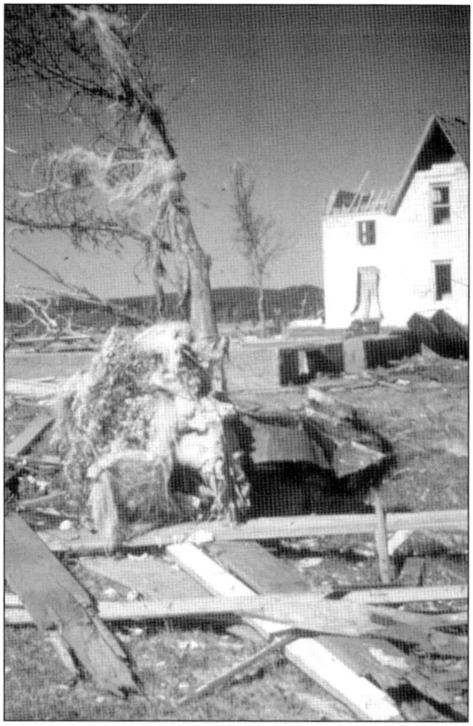

Amid the remains of this home was a pair of wringer washing machines. The survivors were astounded by the randomness of the destruction. Some belongings were never seen again, while others seemed to be untouched. A combination phonograph and radio in one home still worked fine, in spite of its cabinet being smashed to bits, while the television next to it did not even have a mark. (Courtesy of Joan Shong.)

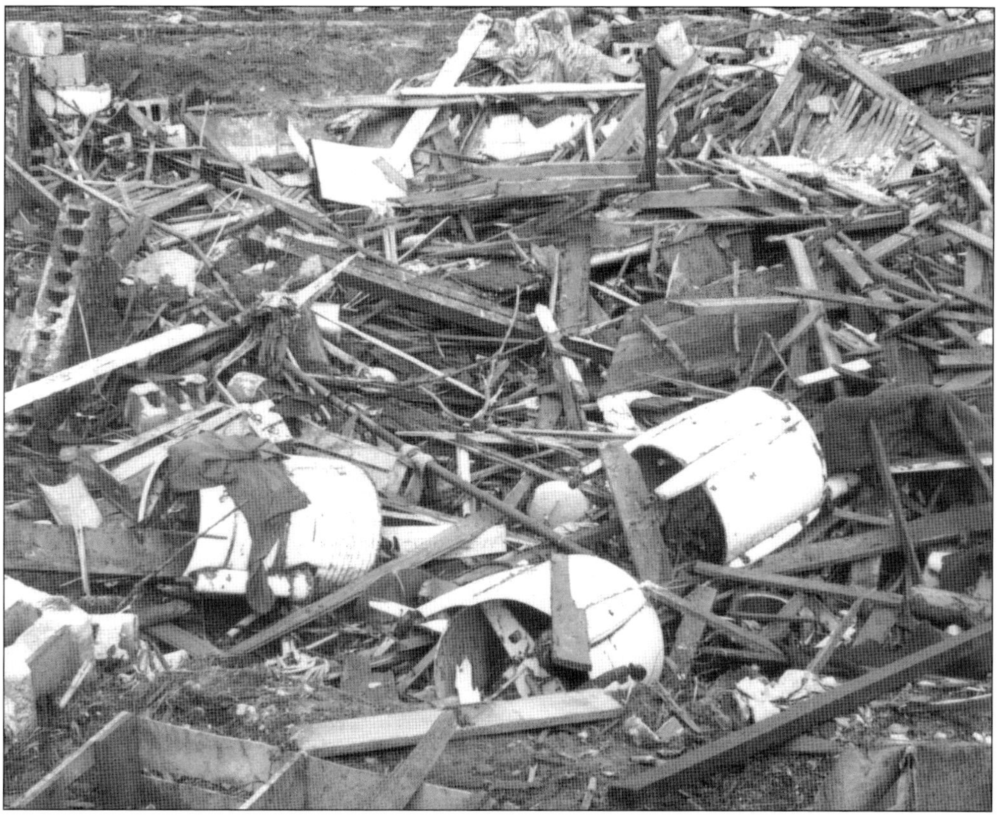

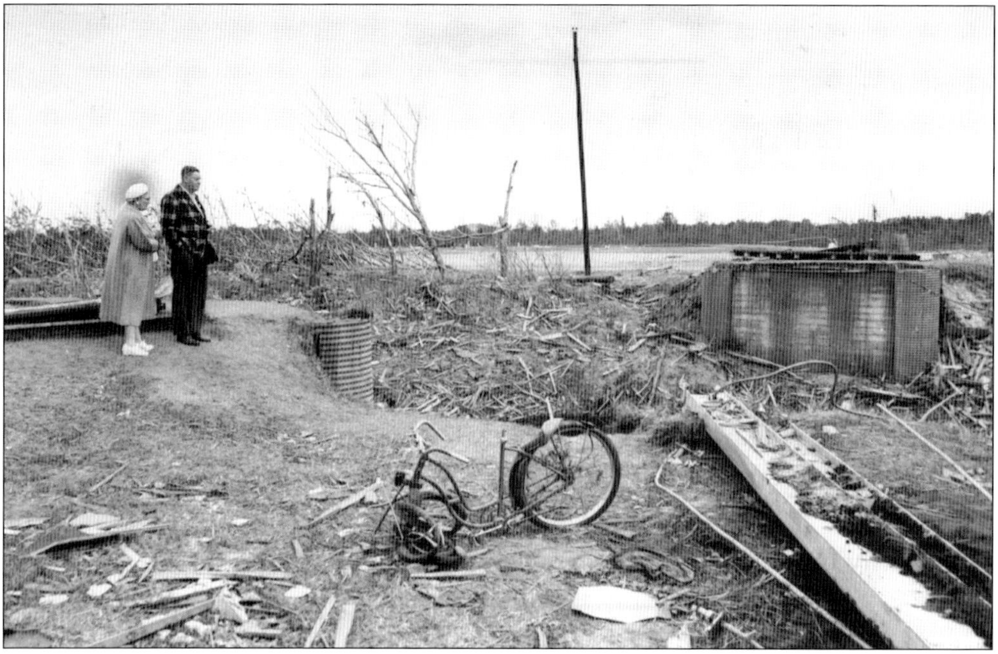

Hundreds of people drove to Colfax in the days following the tornado to see the destruction firsthand. George Sorenson of Eau Claire and his wife are seen here looking at what was left of the 18 Mile Creek Bridge. (Author's collection.)

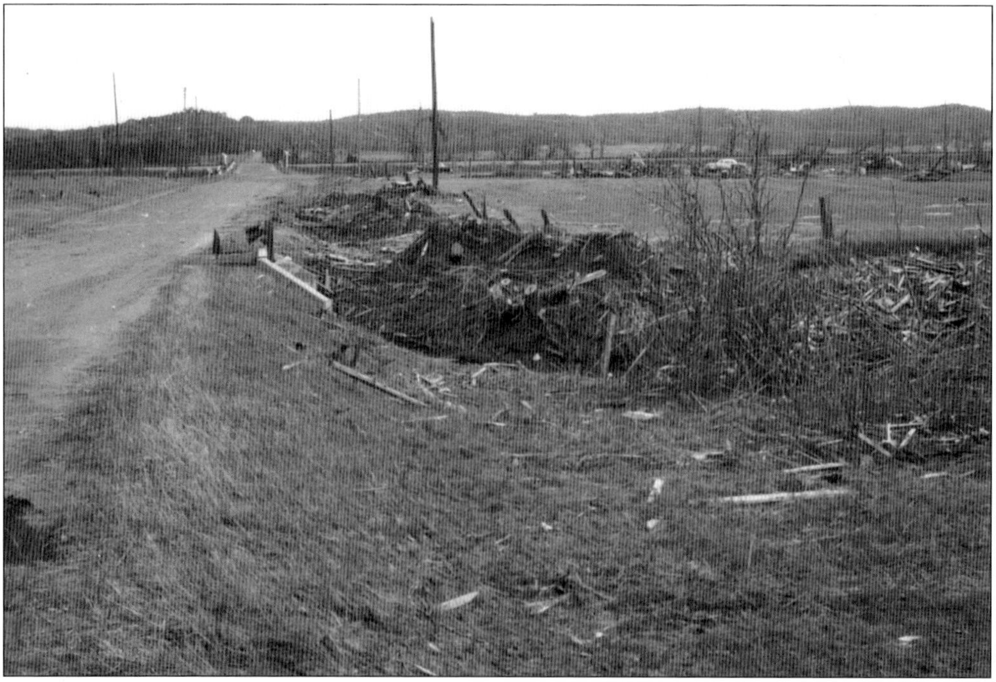

Looking south on Highway M, the landscape appears to be a war zone with all the damage and downed trees. Survivors found refuge in any way they could. Two boys found themselves stuck in manure as the tornado went over them, shredding their clothes and demolishing buildings around them, yet allowing them to survive to tell about it. (Courtesy of Joan Shong.)

This car belonged to Mildred Gerber Slaga. It looks like it was tossed around by the storm and landed here on the north side of the village. Mildred Gerber Slaga of Pomona, California, lost her life in the storm. She had been in Colfax visiting her mother, Nora Gerber, who was also killed. (Courtesy of Joan Shong.)

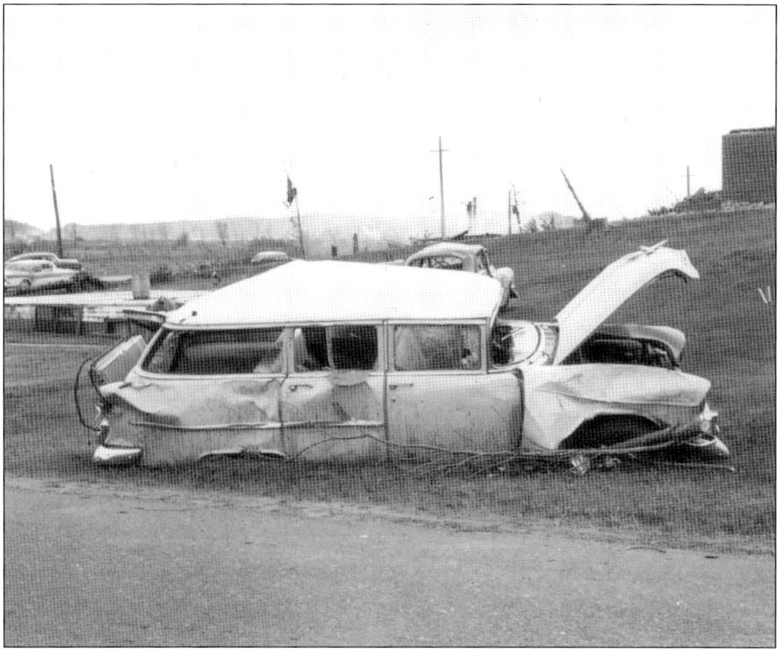

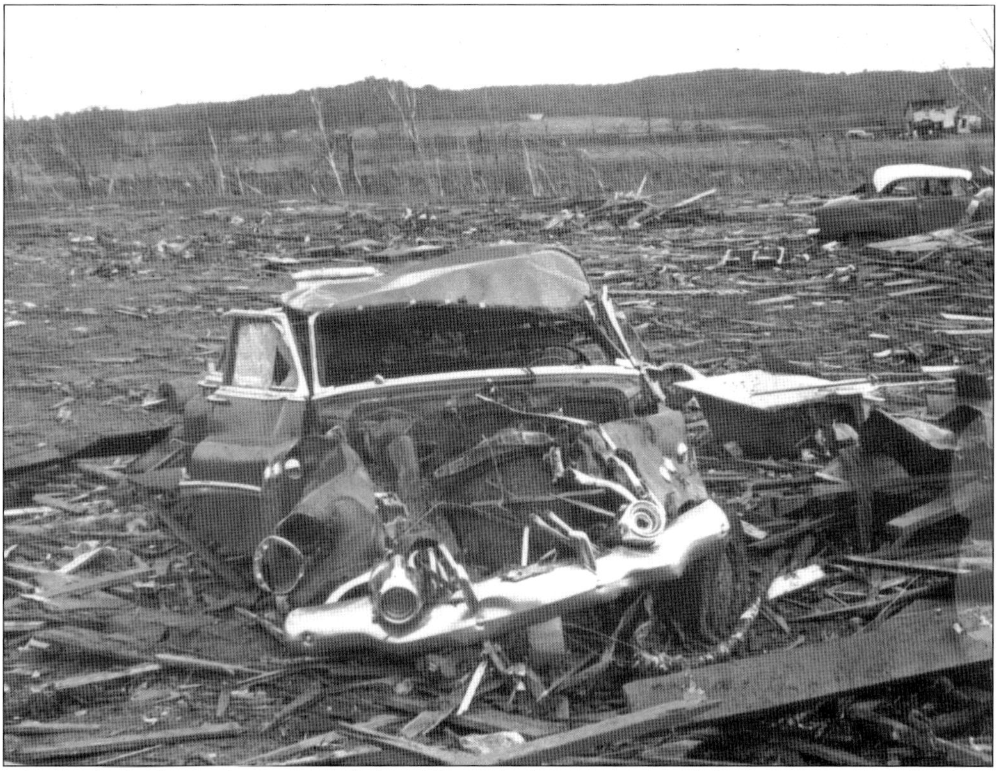

Those who had cars that were still drivable made their way around the community to check on others. Neighboring farmers helped each other out with chores and pulling together to share food. Arlene Hones, who had been baking bread at the time of the storm, was never able to make bread again without thinking about the tornado. (Courtesy of Joan Shong.)

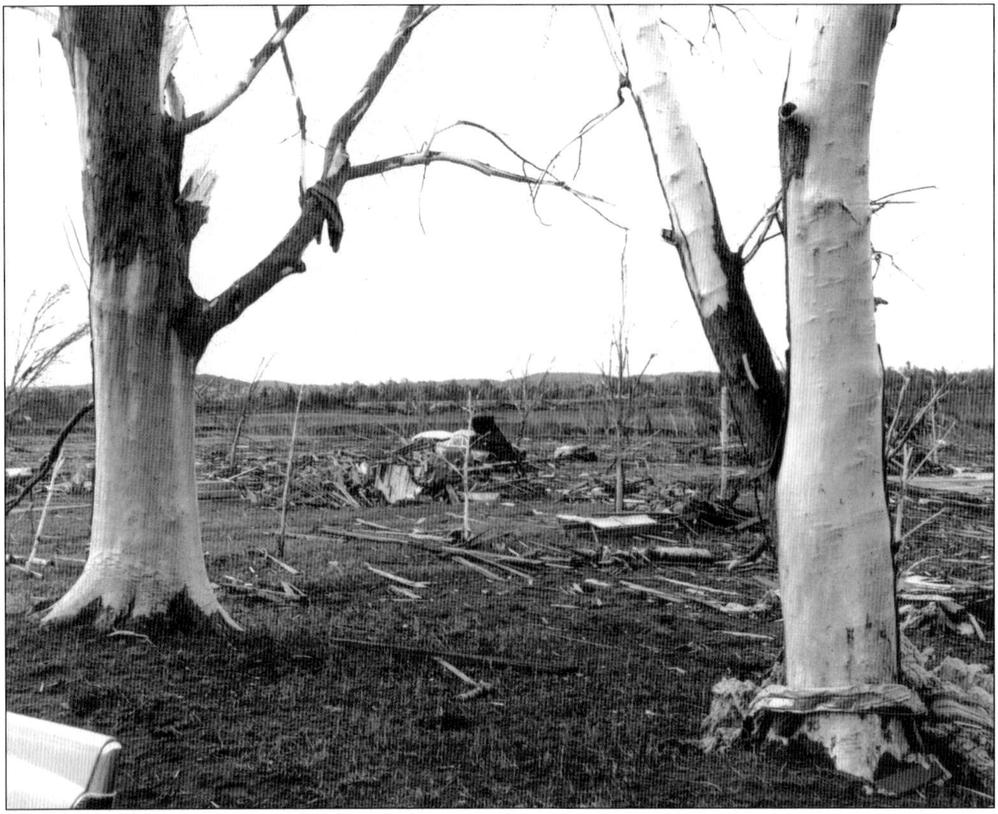

These trees on the north side had their bark peeled off by the force of the winds. Sylvia Puhl Scheff recalls watching the sky from her childhood home on the south side: "The word 'eerie' stays in my head. I remember the colors—dark purple, blackish blues, sickening yellow, putrid colors." (Courtesy of Ron Blakely.)

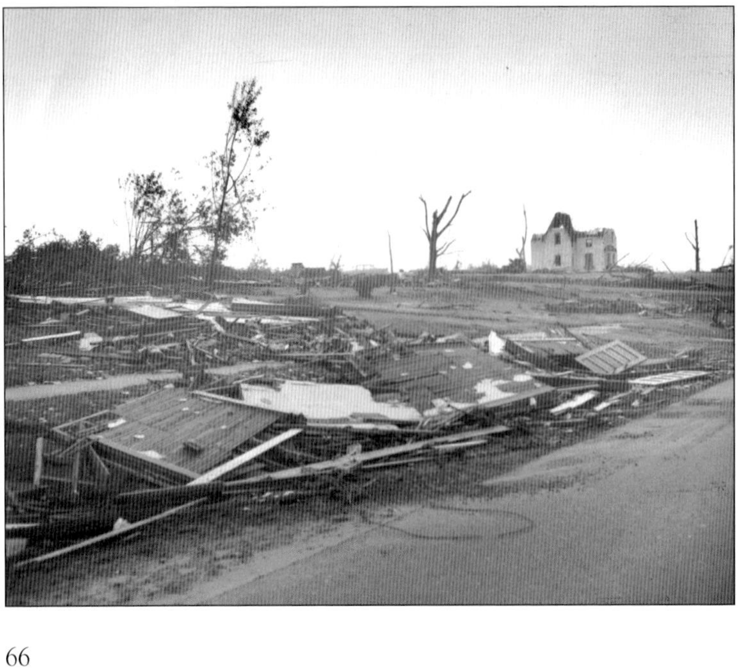

The home of Clarence and Minda Burling can be seen in the background of this photograph. It was sometimes difficult to remember what the homes and farms had looked like prior to the tornado. For years, its path through the woods was easy to see. (Courtesy of John Russell.)

This car and the bridge that spanned 18 Mile Creek met their match with the tornado. A two-ton Sno-Flake Foods delivery truck driven by Ron Husby went missing in this area. Only the chassis, the motor, and the rear dual wheels were found several days later. No other parts were ever located. (Courtesy of Ron Blakely.)

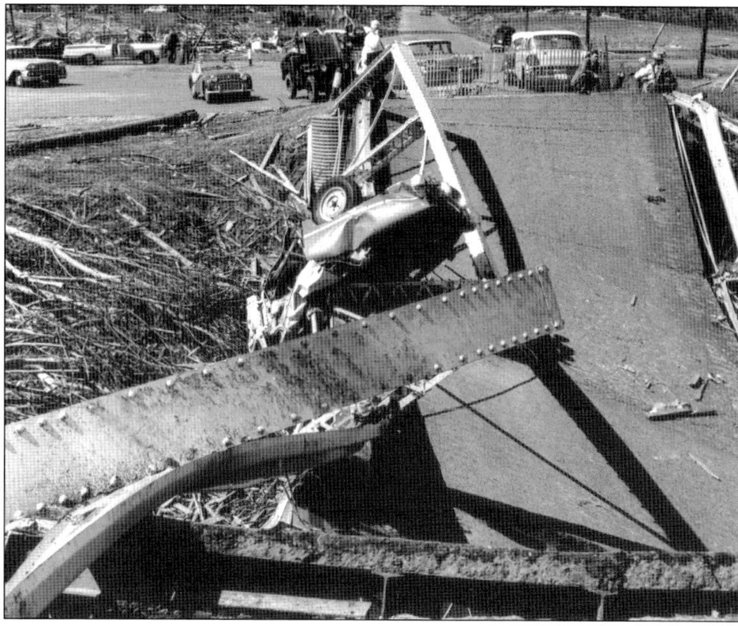

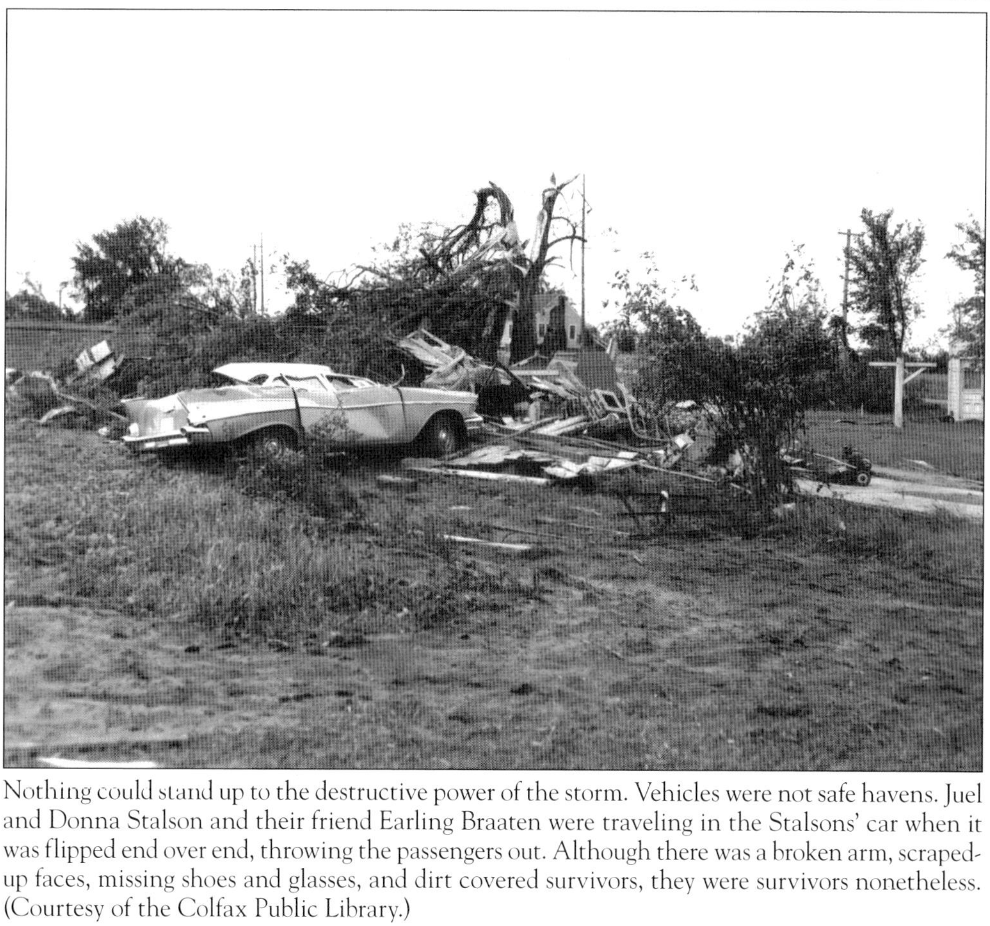

Nothing could stand up to the destructive power of the storm. Vehicles were not safe havens. Juel and Donna Stalson and their friend Earling Braaten were traveling in the Stalsons' car when it was flipped end over end, throwing the passengers out. Although there was a broken arm, scraped-up faces, missing shoes and glasses, and dirt covered survivors, they were survivors nonetheless. (Courtesy of the Colfax Public Library.)

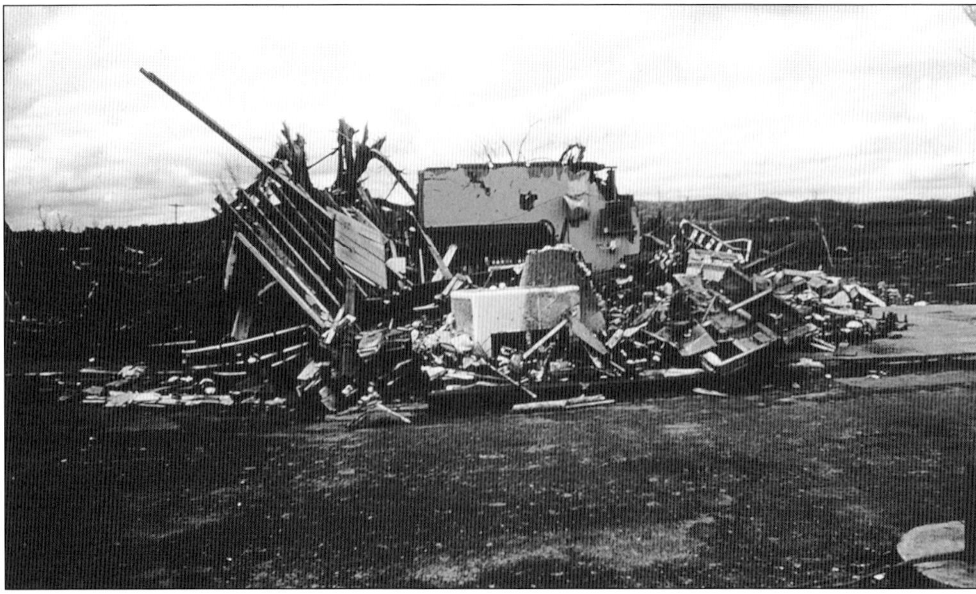

There was not much left of the Gilberts' Four Corners Store on the corner of Highway M south and University Avenue. The tornado left 28 dead, 148 hospitalized, 250 treated and released for injuries, 259 homes destroyed, 426 homes damaged, 173 farm buildings destroyed, and 706 farm buildings damaged. (Author's collection.)

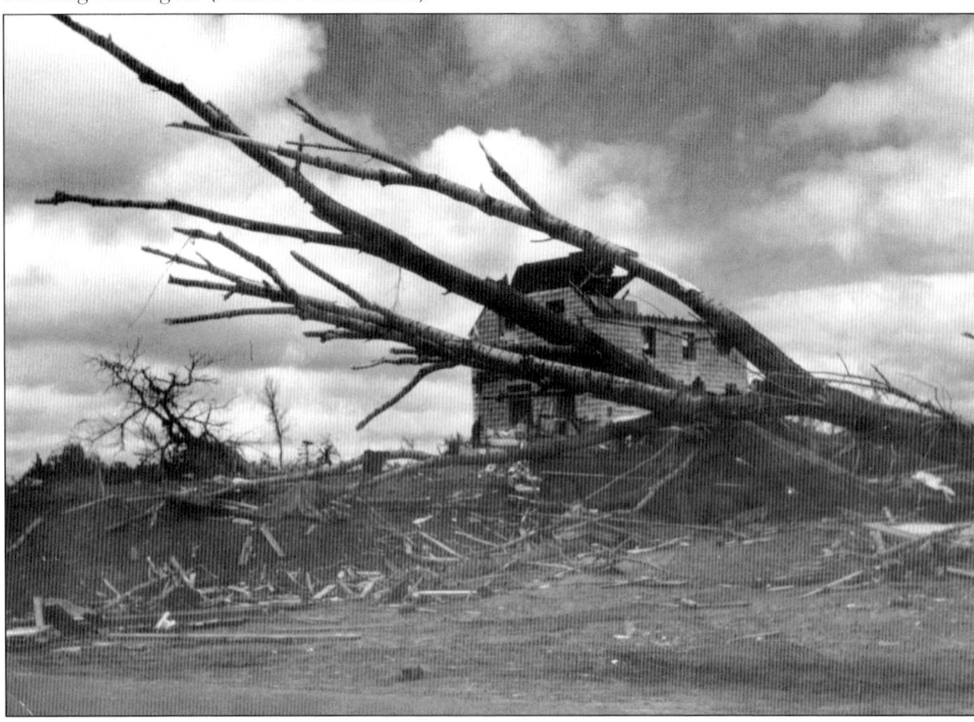

Just a few small saplings stand beside the Burling home on University Avenue. Larger trees were left holding up the remains of some homes. When people took refuge in their cellars, they noted that as a result of the suction from the tornado, their hair stood straight up on end. (Courtesy of John Russell.)

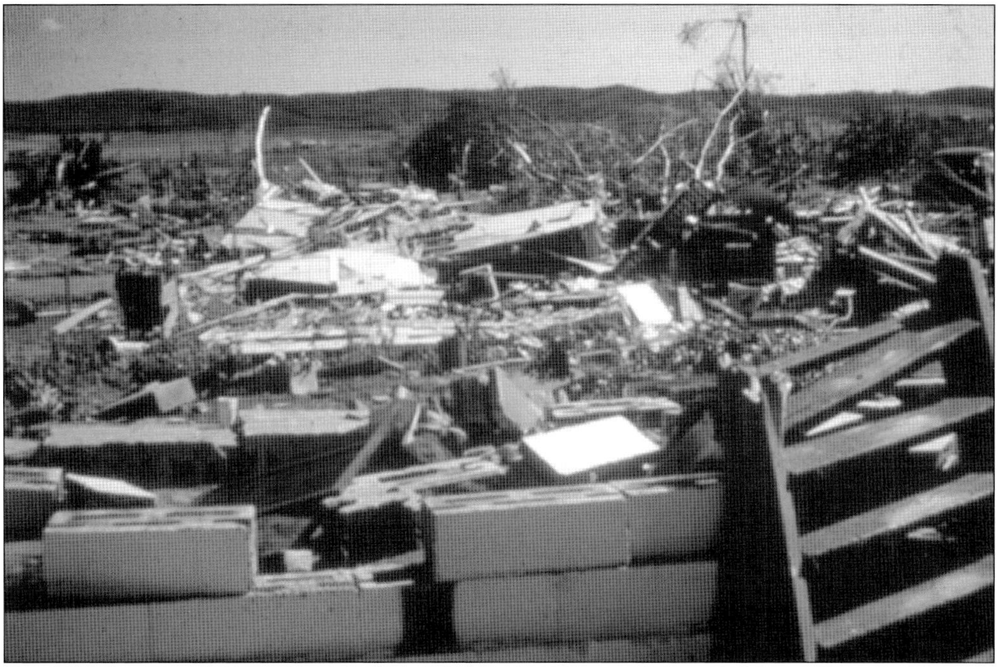

This was the typical scene that many people saw as they climbed out of their basements for the first time after the tornado—no houses, no trees, no cars, no people anywhere. It was totally flat in every direction, recalls Jean Burling Alf. (Author's collection.)

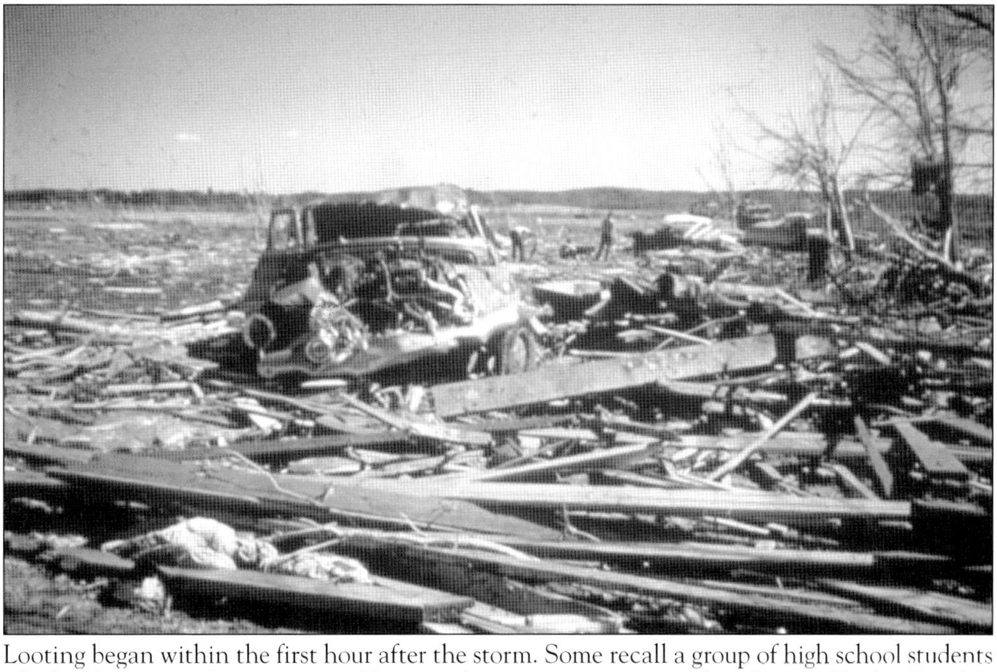

Looting began within the first hour after the storm. Some recall a group of high school students who had been attending a prom in Minneapolis coming over to see what they could take. Families were already shocked and confused as to what had just happened, and now they had to protect what little they had left. Once the National Guard got to town, they closed all the roads coming in. (Author's collection.)

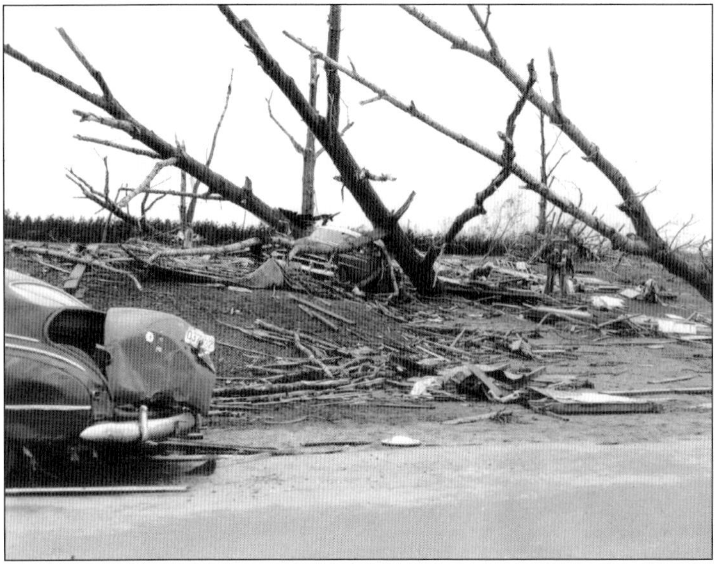

Dr. Gordon Neumann called the Red Cross as soon as he was able. They said they would have to wait until the morning, so "Doc" took matters into his own hands and loaded up the injured in cars to be transported to the hospital in Eau Claire. This is a scene from the north side of the village. (Courtesy of the Colfax Public Library.)

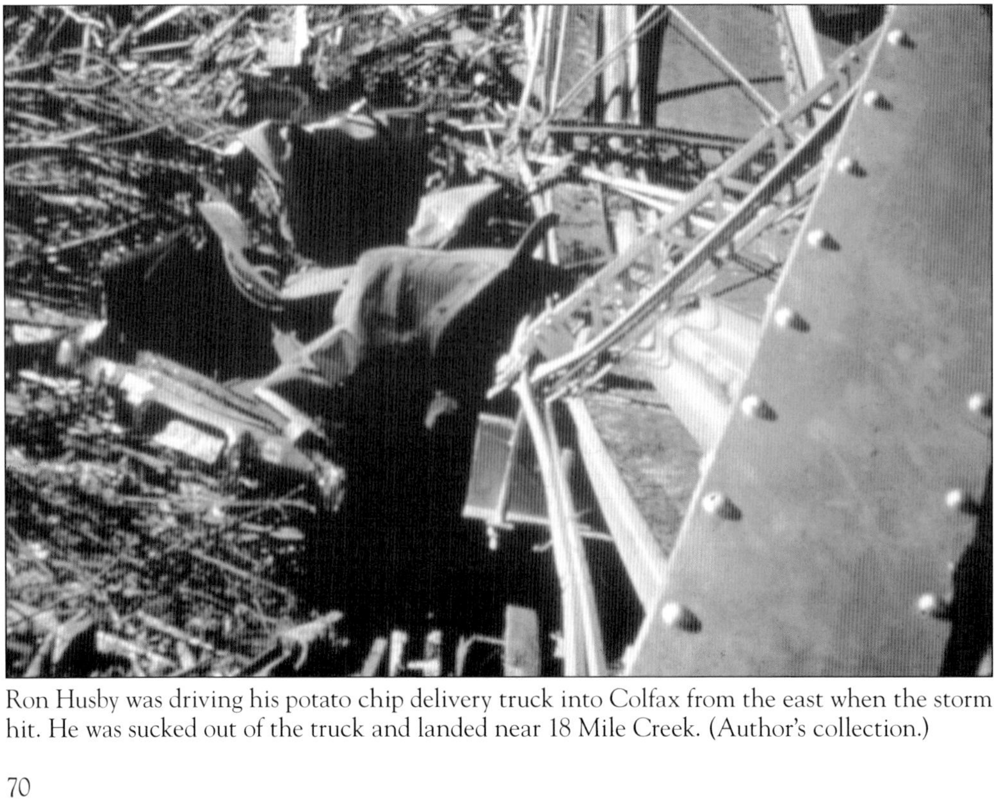

Ron Husby was driving his potato chip delivery truck into Colfax from the east when the storm hit. He was sucked out of the truck and landed near 18 Mile Creek. (Author's collection.)

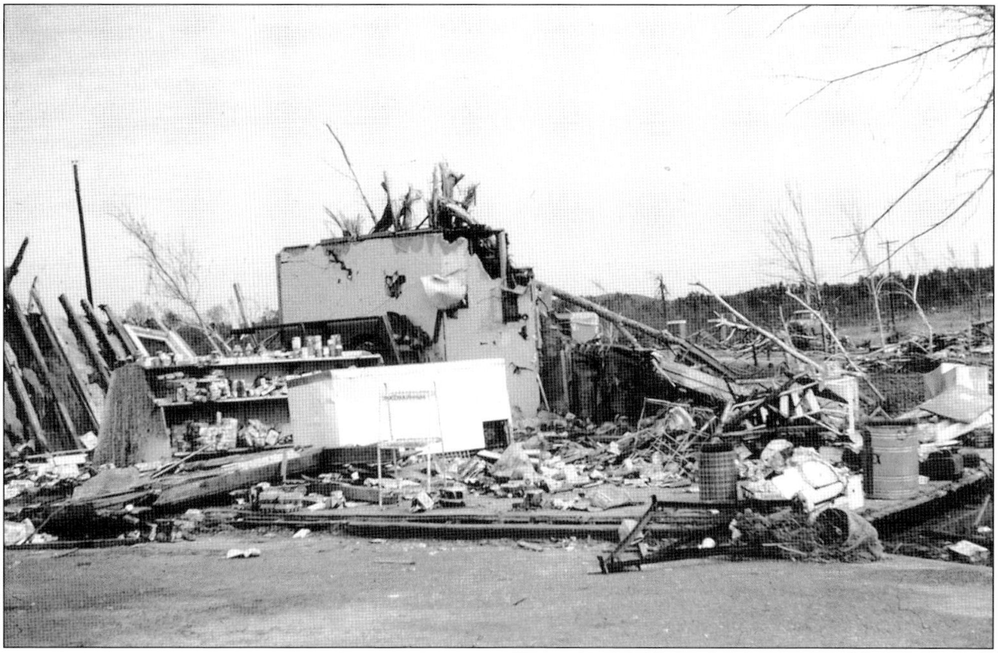

Some of the canned food items still remained on the shelves at the Gilberts' Four Corners Store, while others were not able to withstand the wind and force and were tossed among the litter. The Gilberts' car was also no match for the power of the storm. (Courtesy of Ron Blakely.)

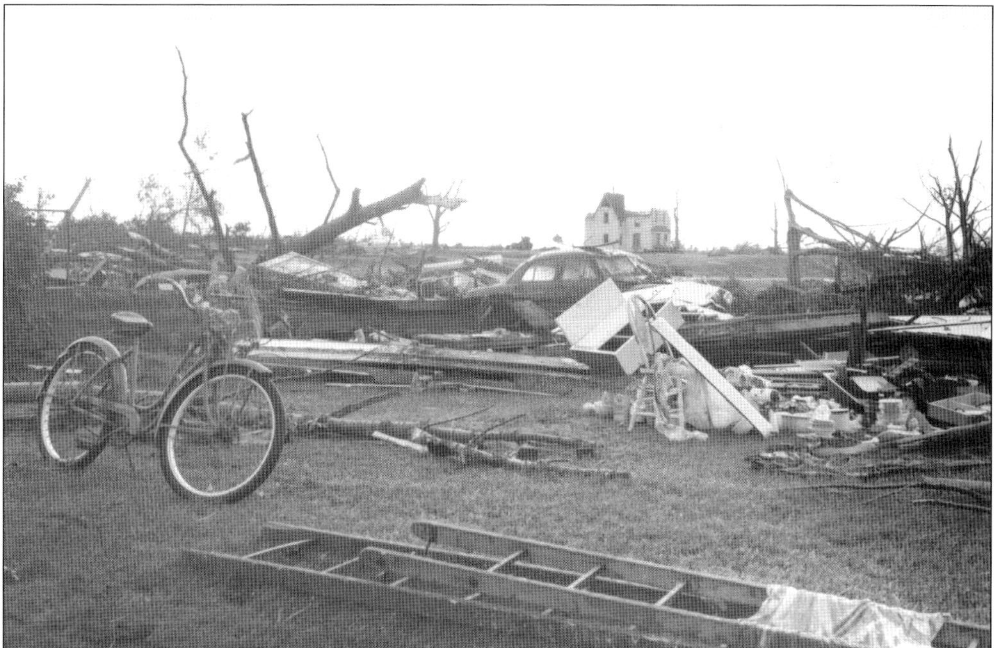

Few items were salvageable in this photograph taken on the north side of the village. Most of the homes did not have central air conditioning, so they had their windows open prior to the storm. Because of that, some survivors remembered belongings lifting into the air and floating around in a way that seemed unnatural. (Courtesy of John Russell.)

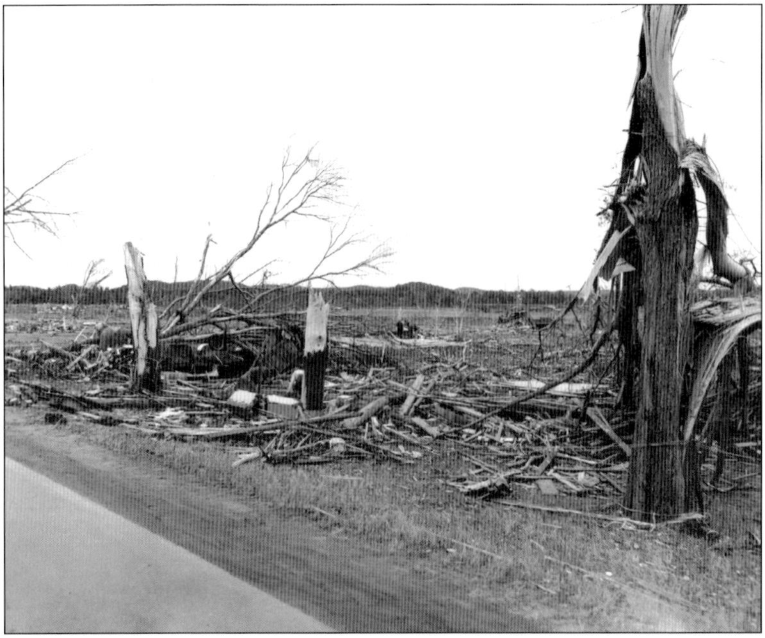

Pictured is a view of the damage on the north side of the village. Sifting through the unrecognizable piles of debris was a daunting task. One never knew what they would find, like a truck wrapped in a tree, trees with their bark completely removed, or perhaps a kitchen sink. (Courtesy of the Colfax Public Library.)

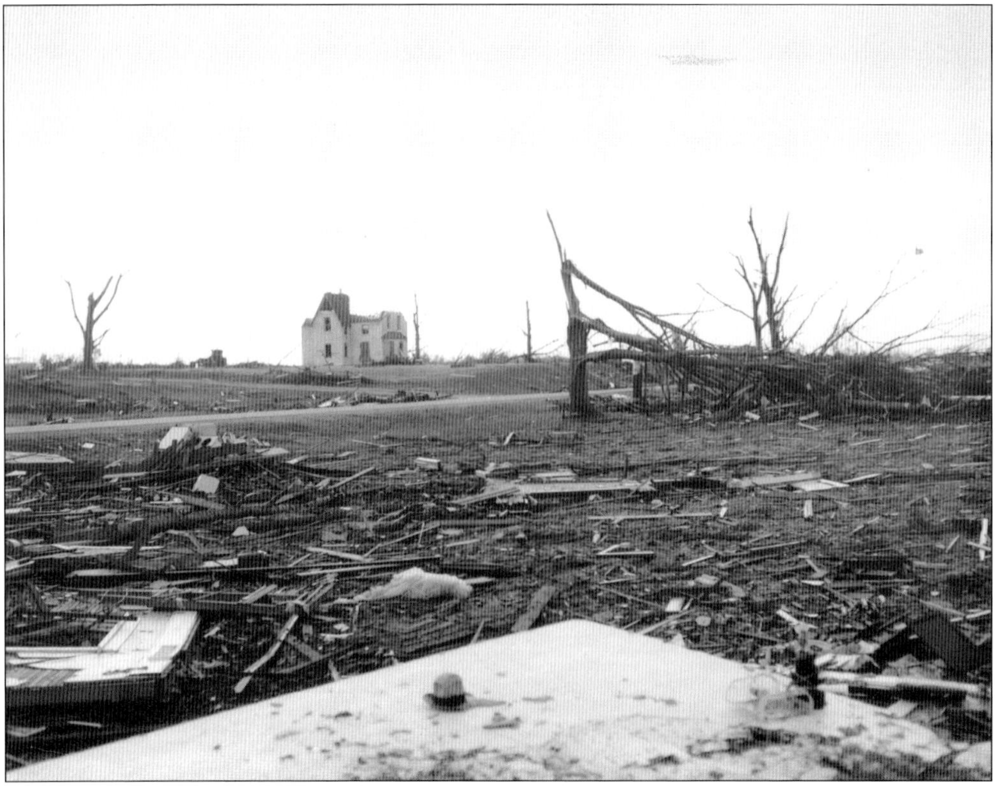

A man's hat landed on this concrete slab after the storm. There is a story of a Colfax resident's social security card being found near Cadott, Wisconsin, after the tornado. (Courtesy of John Russell.)

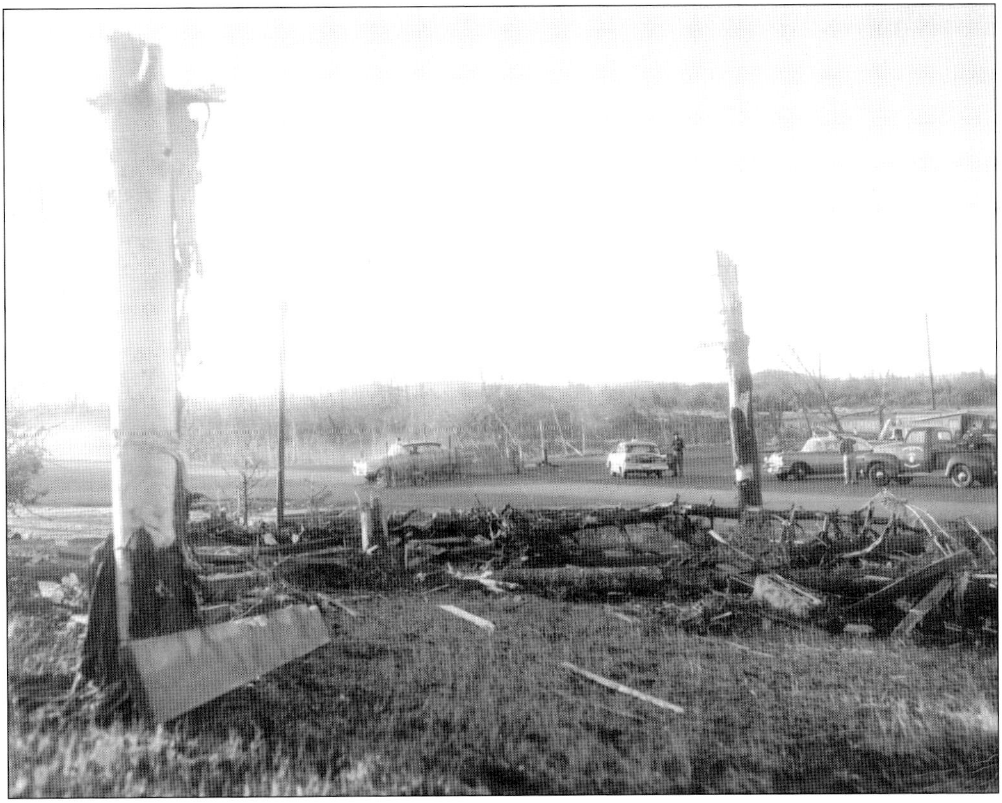

Hundreds of trees were knocked down and left in piles. The village was almost unrecognizable. (Courtesy of John Russell.)

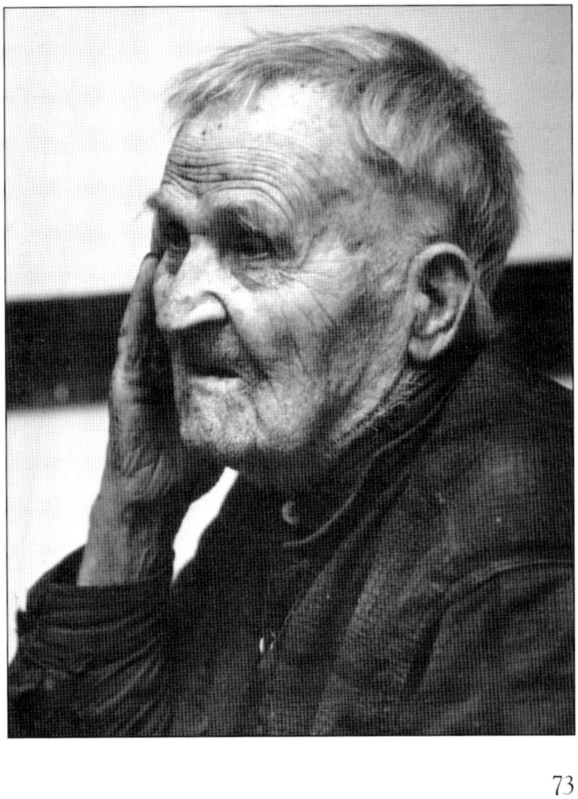

Here sits a dazed Ole Engen, who lived with Clarence and Minda Burling at the time of the tornado. Neither Engen nor Clarence were able to get to the basement in time, and Clarence got hit by the refrigerator and blacked out for a moment. (Courtesy of Ron Blakely.)

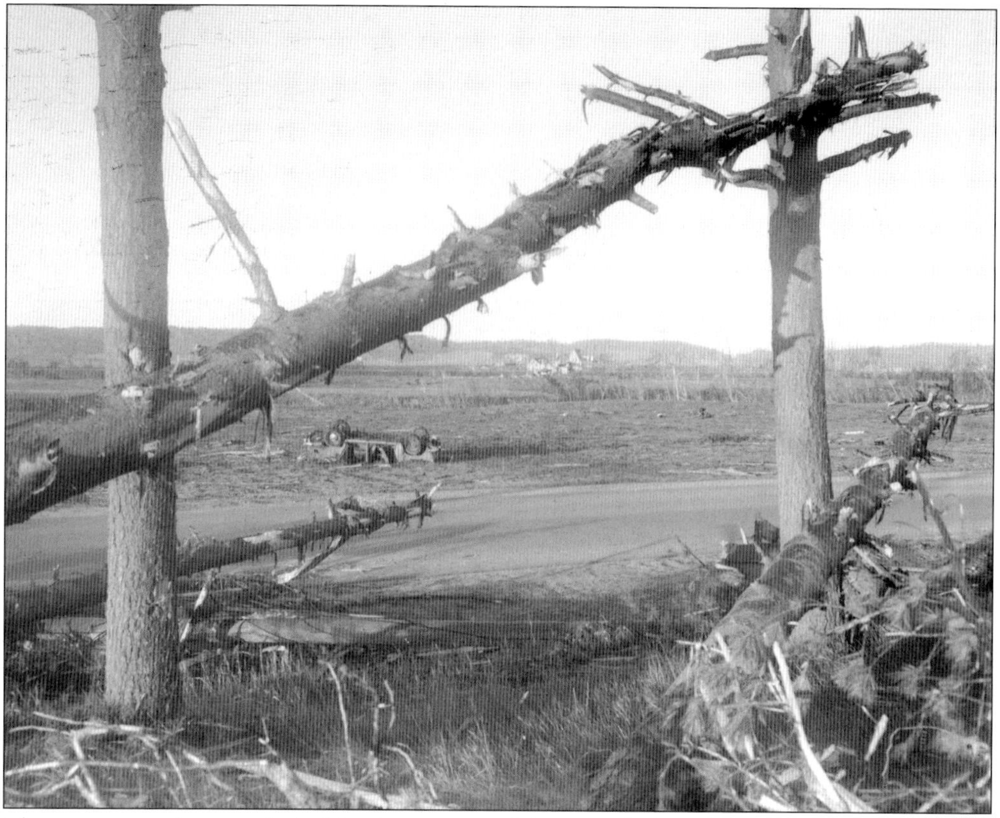

These trees stand as a symbol of the devastation of the tornado. Residents assessed their personal losses, but then reached out to help neighbors. Help came in from the local area and surrounding states. Men from northern Minnesota with chainsaws in hand came to help clean up the fallen trees. (Courtesy of John Russell.)

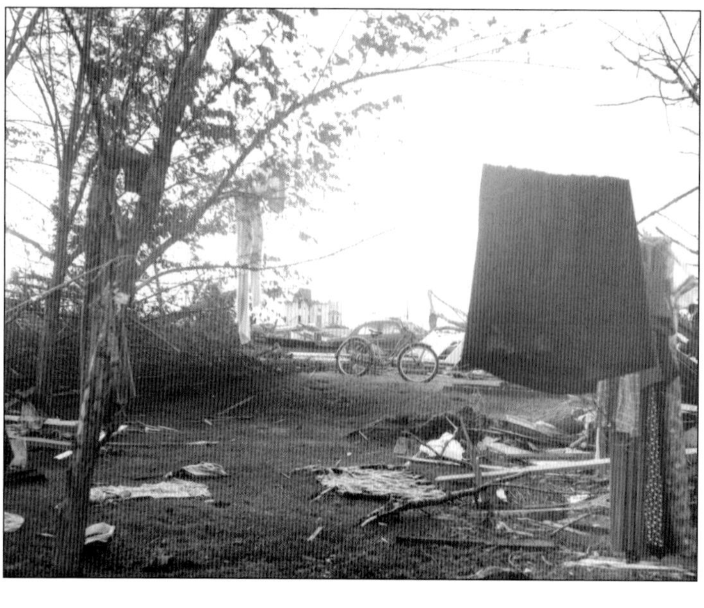

These pieces of clothing and fabric were scattered around the yard of a home on the north side of Colfax. Survivors remembered sand and plaster working its way out of their skin in the weeks following the storm. Property damage in the community was estimated to be upwards of $2 million. (Courtesy of John Russell.)

At the Steve Figura home, this view looks south from University Avenue showing what was left of the Odd Lindberg, Phillip Felland, and James Schindler farms in the background. It would take a lot of strength to recover, but giving up was not an option. (Courtesy of the Colfax Public Library.)

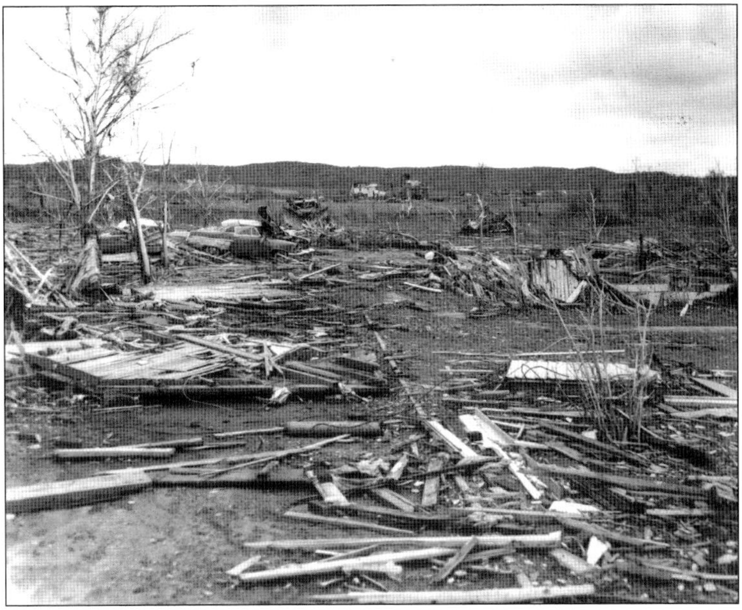

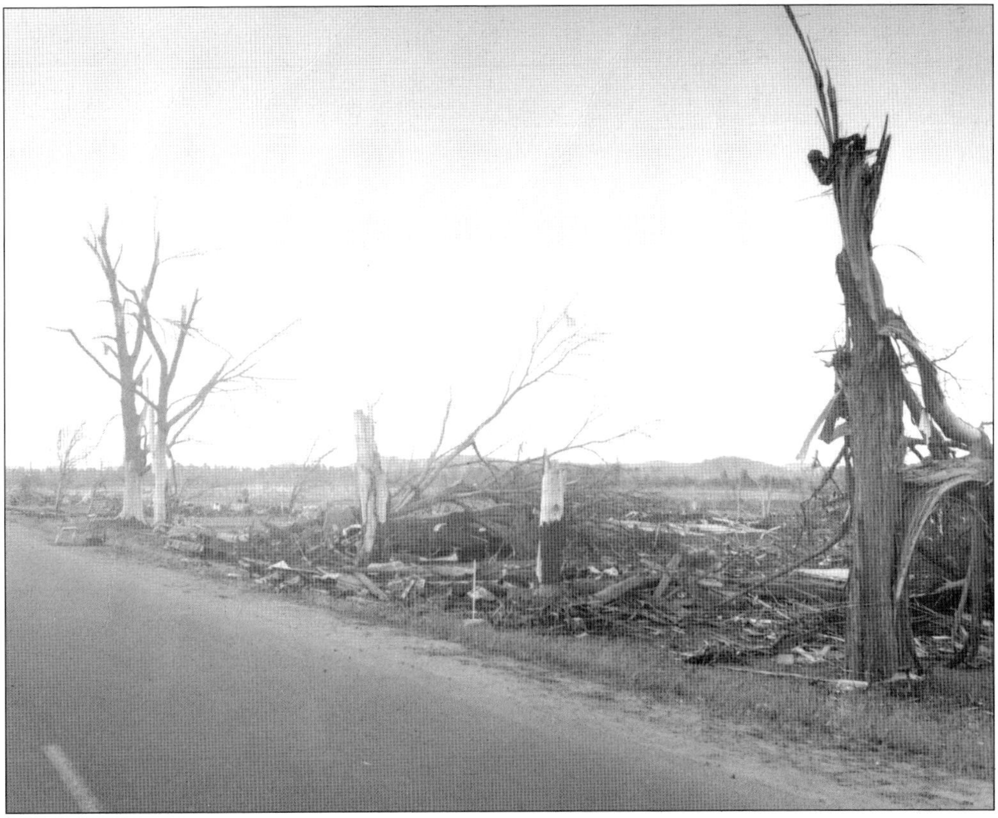

Only a few trunks and branches were left of the hundreds of trees within the village limits. Because so many trees were down, it was impossible to get into the village. Residents immediately got out chainsaws to clear roads so the injured could be taken to local hospitals. (Courtesy of John Russell.)

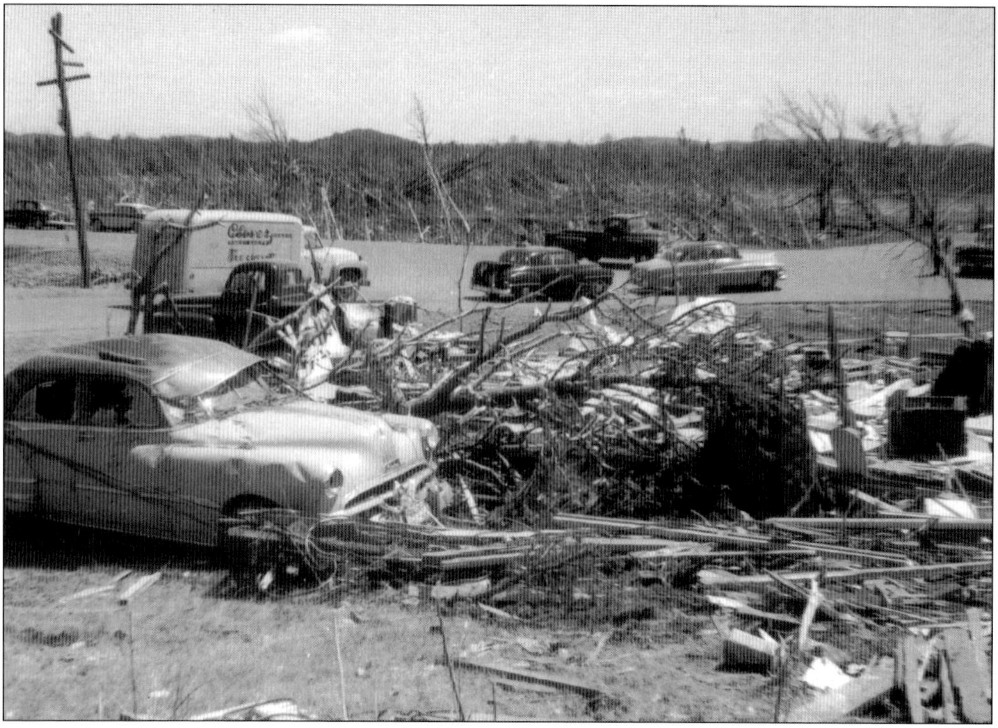

Pictured is another horrifying scene of the mess that the tornado left. North of town at the farm of Roger and Arlene Hones, a piece of paper was found belonging to Ole Repaal in the pasture. Repaal's farm was south of their pasture. (Courtesy of the Colfax Public Library.)

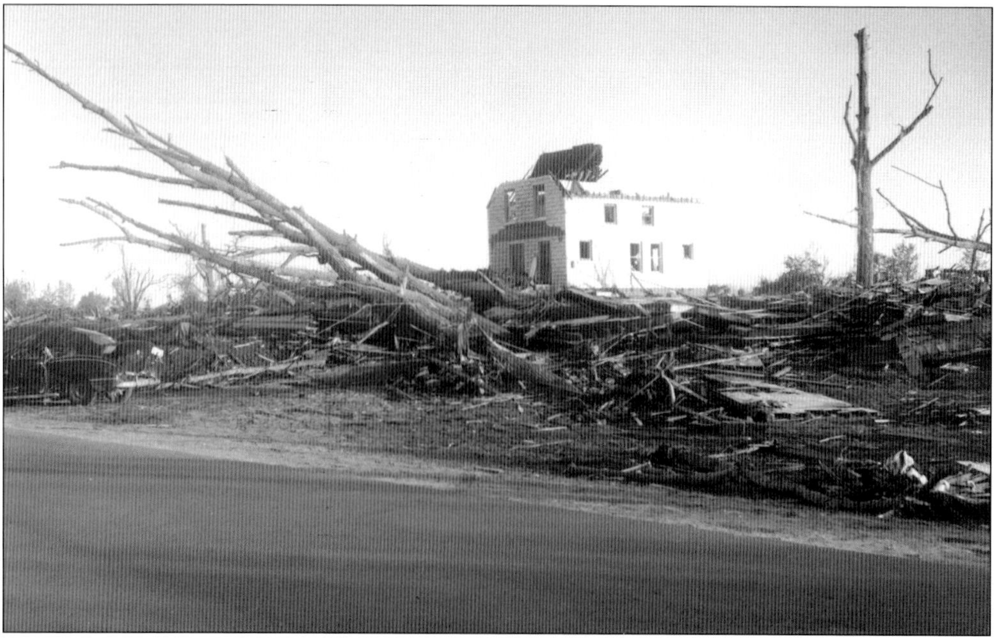

Some curtains are still hanging out of the windows of the Clarence and Minda Burling home on University Avenue. Paperwork from inside homes was found wedged in trees in the yards. (Courtesy of John Russell.)

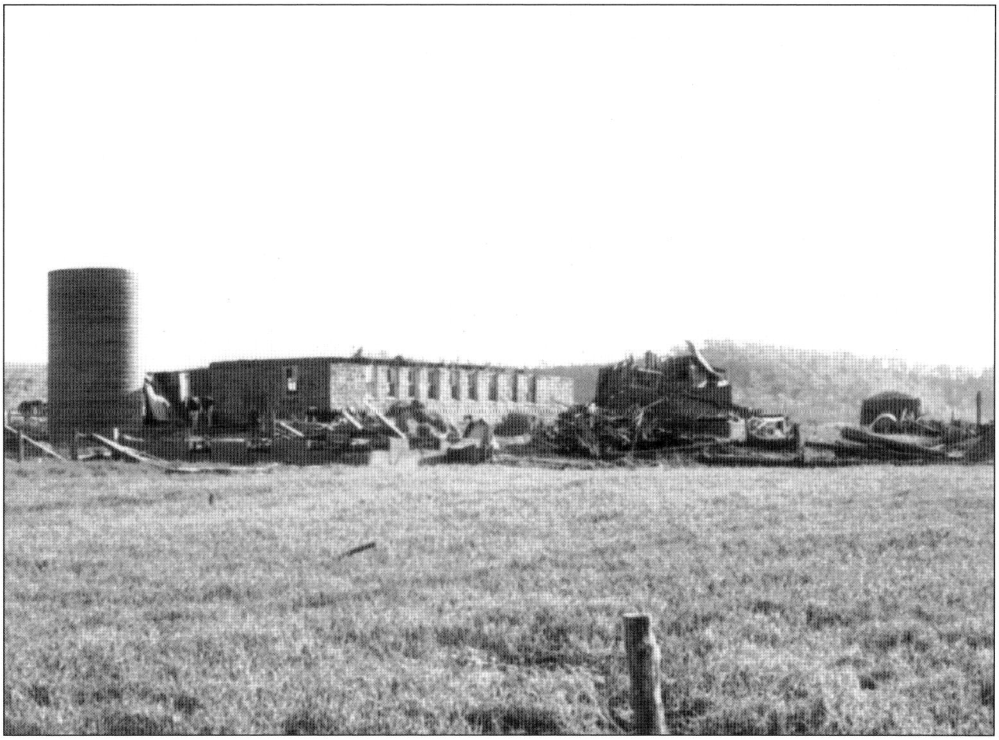

A few stray cattle are seen beside what is left of the barn they once called home. The entire top portion of the barn was ripped off. Because the storm happened in early June, farmers were able to replant and recover for the season. (Courtesy of Joan Shong.)

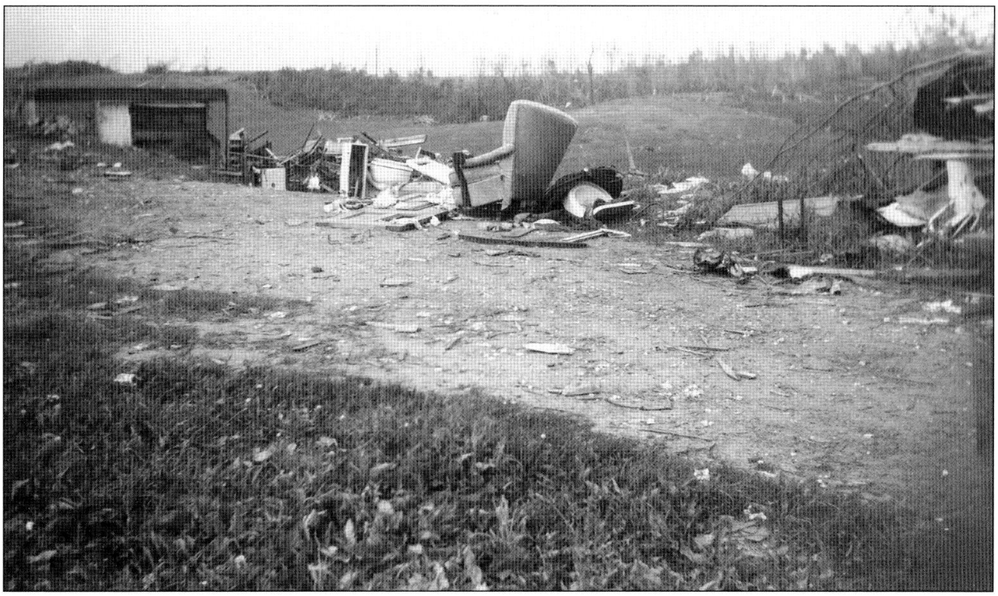

The bathroom sink and toilet that were once part of the Alvin and Clara Fjelstad home were definitely relocated as a result of the tornado. The living room chair also appears to have some damage. The Fjelstad home was just east of the village. (Courtesy of Diane Haugle Hodgson.)

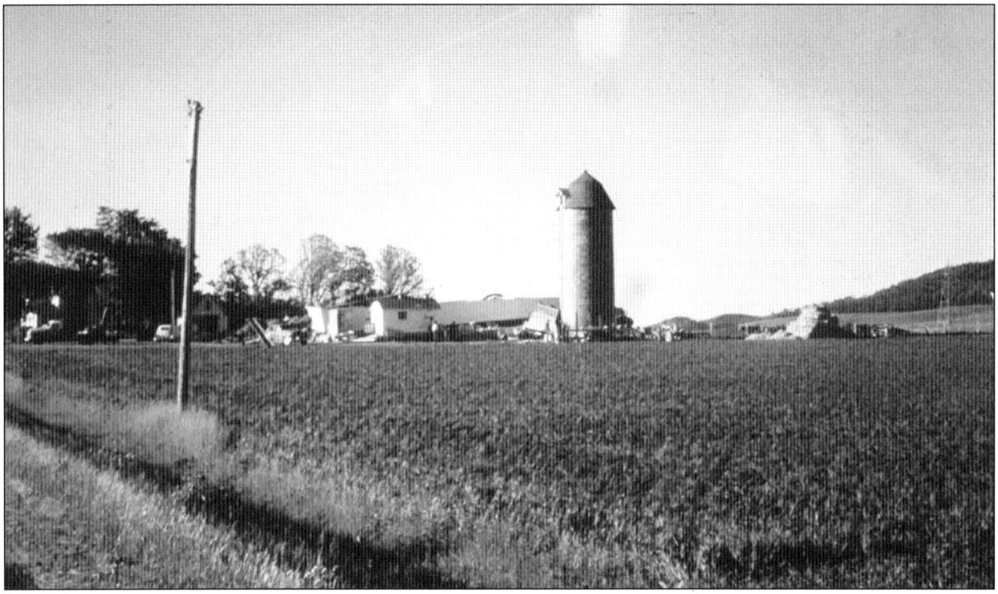

Donald and Dawn Bergeson's farm, northeast of Colfax on Highway A, also had major damage. The tornado started at about 6:30 p.m. near Woodville, Wisconsin, in St. Croix County and lasted until about 8:00 p.m. when it finally lifted in Clark County just west of Withee, Wisconsin. It touched down in Colfax at 7:07 p.m. (Courtesy of Lyle Christenson.)

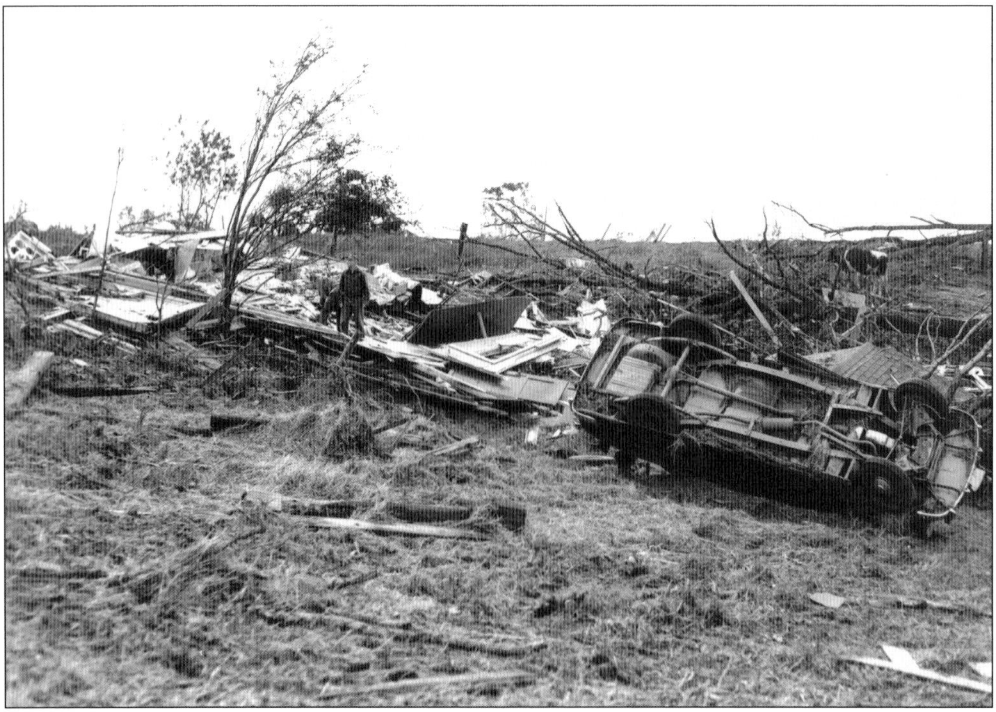

Countless hours were spent sifting through what remained after the storm left town. Recovery of materials that could be used again was essential, as well as discovering lost personal belongings to renew a feeling of hope. Even the animals needed a little hint of normal. (Courtesy of the Colfax Public Library.)

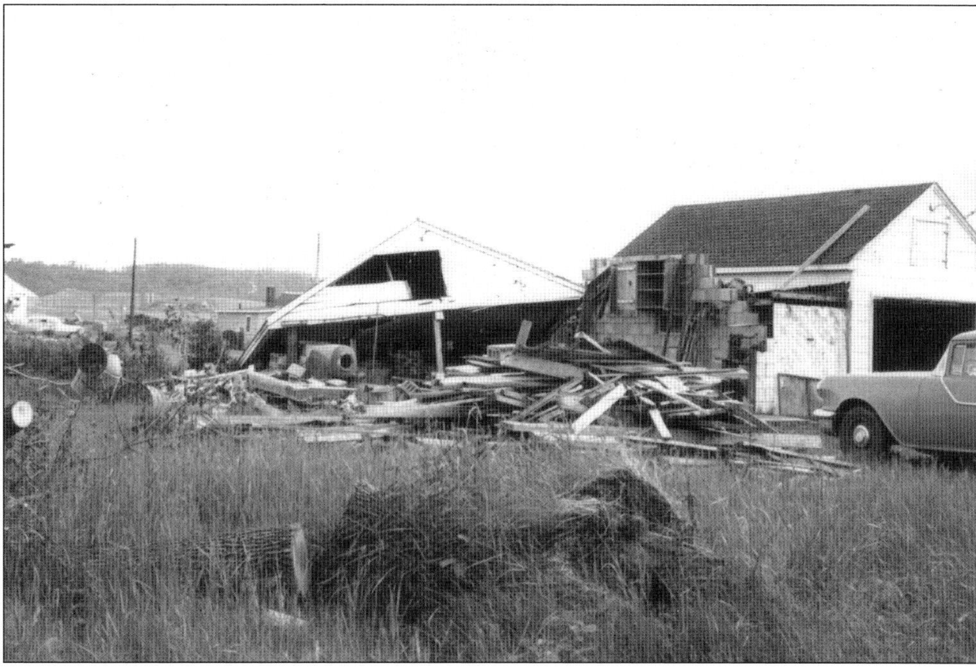

A pair of ladders are leaning up against the only wall left standing of what had been a garage. Everything that could be salvaged was, including furniture, boards and other building supplies, clothing, and personal belongings. (Courtesy of Joan Shong.)

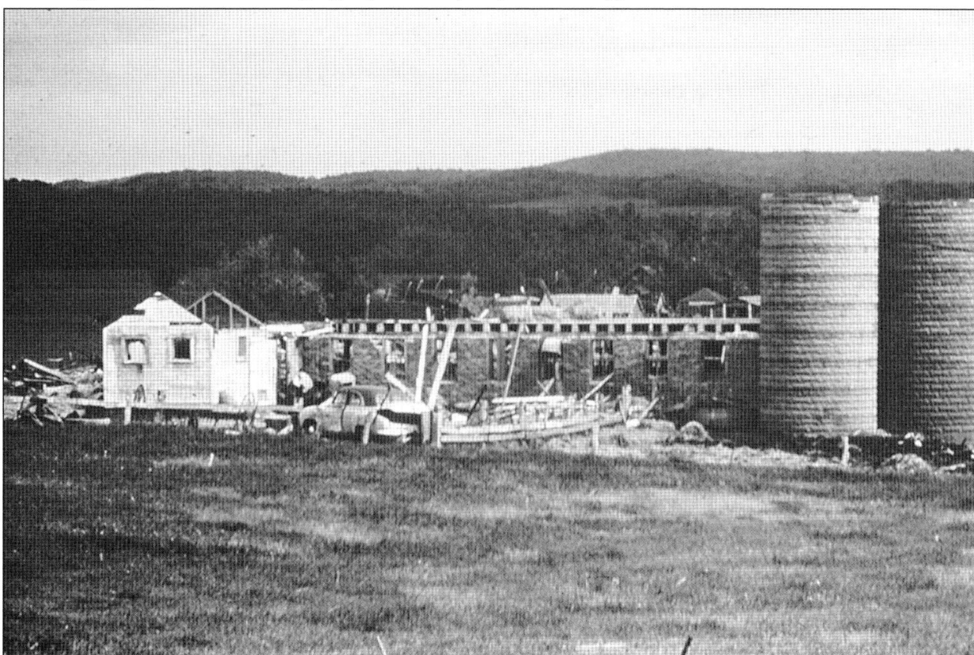

This photograph shows Frank and Arlene Henderson's farm on the south edge of the village. When the storm began in the Baldwin area, there were actually three smaller tornados that could be seen from miles away. The three combined into the F5 tornado that entered Colfax. (Courtesy of Diane Haugle Hodgson.)

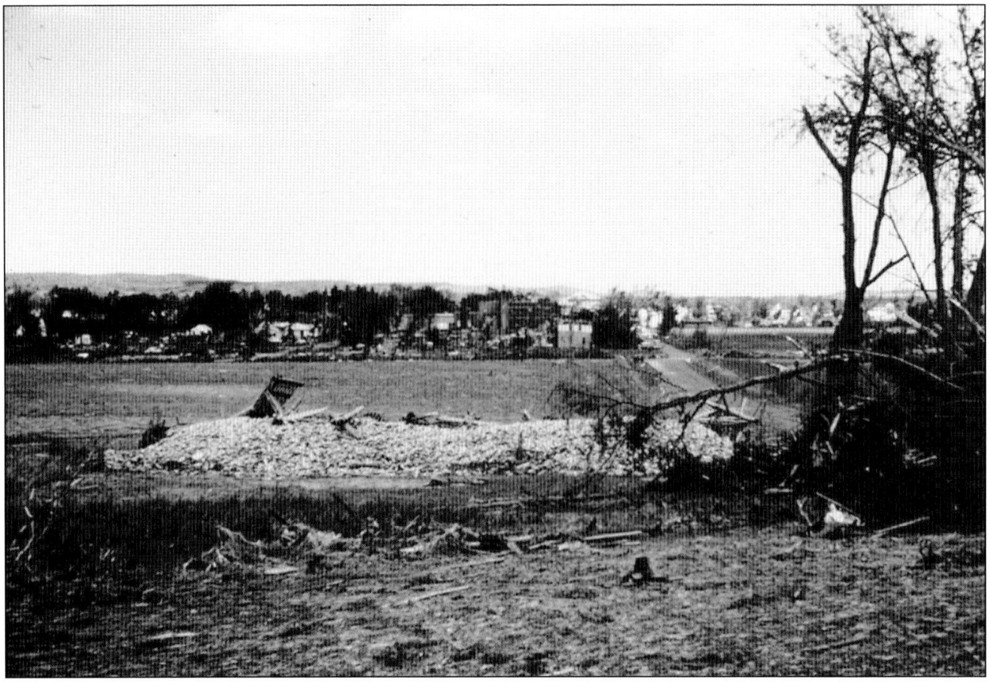

Herb and Mildred Ziebell lost their corn crib, and its contents lay strewn about. This view looks north from the south end of Dunn Street, with the creamery and the school in the background. Herb, who was the local police chief, was kept busy all around town after the tornado. (Courtesy of Diane Haugle Hodgson.)

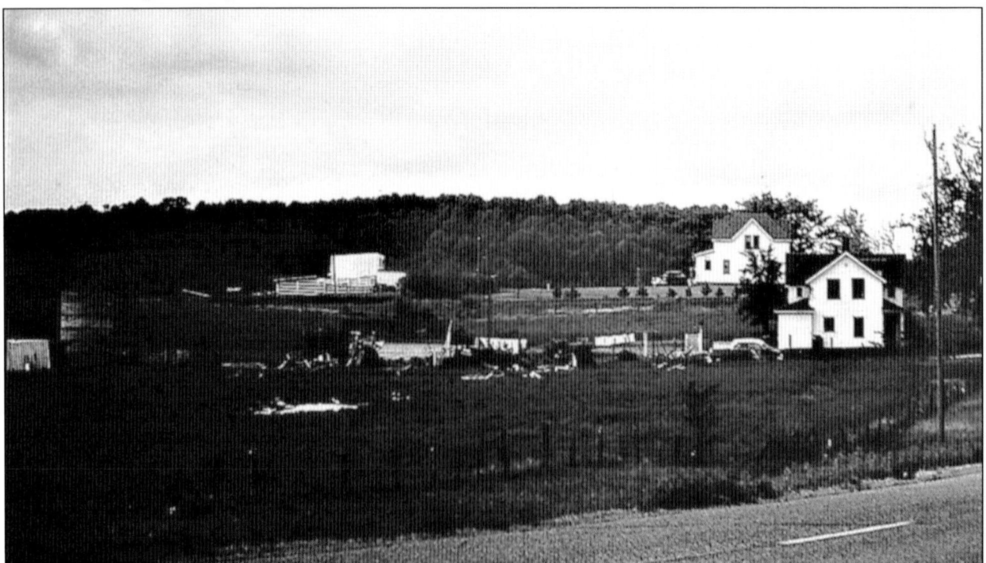

The white house at right belonged to Gaylord and Esther Thorson, who lived south of town near Marvin Volkman's Meat Market. Gaylord was in Milwaukee at the time of the tornado, and when he returned to his hotel after supper, the desk clerk asked him if he knew that Colfax had suffered from the tornado. He drove straight home to find his family fine and his home slightly damaged. (Courtesy of Diane Haugle Hodgson.)

Two

Recovery and Rebuilding

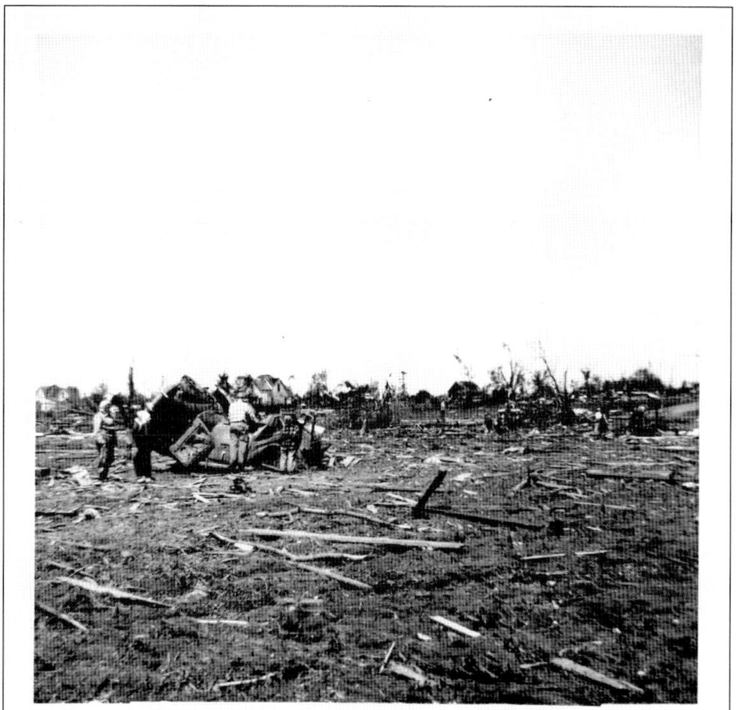

This tangled mess was once two automobiles. They were twisted together by the storm and landed in a field across the road from the Fjelstad home on the north side. They are being surveyed by curious people to see if anything could be salvaged from the pile of metal. (Courtesy of Thelma Mickelson Kettle.)

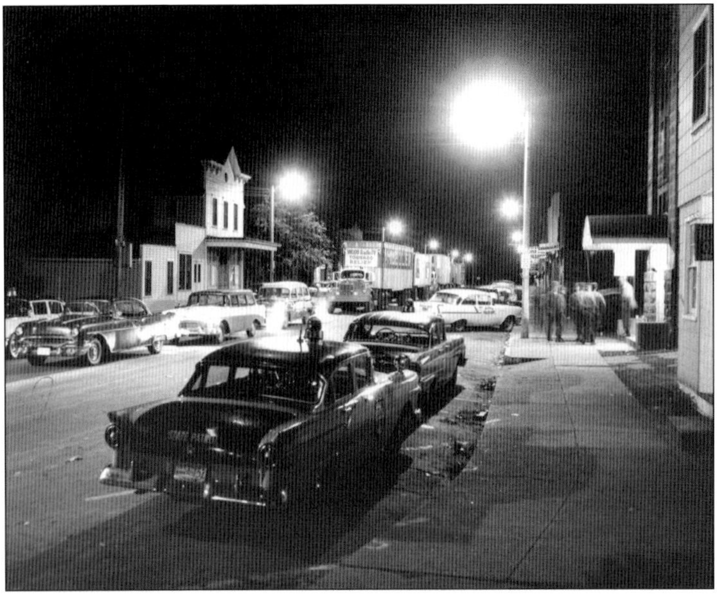

After a command post was set up in the Colfax Municipal Building, there were lists made of those injured or missing. People who had working cars or trucks helped transport the severely injured to hospitals, while the less severely injured were treated in the basement of the Colfax Municipal Building until they were able to be transported to area hospitals. (Courtesy of John Russell.)

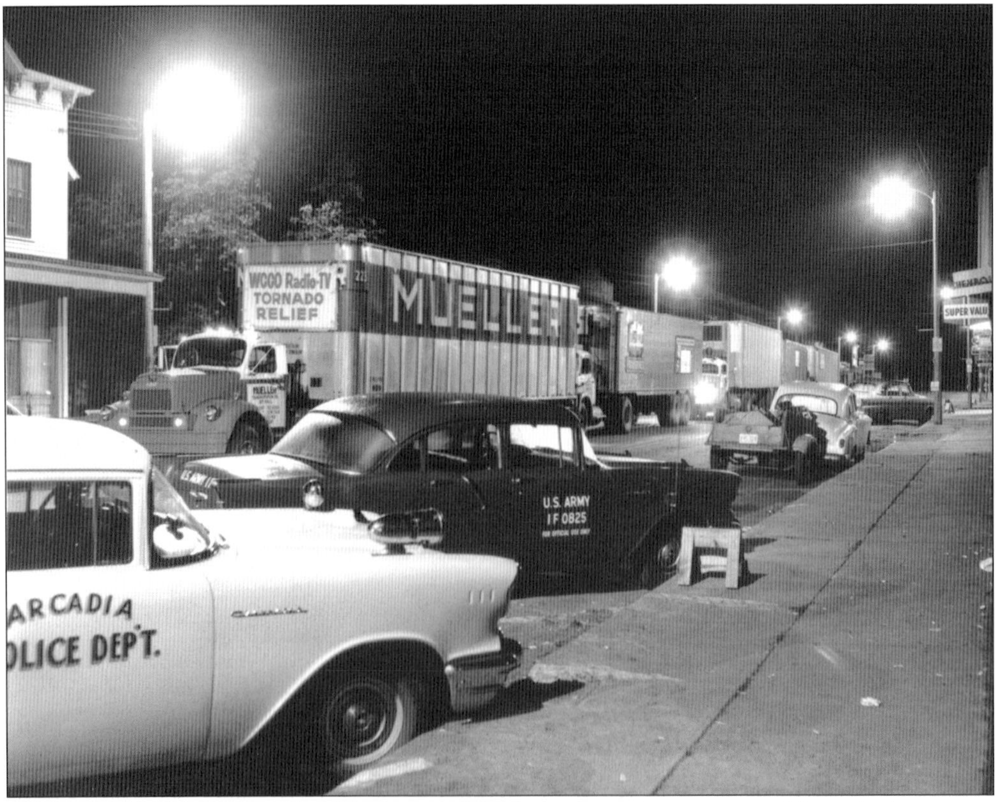

The downtown district suffered little damage. As early as the evening of June 4, there were agencies showing up to help in whatever way they could. Seen here is a police car from Arcadia, Wisconsin, a car from the US Army, and five semi trucks with donations from WCCO Radio out of St. Paul, Minnesota. WCCO Radio listeners had collected over 50 tons of food and clothing to contribute to the relief efforts. (Courtesy of John Russell.)

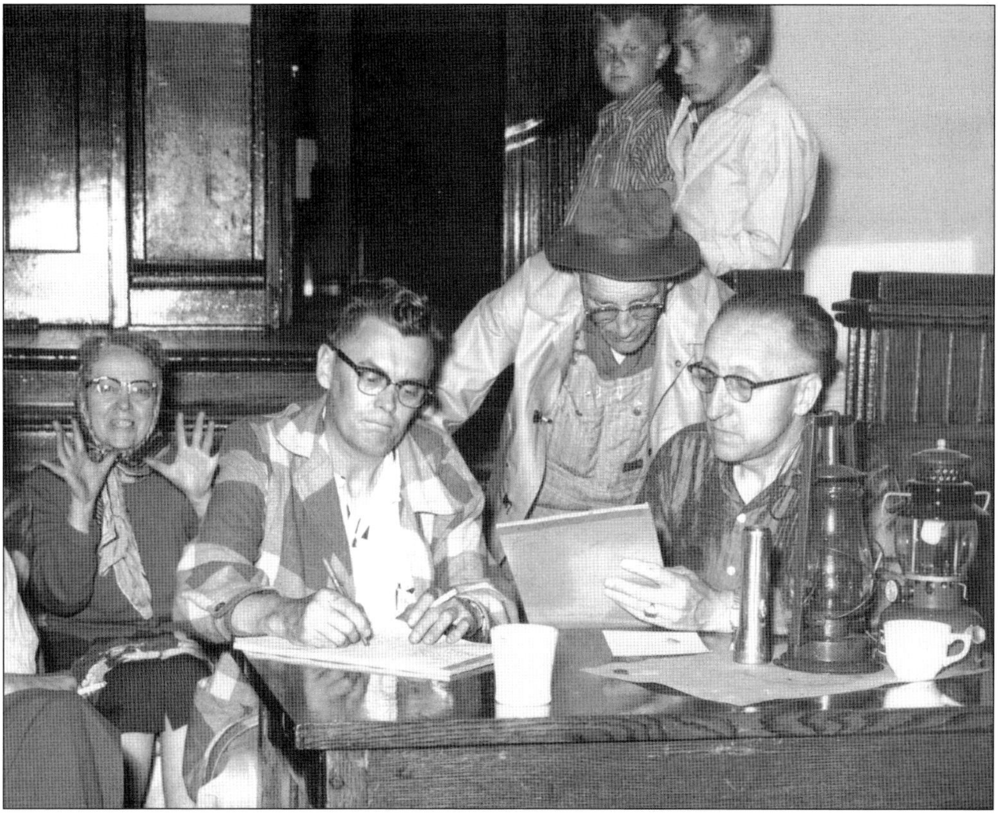

Many people sprang into action after the storm had passed. Pictured here just inside the front doors of the Colfax Municipal Building are, from left to right, Emma Everson, Noel Hilson, Bill Everson (village mayor at the time), and Sliver Pooler. The two boys in the back are Donnie and John Hill. The municipal building was the center for communication to determine the injured, survivors, and the missing. (Courtesy of Ron Blakely.)

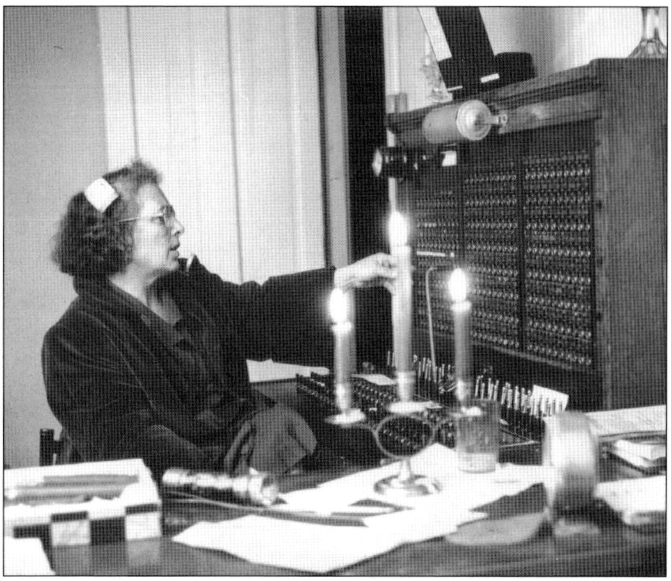

Nora Wiseman is shown trying to keep the telephone lines open to the outside world by candlelight. Due to the difficulty of driving because of the fallen trees and other debris, the telephone lines were essential to allow concerned family to check up on their loved ones. It was reported that the Red Cross distributed more than $150,000 in assistance to those who had suffered losses as a result of the tornado. (Courtesy of Ron Blakely.)

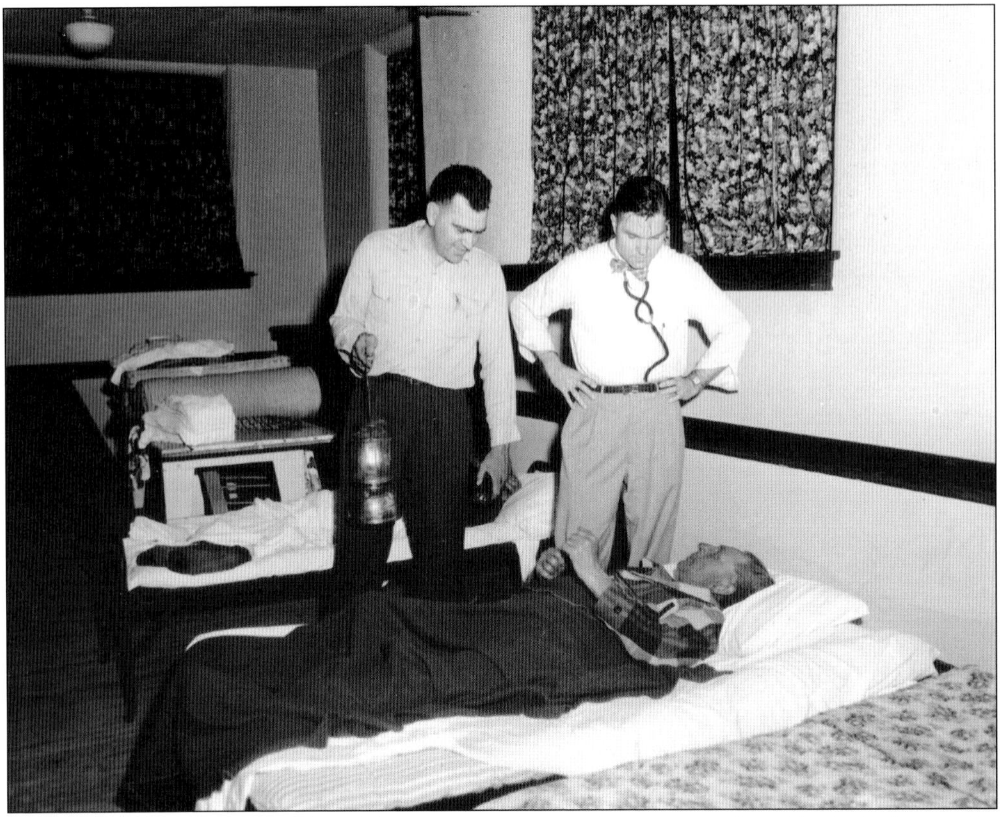

People who were injured and unable to get to a hospital were treated and looked after in the basement of the Colfax Municipal Building. Shown here is veterinarian Dr. John Thomas (left) and Dr. P. Murphy (right) checking on their patient Bill Stockland. (Courtesy of the Colfax Public Library.)

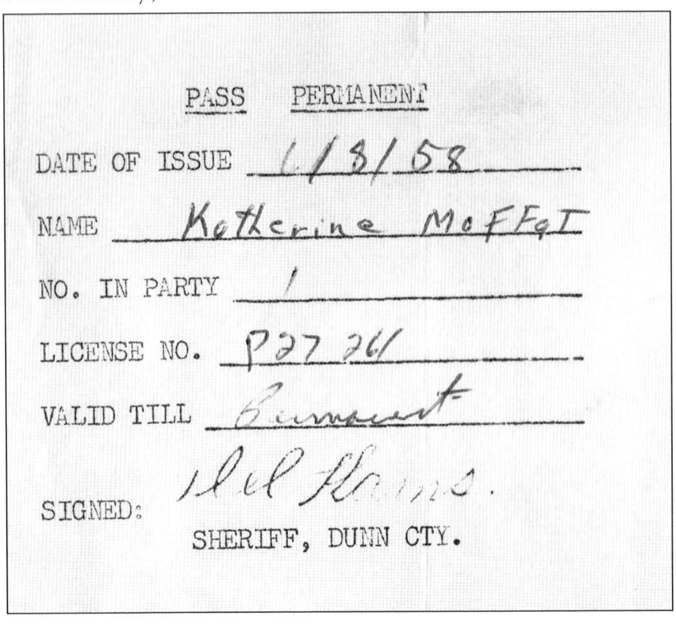

PASS PERMANENT

DATE OF ISSUE 1/8/58

NAME Katherine MoFFaT

NO. IN PARTY 1

LICENSE NO. P27 261

VALID TILL Permanent

SIGNED: Del Hams.

SHERIFF, DUNN CTY.

The National Guard and local sheriff units were called in to help direct traffic and keep the roads open for vehicles to get injured people to hospitals. Here is a pass issued to Katherine Moffat. She must have been able to prove that she had relatives or something within town that she needed to go check on or help. (Author's collection.)

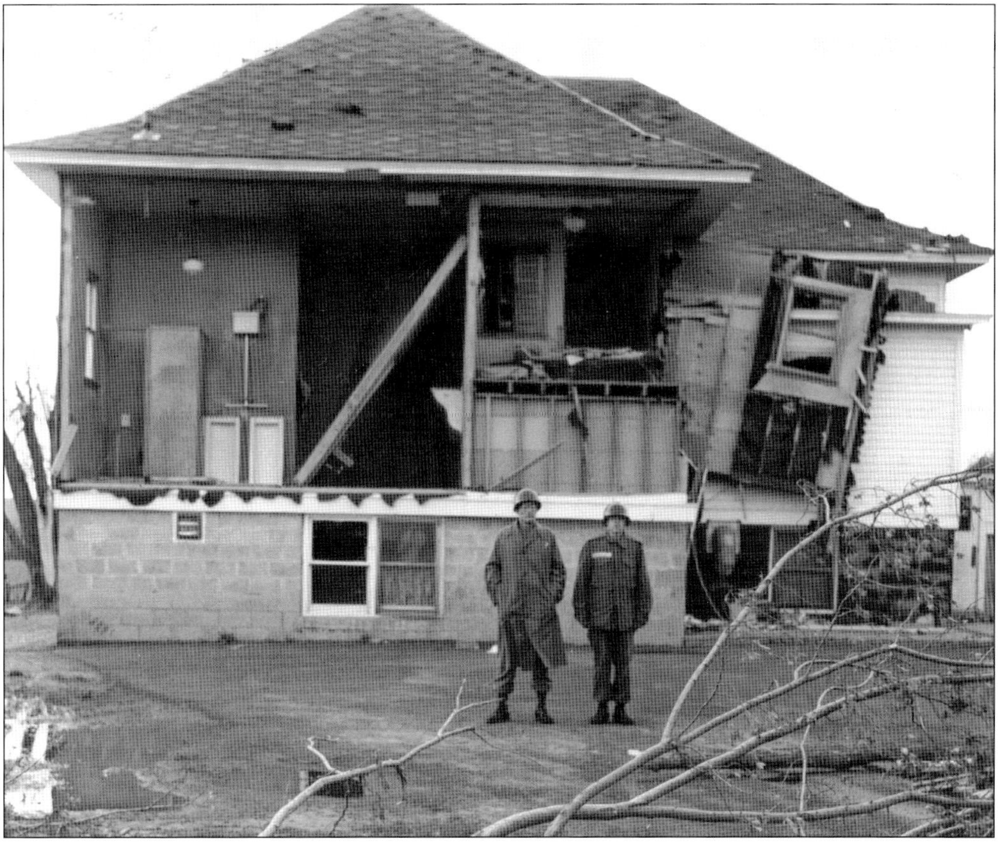

The Knapp Settlement School southwest of Colfax was also hit by the tornado. The storm tore off an entire wall of the school, exposing the boy's restroom and nurse's office. Two National Guard members stand guard watching over the area. The National Guard brought in about 175 members the night of the storm to help with recovery and to stop the looting that had started as early as the night of the storm. The National Guard was on duty in Colfax until Sunday. (Courtesy of Ron Blakely.)

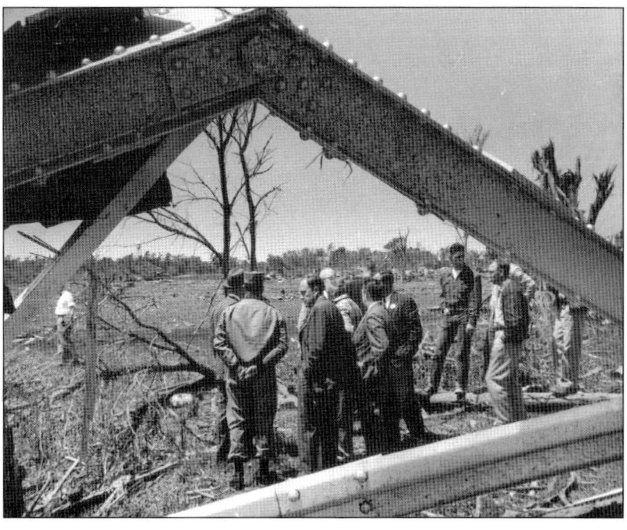

National Guard and state officials visit the ruins. Lt. Col. C.L. Davenport of Elk Mound, Wisconsin, and Capt. Richard Ryan of Eau Claire were in charge of organizing and dispersing the National Guard throughout the area during the relief efforts. (Courtesy of Ron Blakely.)

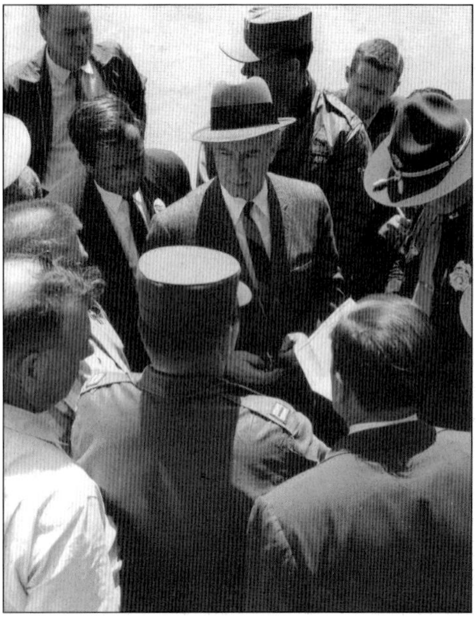

Wisconsin governor Vernon Thompson visited the areas affected by the tornado by car and airplane the day after. He proclaimed it a disaster area, which made aid available to help with cleanup and rebuilding. Thompson also activated the National Guard the night of the tornado to aid in securing the area. (Courtesy of Ron Blakely.)

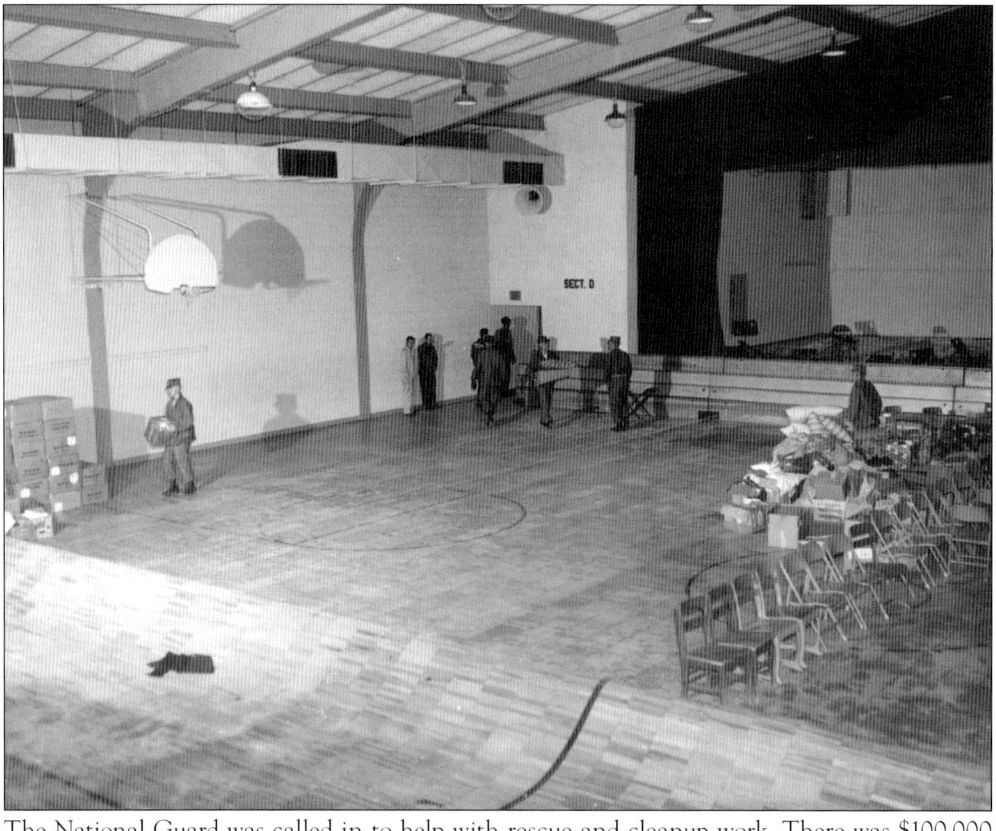

The National Guard was called in to help with rescue and cleanup work. There was $100,000 worth of damage done to the Colfax School, most of which was to the gymnasium floor. The roof leaked and the floor swelled as much as three feet down the center. The floor had just been installed. (Courtesy of John Russell.)

The National Guard was called in to help with rescue and cleanup work. They unloaded the semi-trailers that were filled with donated goods from around the area. The drivers donated their time to the cleanup effort and brought goods to Colfax one day after the tornado. (Courtesy of John Russell.)

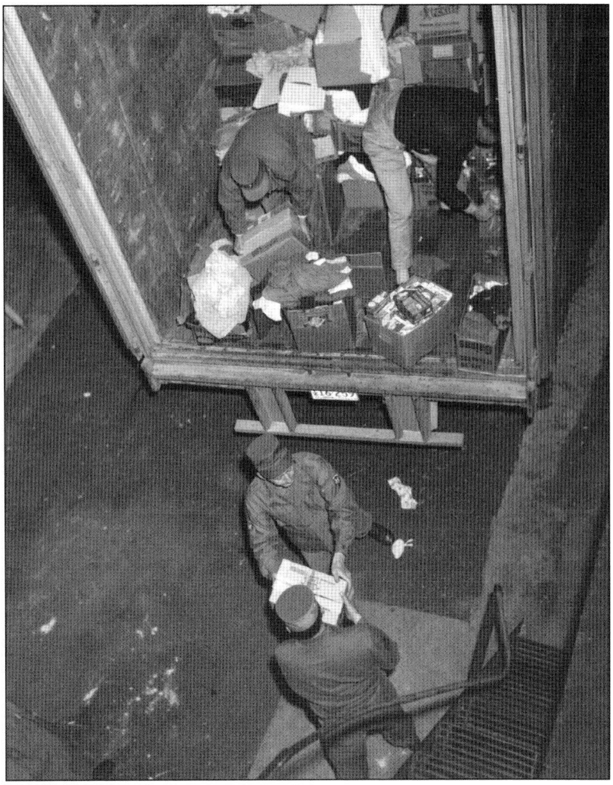

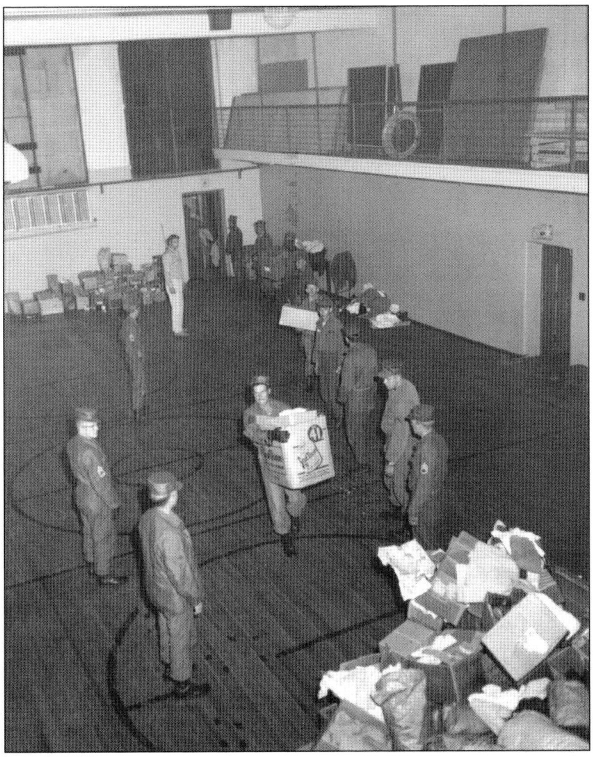

The National Guard is pictured here hauling boxes of supplies into the gym at the high school. The tornado left the community bewildered and confused. However, thanks to the efforts of numerous organizations and surrounding community members, cleanup was not as difficult as it could have been in spite of the horrendous tragedy. (Courtesy of John Russell.)

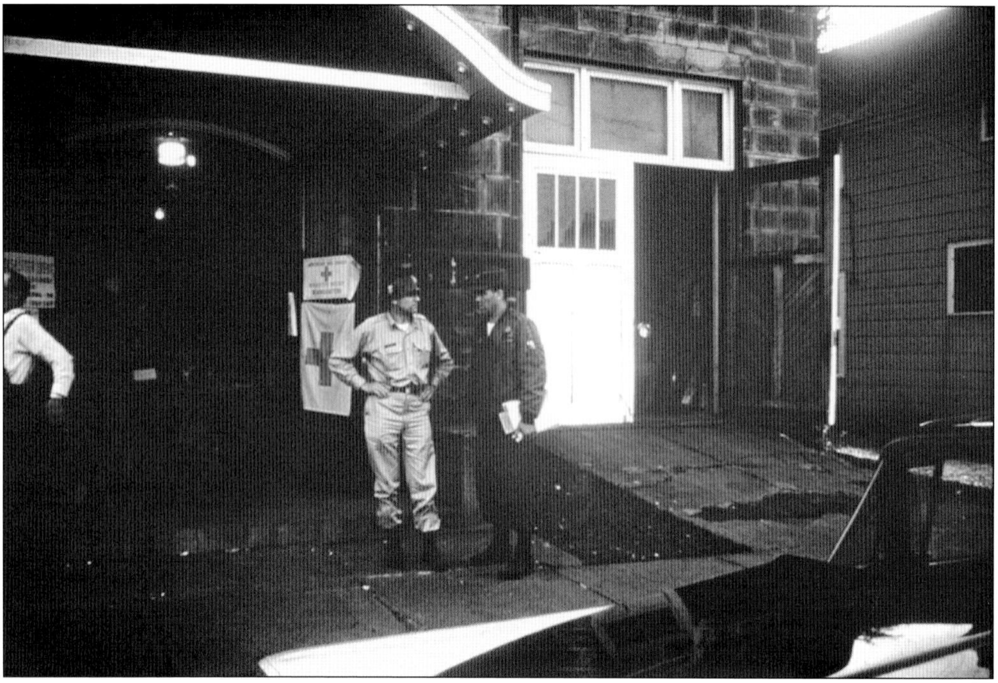

Volunteers from the Red Cross and the National Guard used the municipal building as their headquarters to be able to efficiently and effectively communicate and assist community members in need. On the left is the entrance to the building, and on the right is the garage housing an unharmed firetruck. (Courtesy of Diane Haugle Hodgson.)

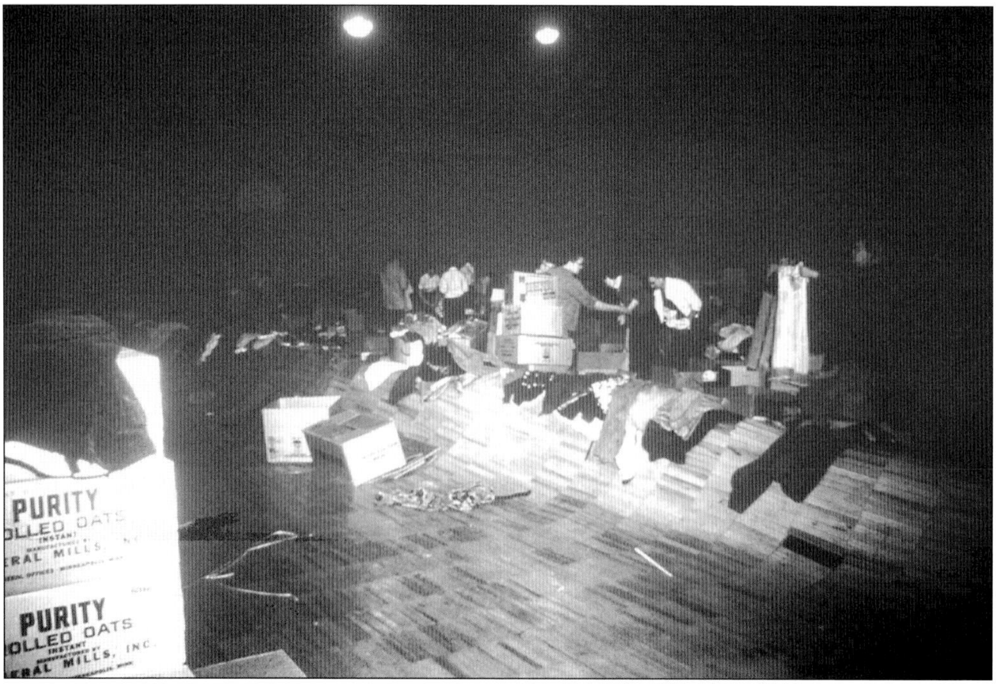

The Colfax School was still standing after the storm but had damage to the roof in several places, but the majority was over the gym. (Courtesy of Diane Haugle Hodgson.)

Here is an inside look at Colfax High School, which served as a central location for distributing much-needed personal goods to the survivors. The losses suffered by community members were eased by the generosity of strangers willing to donate everything from clothing to kitchen appliances. (Courtesy of Diane Haugle Hodgson.)

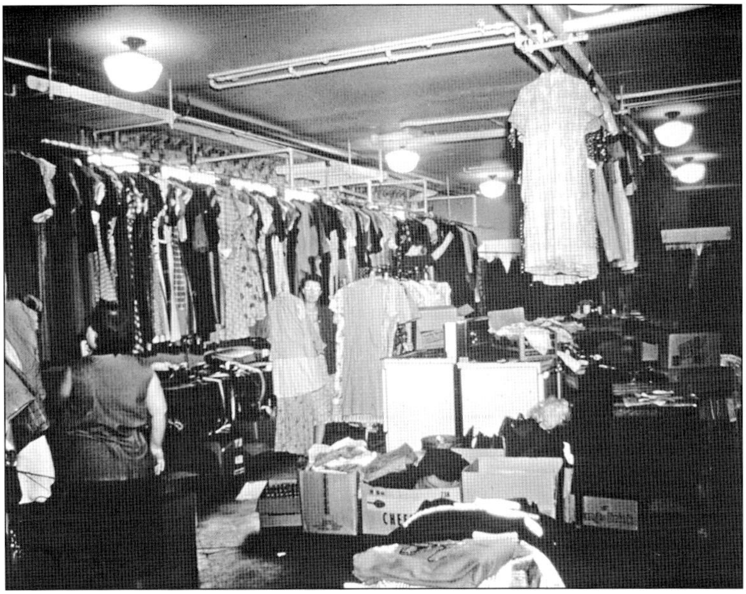

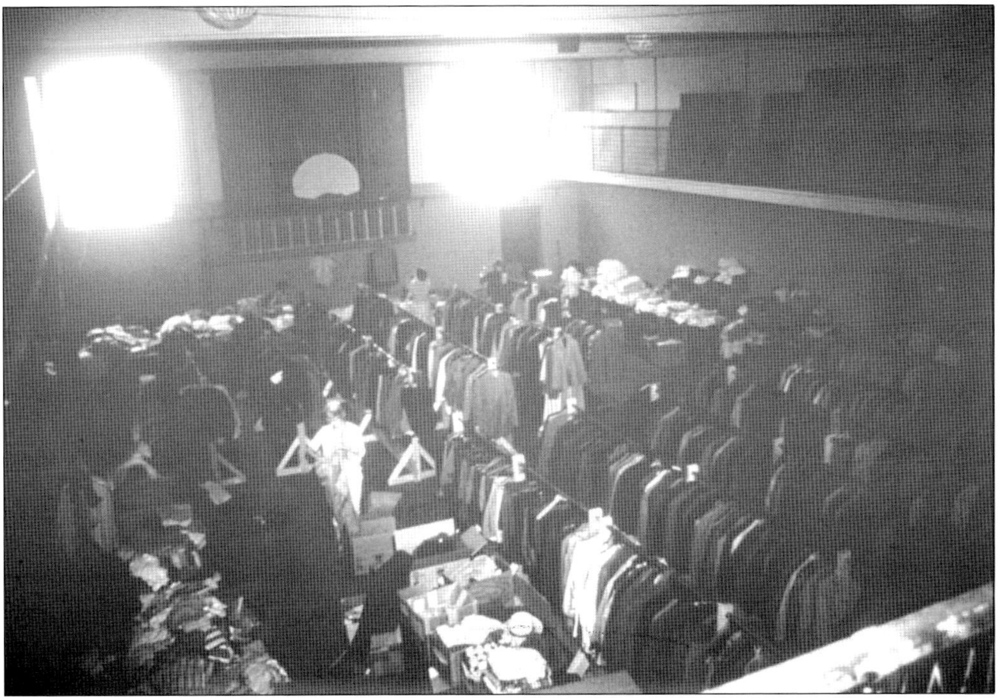

These ladies are busy in the high school sorting clothing that had been donated to the victims. Donations of money, clothing, food, and just about anything that was needed came pouring into the community as soon as an hour after the tornado hit. (Courtesy of Diane Haugle Hodgson.)

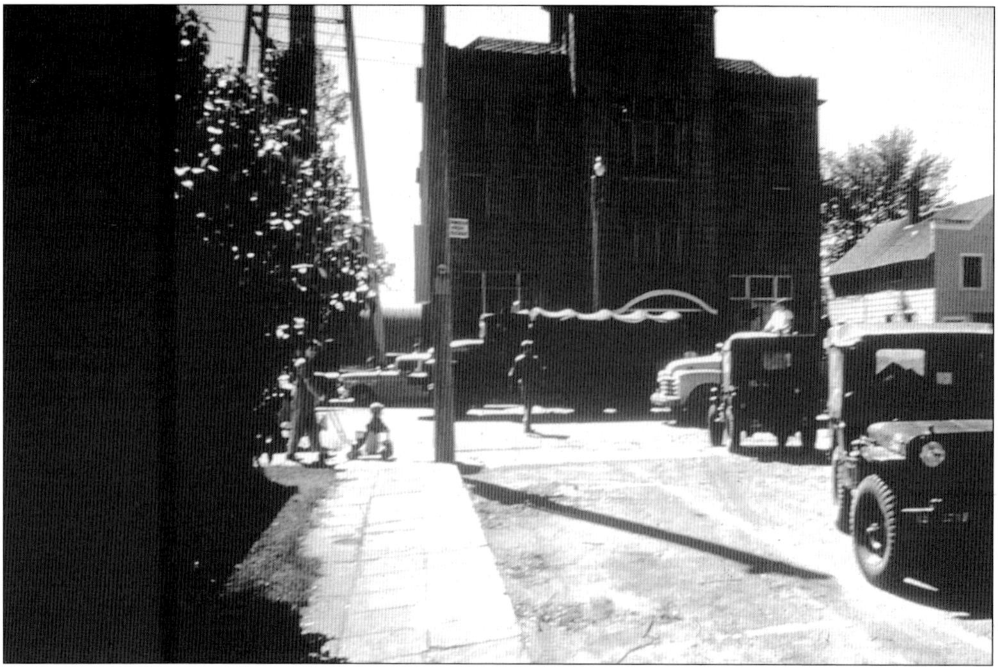

The municipal building acted as the headquarters for the recovery efforts. Not only were the injured treated and survivors accounted for there, it was also where the National Guard spearheaded its rescue efforts from. Its central location between the damaged areas made it an ideal location. (Courtesy of Diane Haugle Hodgson.)

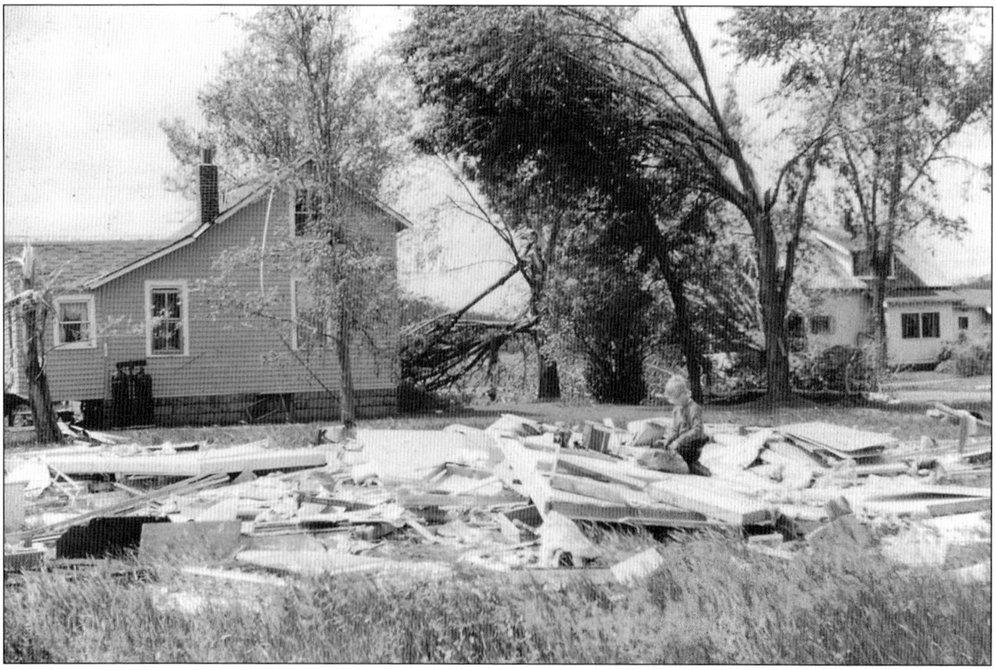

Carefree children found all sorts of new things to explore following the tornado, although fears would creep in when the weather changed. What was once a strong structure has now become a playground for this unassuming youngster. (Courtesy of Diane Haugle Hodgson.)

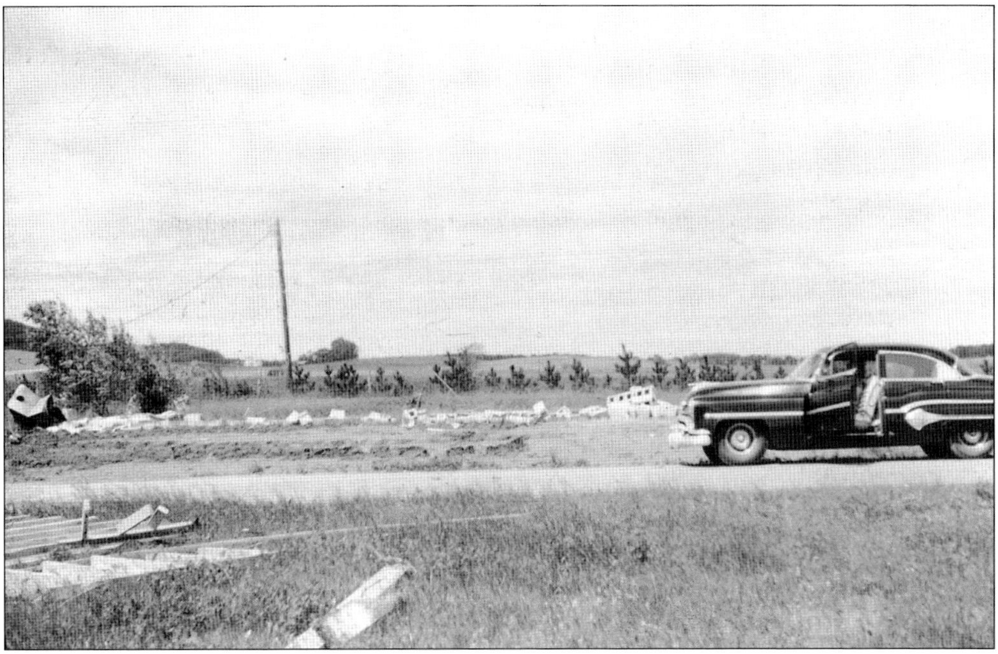

There is nothing to be seen of what was once the family home of Juel and Doris Haugle. It is difficult to even imagine what the home and grounds looked like before. This was a common scene all across the village following the tornado. (Courtesy of Diane Haugle Hodgson.)

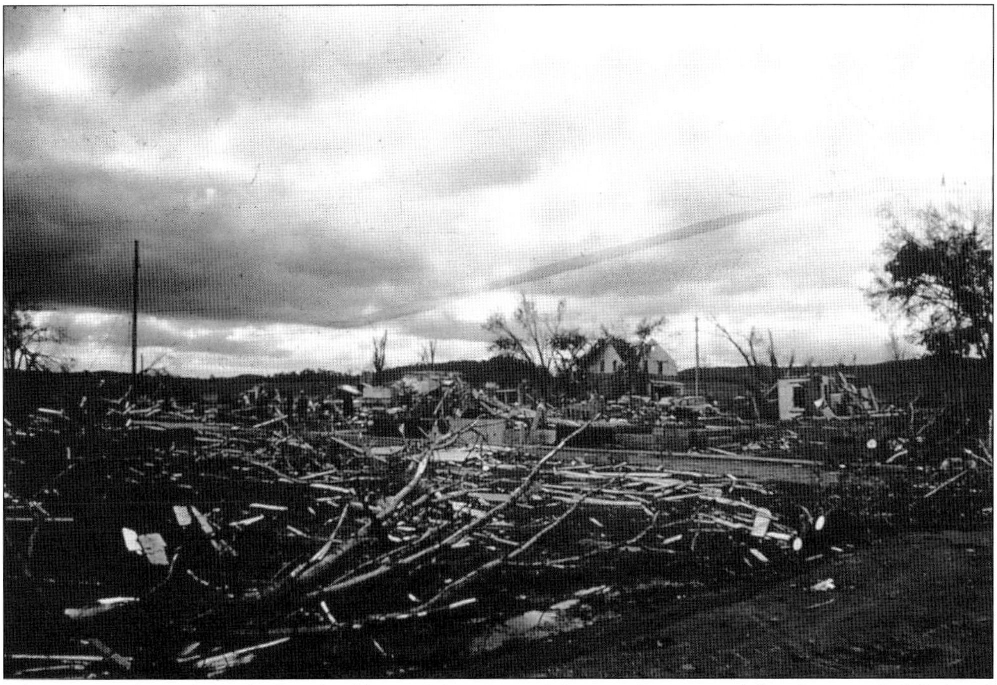

There is nothing left of what had been Mary Lunn's home. In spite of the damage left behind from the tornado, residents did not let themselves be deterred by the rebuilding process. Several residents ended up working extra shifts to save enough money to rebuild. (Courtesy of Diane Haugle Hodgson.)

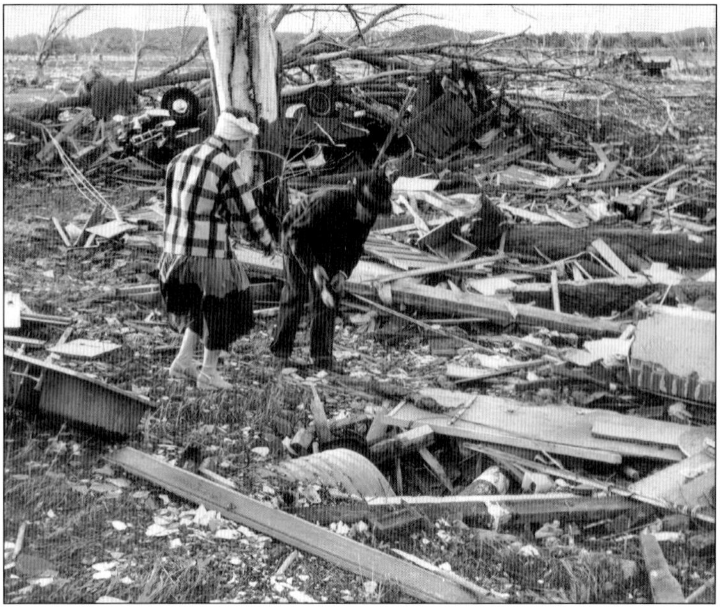

Sifting through rubble are Millie and Frank Langle on the north side of the village. One home had two dozen eggs sitting on a counter unharmed, while the rest of the house was gone. There was also a story of an attached garage being removed from its house and the car that was inside it left unscratched. (Courtesy of Ron Blakely.)

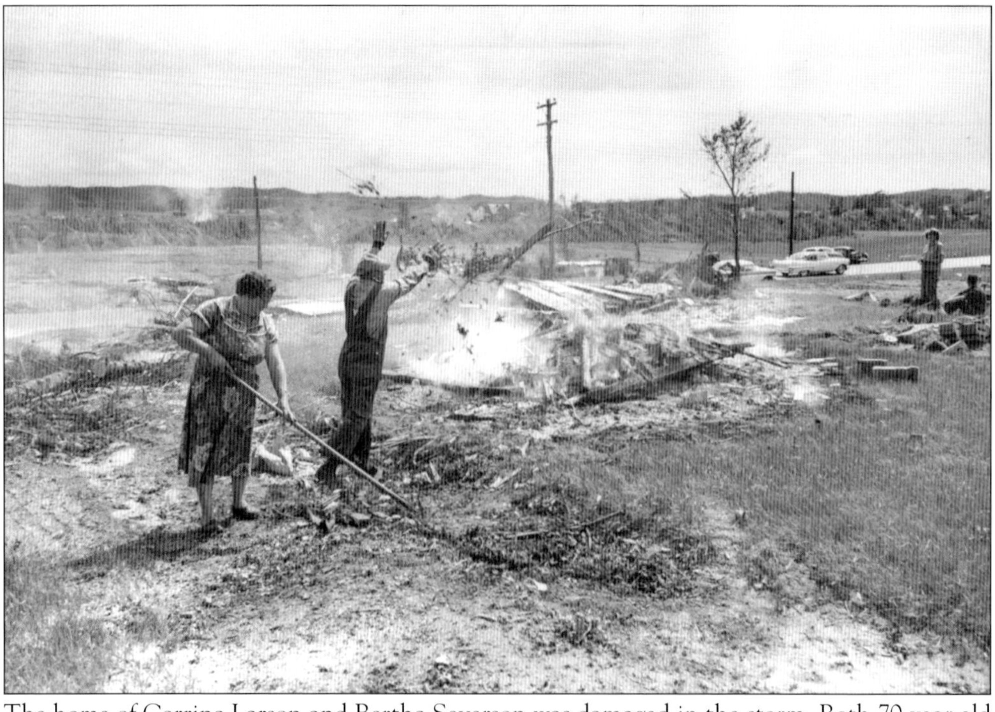

The home of Corrina Larson and Bertha Severson was damaged in the storm. Both 70-year-old women were seriously injured in the twister. Shown here are Alvin and Eve Olson cleaning up some of the wreckage. This is another example of how the community came together to help each other out in spite of what appeared to be a bleak situation. (Author's collection.)

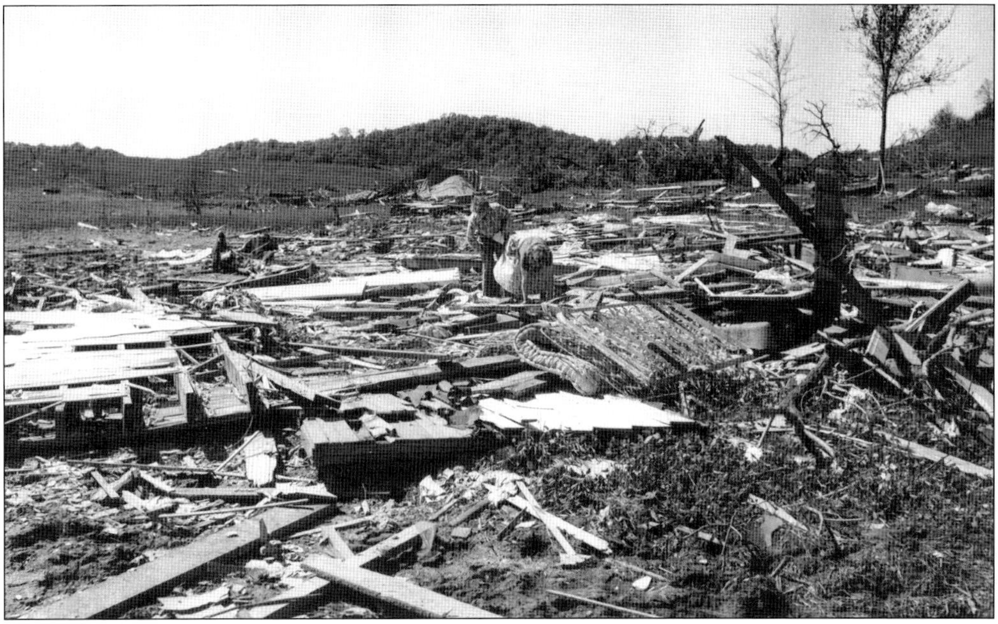

There was nothing left but the corn crib on the Dan Emmerton farm just southwest of the village. A neighbor and Mary Emmerton (left) are sifting through the aftermath of the tornado searching for bedding and other items that could be salvaged. The remains of the Emmerton farm were scattered over a quarter mile. (Author's collection.)

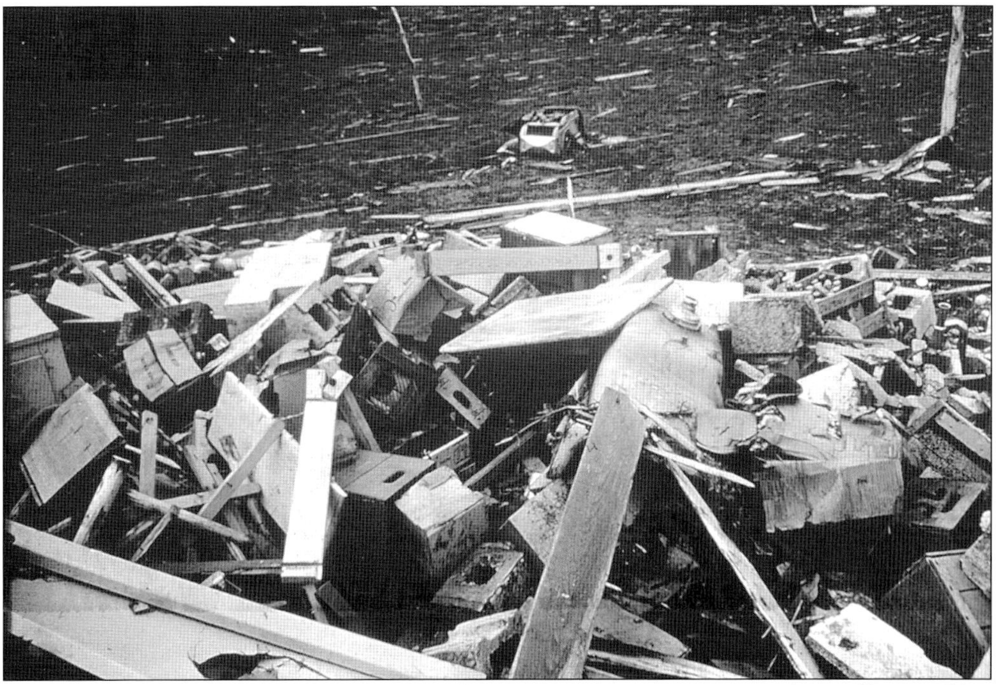

This photograph shows what was left of Gilberts' Four Corners Store. Gordon Gilbert and his wife, Ethel, survived the tornado by hiding underneath their kitchen table. They suffered the loss of their home and their family business, much like others in the area. However, they considered themselves lucky to have survived. (Courtesy of Diane Haugle Hodgson.)

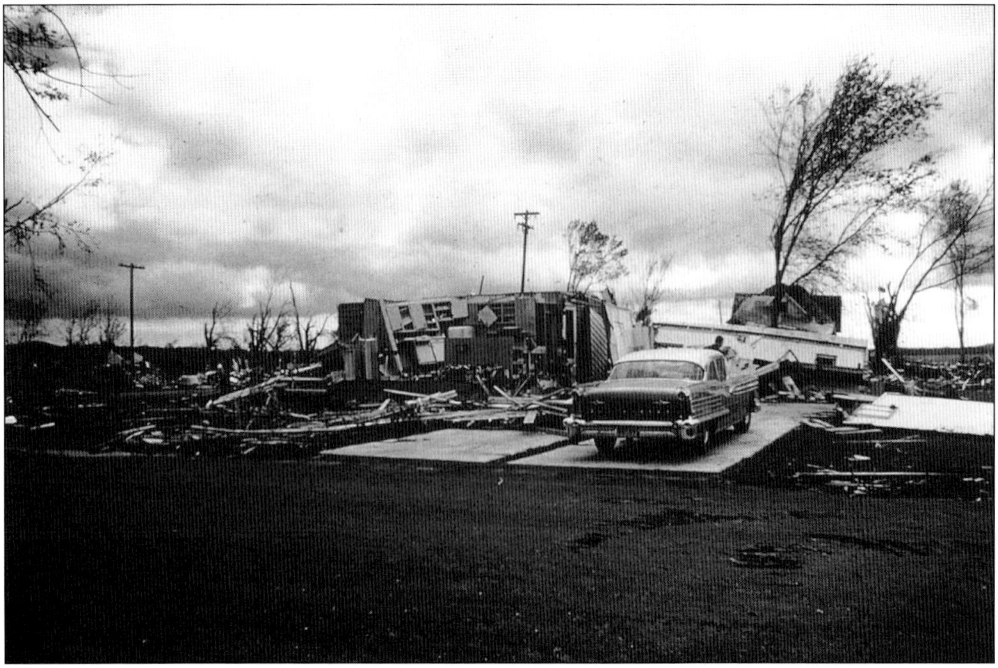

The home of Chuck Billie is left unrecognizable except for his car, which seems to have made it through the storm without a scratch. The tenacity and optimism of the residents held them back from nothing. Rebuilding was not a question, and they moved forward to other milestones in life such as marriage, childbirth, and going off to college. (Courtesy of Diane Haugle Hodgson.)

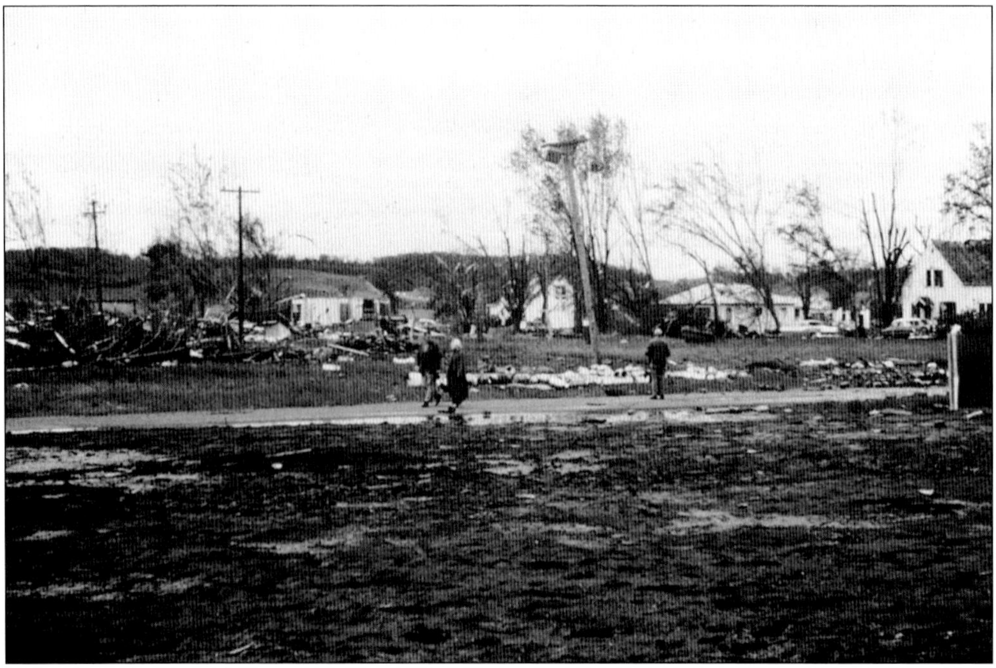

Pictured is a view from what was left of the Colfax Creamery. Although the creamery and other local businesses were damaged, the owners took all that they could to donate to the efforts of the Red Cross to help their community. (Courtesy of Diane Haugle Hodgson.)

It was a long, hard job cleaning up after the twister swept through. Here, a dead calf is dragged from the wreckage of a barn on the James Schindler farm. Eight of Schindler's 35 cattle were killed when the barn collapsed on them. (Author's collection.)

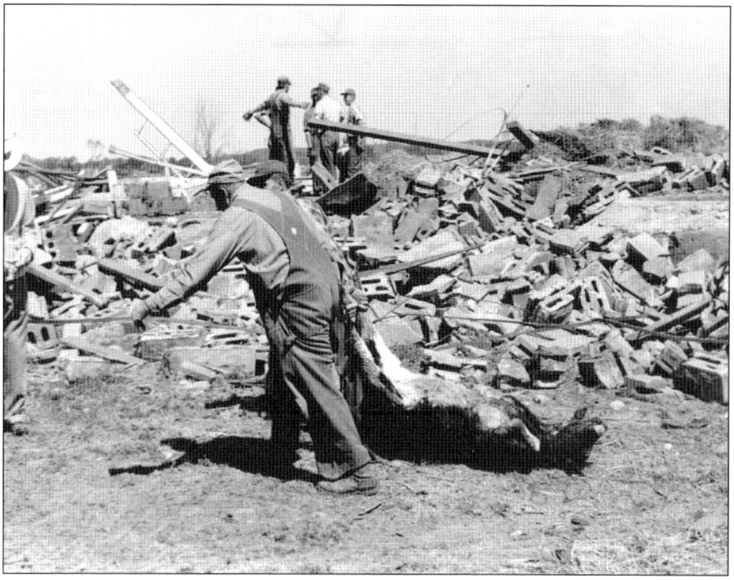

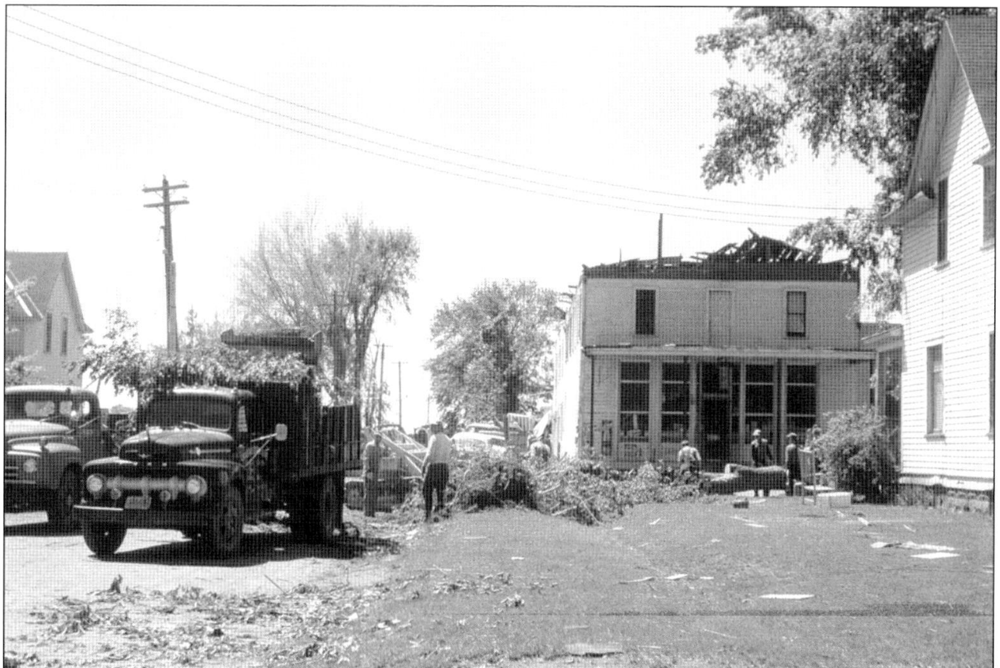

The sun was bright the day after the tornado. It is hard to believe that less than 24 hours before, Colfax was in the middle of a disaster. Many hands pitched in to help clean up after the storm. The roof of Buck Gunderson's store had some major damage. The store was on the south end of town on the corner of Third Avenue and Main Street. (Courtesy of Lyle Christenson.)

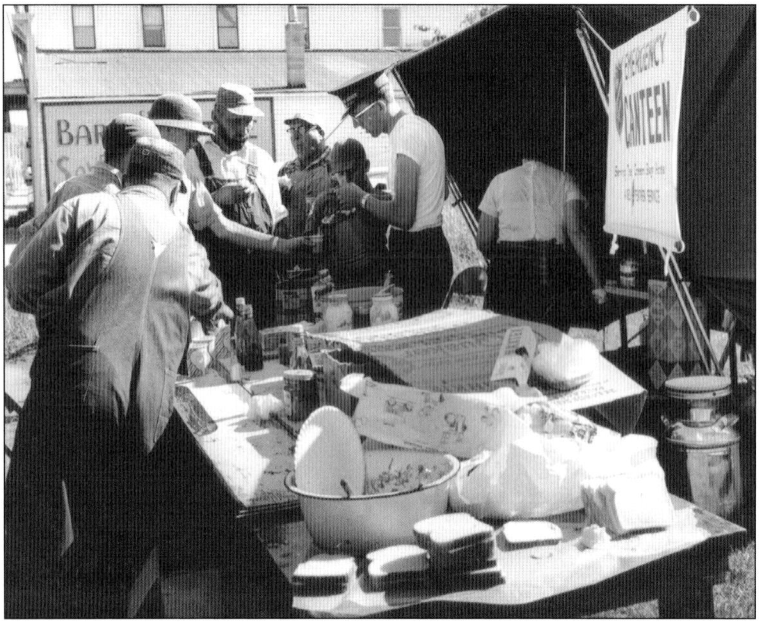

The Salvation Army set up a canteen on the south end of town to provide food and drinks to those in town working on the recovery efforts. The Red Cross spent $300,000 in disaster relief to help the residents of Colfax and the other west central Wisconsin communities affected by the tornado. (Courtesy of Ron Blakely.)

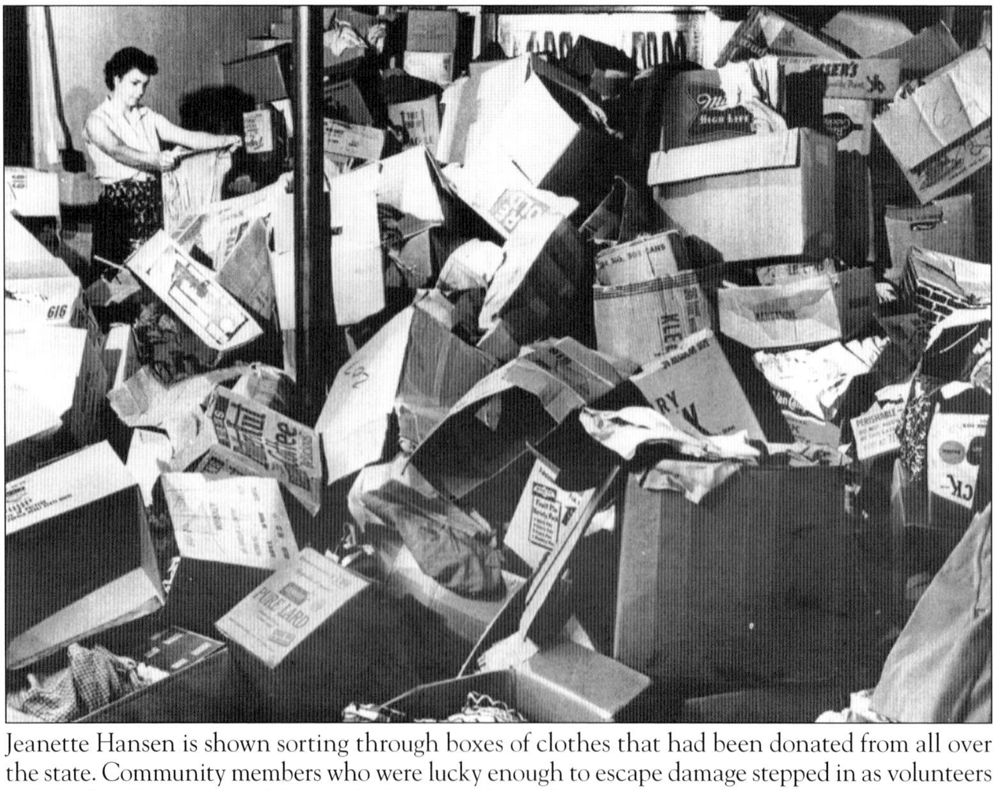

Jeanette Hansen is shown sorting through boxes of clothes that had been donated from all over the state. Community members who were lucky enough to escape damage stepped in as volunteers to help distribute personal items, clothing, meals, medical assistance, and anything else that was asked of them or was needed. (Author's collection.)

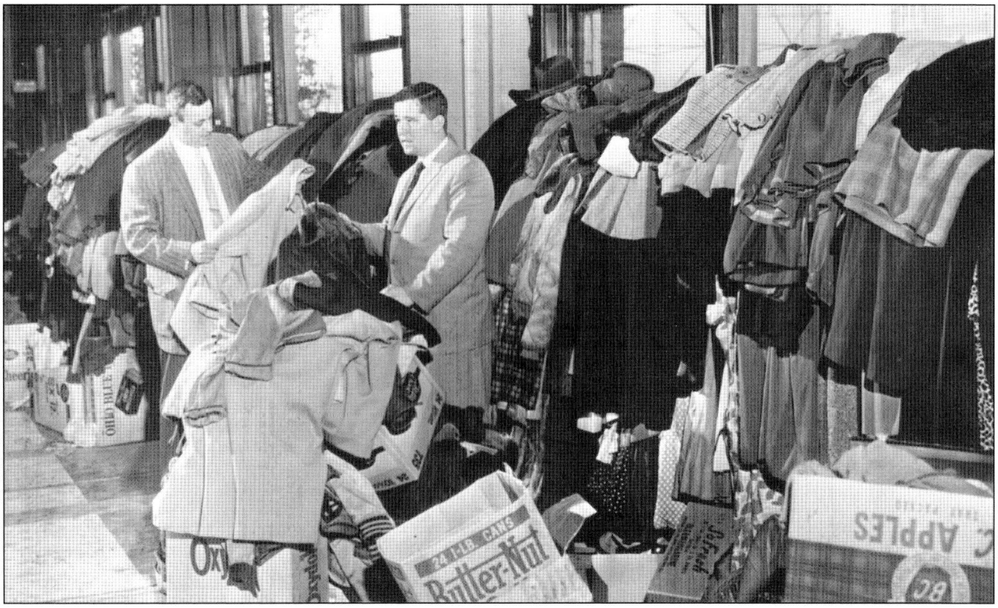

An old office building in Eau Claire was one of many holding and sorting areas for clothing and supplies for the tornado victims. Ken Ross and Jim Gort sorted clothing in the relief center. The Methodist church, as well as the Colfax High School gymnasium, served as clothing distribution centers. The clothing helped the survivors immensely. (Author's collection.)

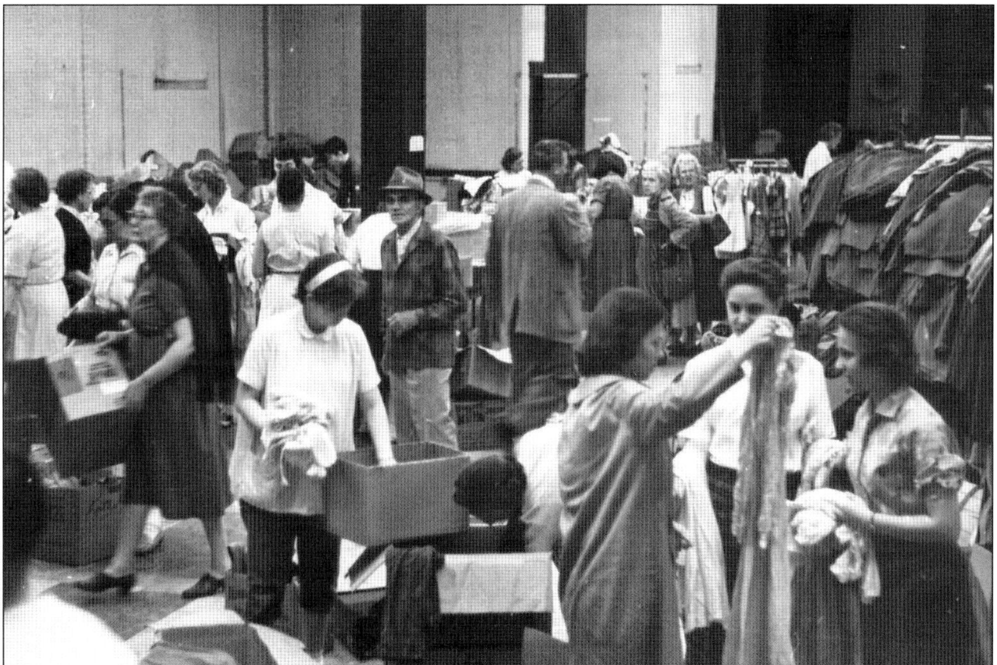

Huge piles of clothing are being checked over and sorted in an old office building in Eau Claire after a spontaneous collection was received by area communities. The local Boy Scout troop set up donation cans around the village and collected approximately $3,300 to go toward the disaster relief fund. (Author's collection.)

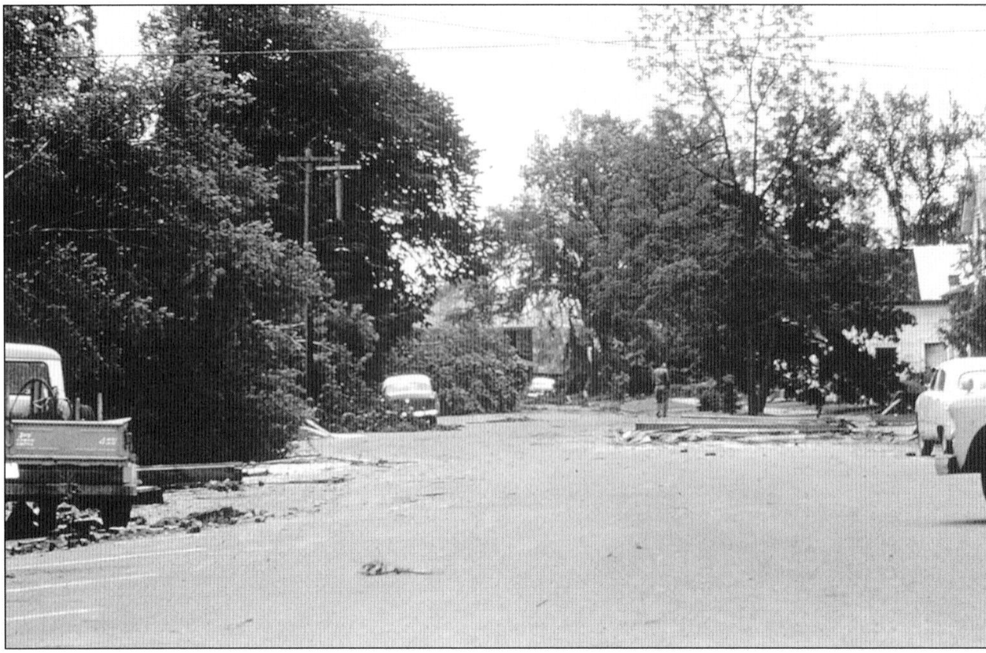

This street scene illustrates the difficulty vehicles had moving through the streets. However, those difficulties did not keep the residents of Colfax from obtaining the assistance they needed for those who were injured. (Courtesy of Diane Haugle Hodgson.)

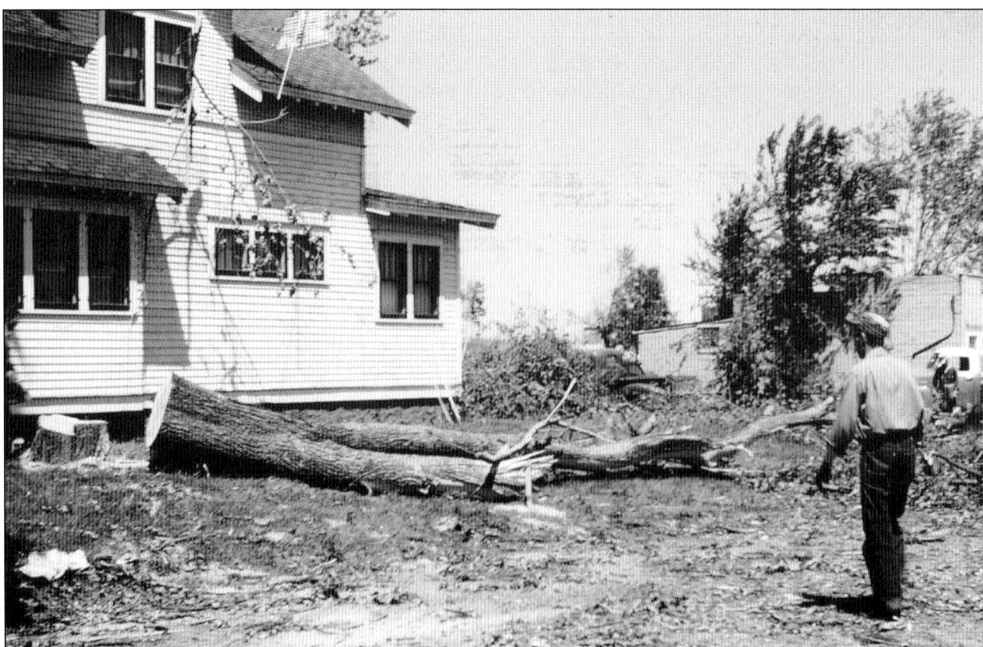

Luckily, in this case, the tree seemed to blow over in the opposite direction of the house, saving it from damage. Villagers were never the same following the tornado, always on the lookout when the weather seemed to turn strange. (Courtesy of Diane Haugle Hodgson.)

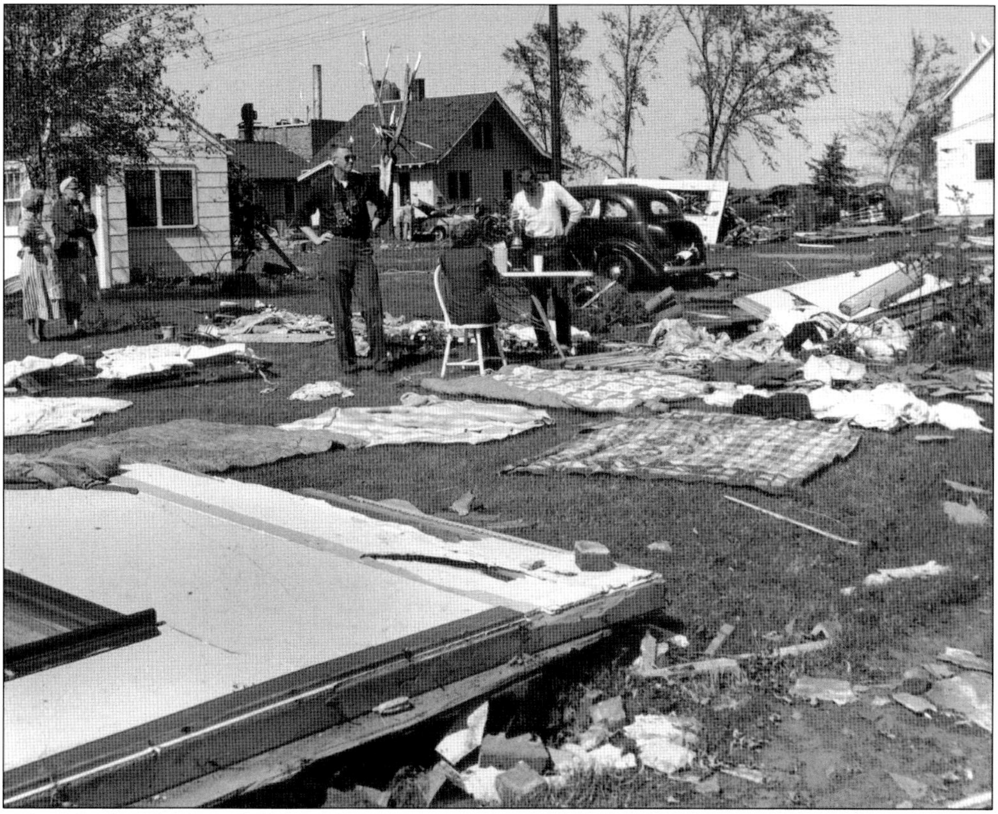

After the dust had settled from the storm, people started to come out of their shelters and began salvaging what they could. These people found a bunch of blankets and spread them out on the lawn to dry while deciding what to do next. This photograph was taken on the southeast side of town. The Colfax Creamery building is in the background. (Courtesy of Ron Blakely.)

Most of the brick facing of this home was stripped off by the tornado. In addition to damage, personal items were also misplaced during the storm. The Hendrickson family found six washing machines in the basement of their destroyed home, none of which belonged to them. (Author's collection.)

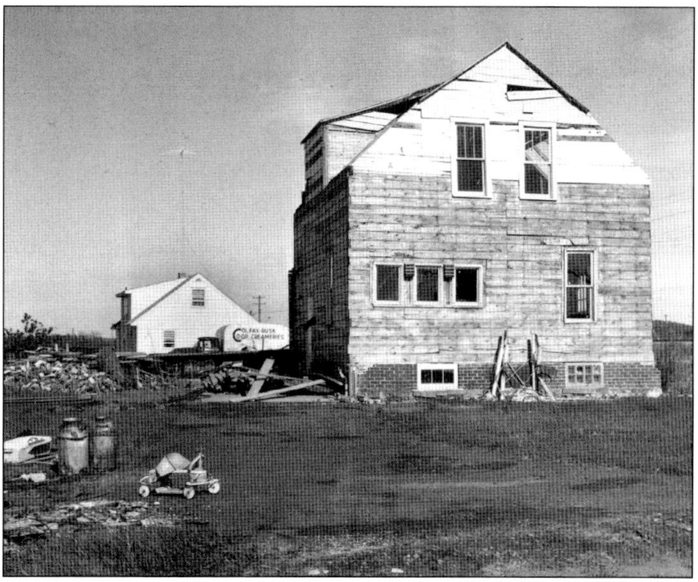

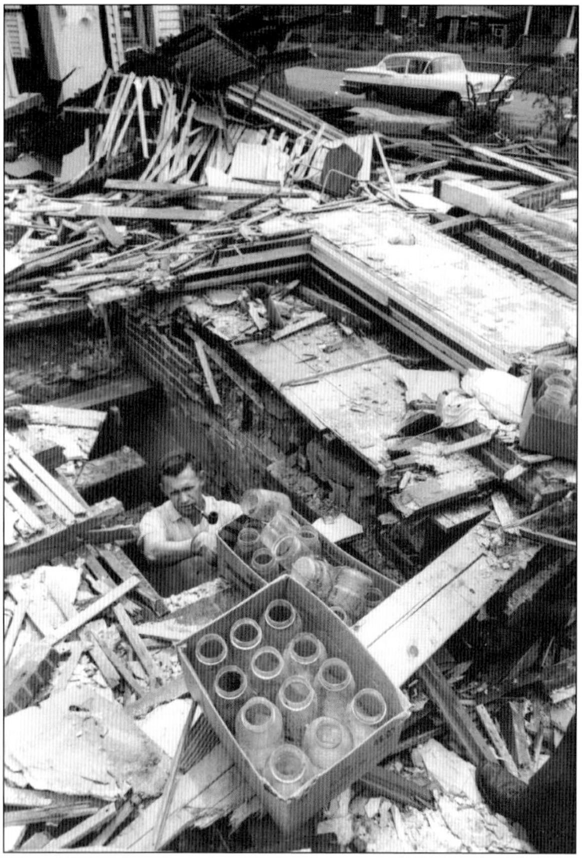

Hilda Knutson had just gotten to the bottom step of her cellar when the twister lifted her home off its foundation. Her son-in-law Byron Dodge, of Barron, is shown here saving as much as he can from the splintered timbers and lathe. The tornado was estimated to have been traveling about 56 miles per hour as it entered the southwest corner of Colfax. (Author's collection.)

The Colfax Lutheran Church suffered little damage from the storm and served as a community mess hall. Over 300 people were served meals on Thursday for lunch and supper. A total of 51,000 meals were served in all. Women from all over the area got together and made quilts for the victims. (Courtesy of Lyle Christenson.)

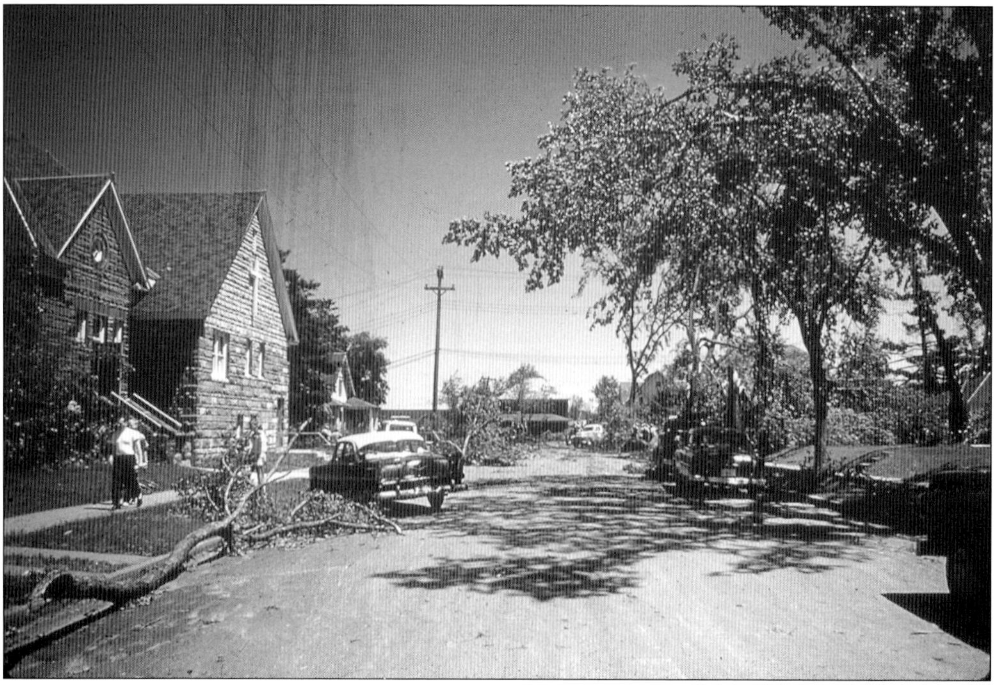

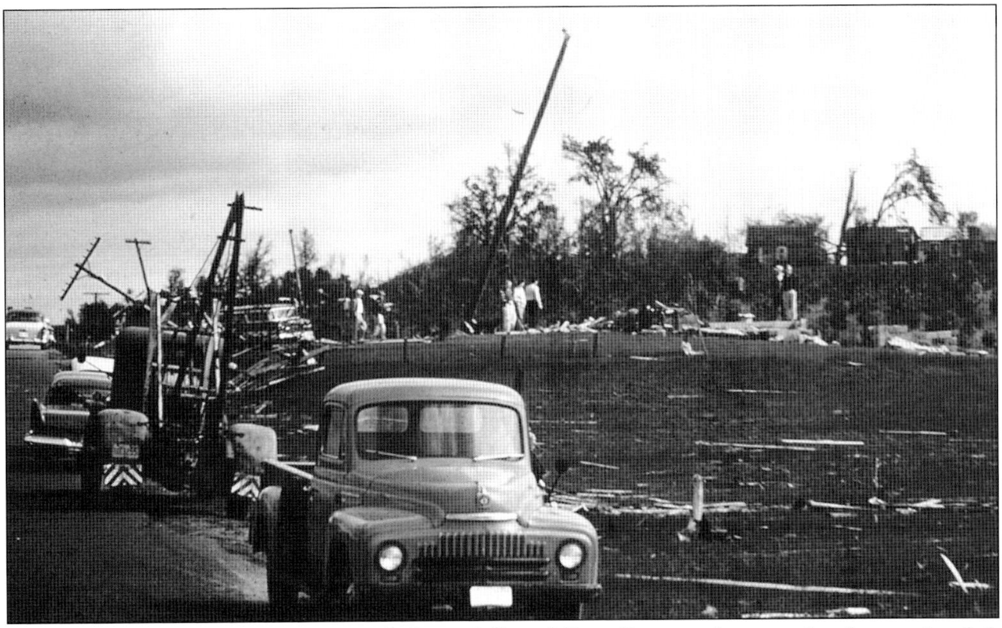

This picture was taken looking north from Gilberts' Four Corners Store at the destruction left behind by the tornado. People are surveying the damage and most likely envisioning what the rebuilding may look like. In spite of the damage and destruction, hope was not lost. (Courtesy of Diane Haugle Hodgson.)

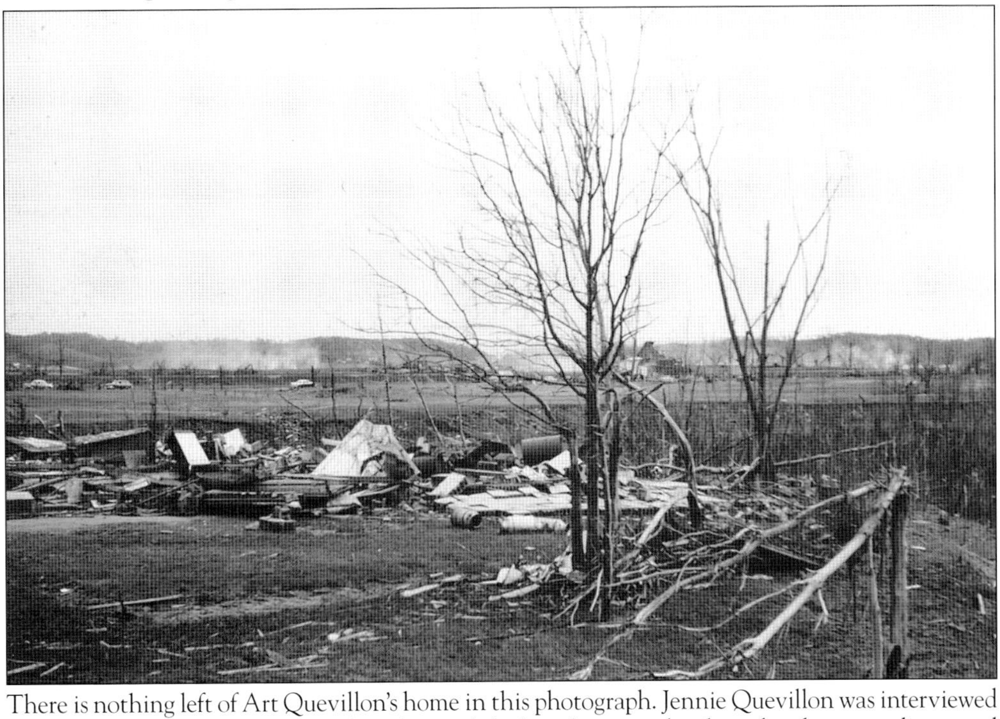

There is nothing left of Art Quevillon's home in this photograph. Jennie Quevillon was interviewed in the newspaper, remembering that the week before the tornado, their daughter was diagnosed with leukemia, and they believed nothing worse than that could happen, but the tornado had a different idea. (Courtesy of Diane Haugle Hodgson.)

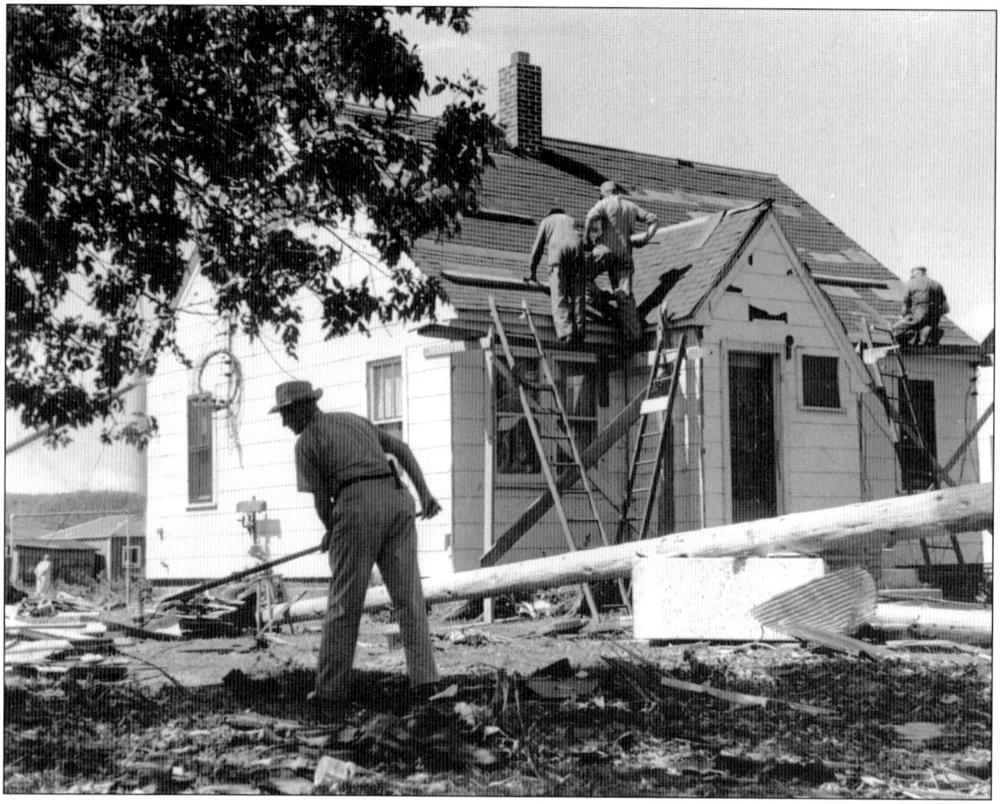

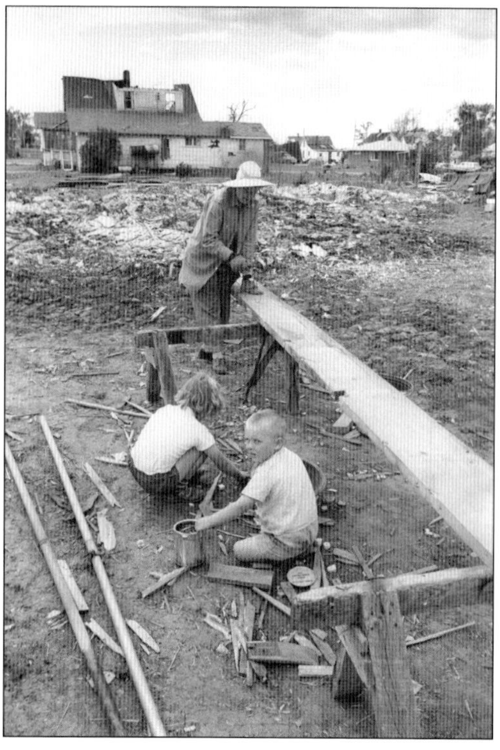

The home of Carl Hagen had extensive roof damage as well as a fallen utility pole in his yard. H.A. Halberson from Elk Mound is shown here raking up rubbish in order to help with the cleanup efforts. According to a local insurance adjuster, one third of the village was destroyed. (Author's collection.)

People tried to salvage as much as they could after the storm. Emma Rose and her two grandchildren, Donna, seven, and William, five, are shown collecting nails to remove the risk of more injury by stepping on them. The Rose home was located in the southeast section of the village. Only the south wall was left standing. (Author's collection.)

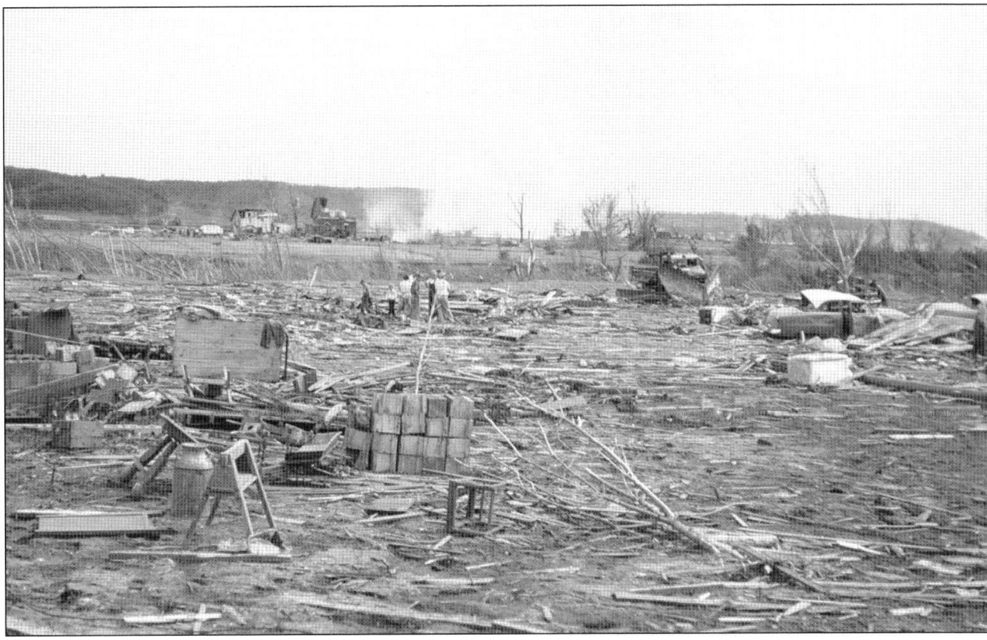

This is all that was left of the Steve Figura home on the north side. What is left of the Odd Lindberg and Phillip Felland homes can be seen along 18 Mile Creek in the background. Steve Figura, who owned a car dealership in town, had left his home just five minutes prior to the storm to go sell a car. His family took shelter in their basement and were unharmed. (Courtesy of Lyle Christenson.)

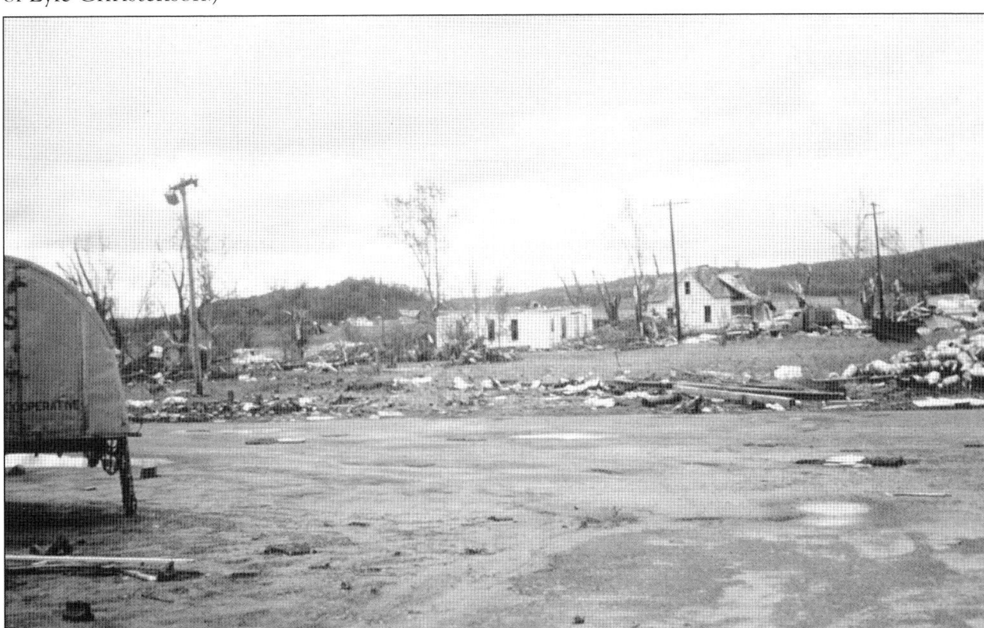

This photograph was taken looking southeast on the south side of town. This was the hardest hit area of town. Every building suffered some sort of damage. The whine of chainsaws could be heard for months. Hundreds of trees were ravaged and left a story of destruction in jumbled piles throughout the community. (Author's collection.)

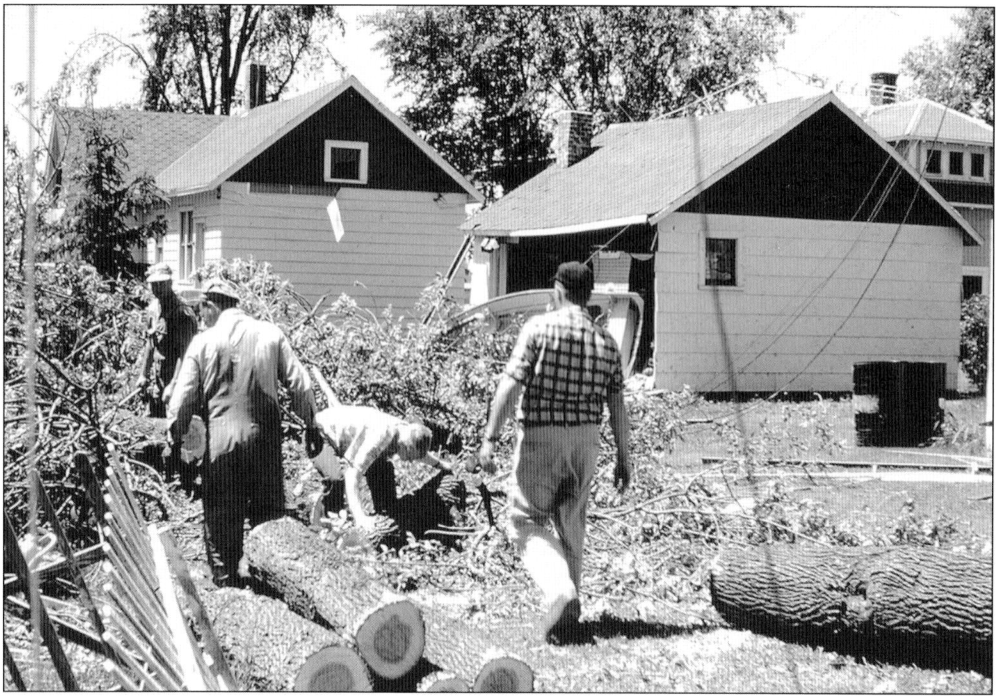

Seen here is the Arnold Solberg home and the backyard of the Walter Schultz property. The newspaper reported that people laughed when Mayor T.A. Everson predicted the village would be rebuilt. The survivors and the citizens proved him right. (Courtesy of Diane Haugle Hodgson.)

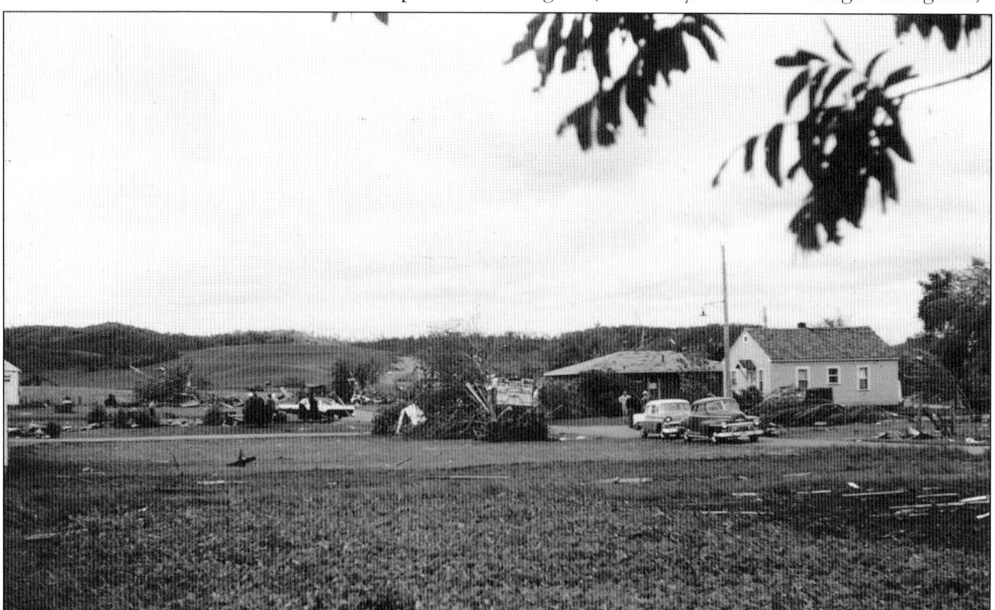

Pictured is a view of the south side and what had once been the site of Duane Haugle's home. It is amazing to think that there were not more people killed, especially when children had been outside playing in the heat and farmers had been in their barns in the middle of chores. (Courtesy of Diane Haugle Hodgson.)

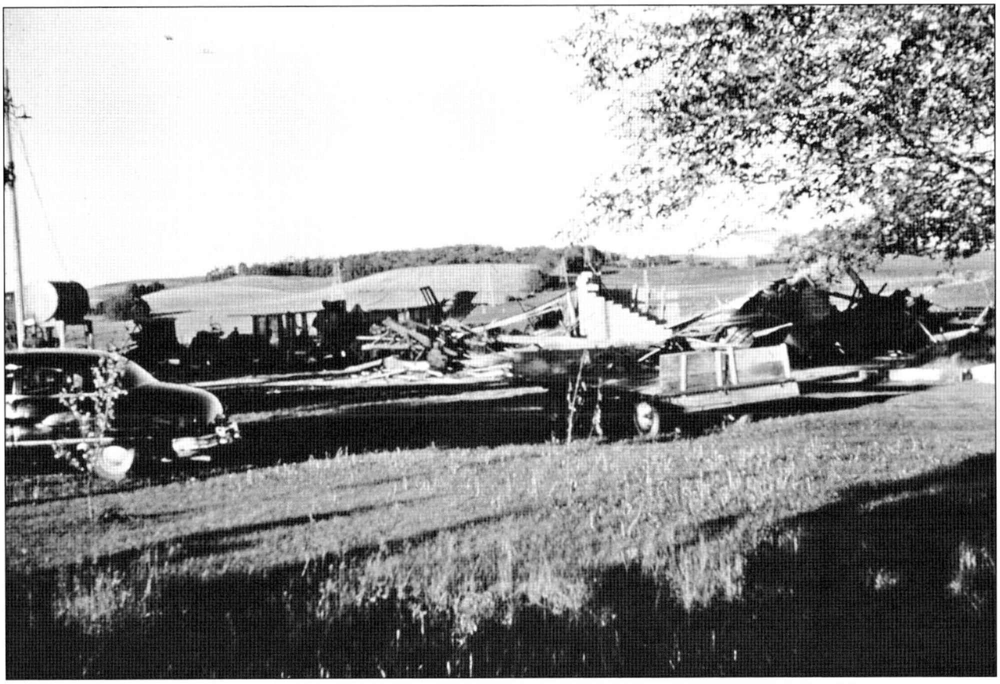

Although Donald Bergeson's home is left as nothing but sticks and debris, rebuilding was never a question. In the three years that followed, 103 new homes were built, stores were reopened, and the bank was remodeled. The people of Colfax would not be left crippled by the tornado. (Courtesy of Diane Haugle Hodgson.)

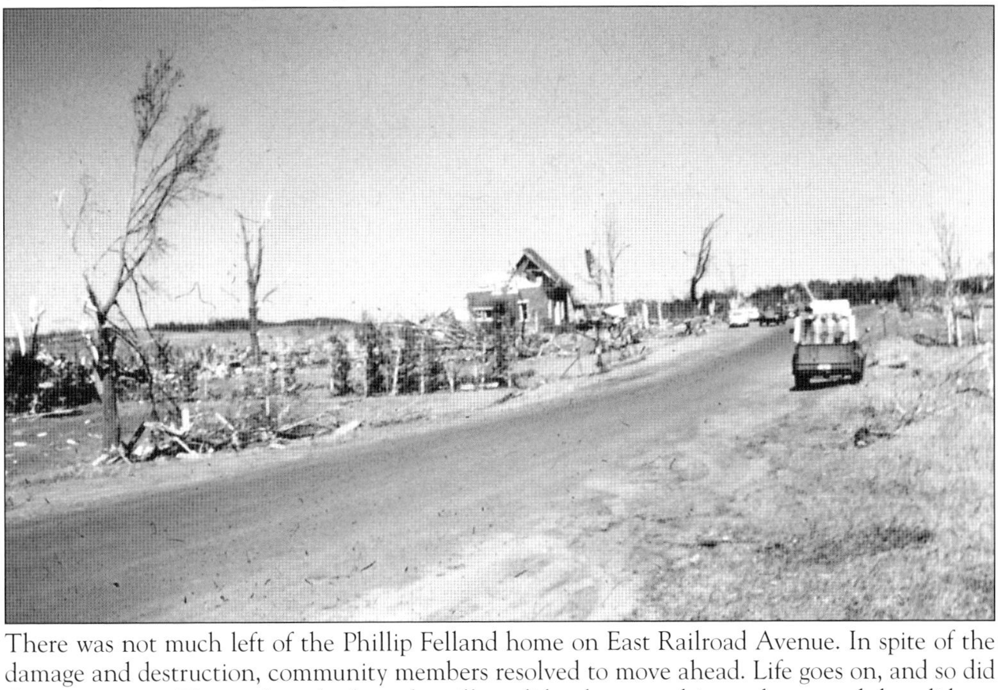

There was not much left of the Phillip Felland home on East Railroad Avenue. In spite of the damage and destruction, community members resolved to move ahead. Life goes on, and so did the community. Those who rebuilt in the village did so because this was home and they did not want to live anywhere else. (Courtesy of Diane Haugle Hodgson.)

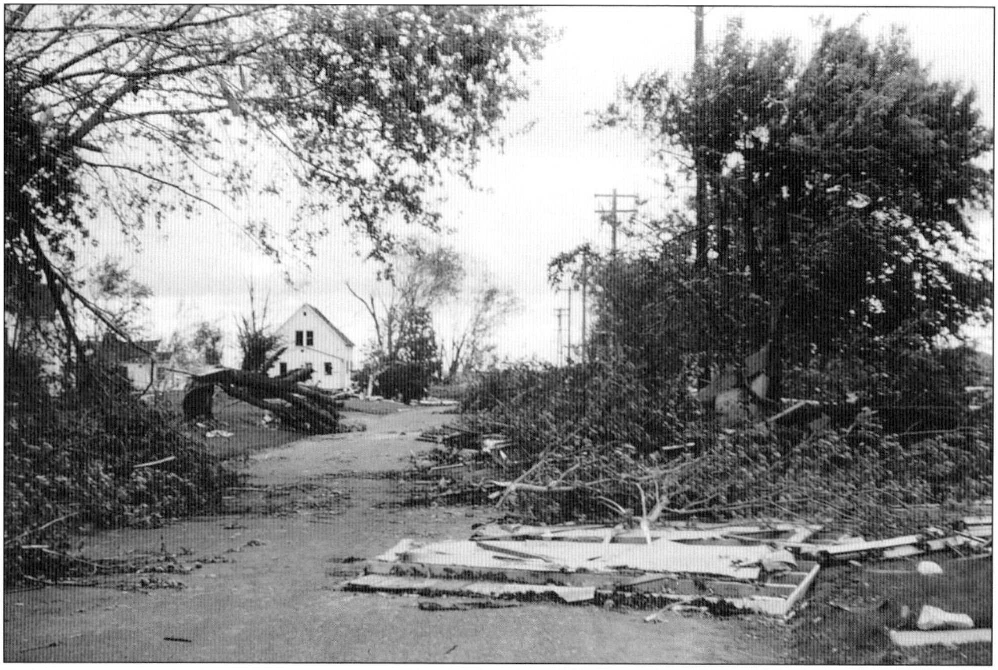

What was once the brand-new garage of Savel Haugle is left in pieces among the branches of mature trees. It seems hopeless that rebuilding and recovery could happen based on this photograph. But in spite of the loss of lives and homes, rebuilding did happen as a result of the resolve of the citizens of Colfax. (Courtesy of Diane Haugle Hodgson.)

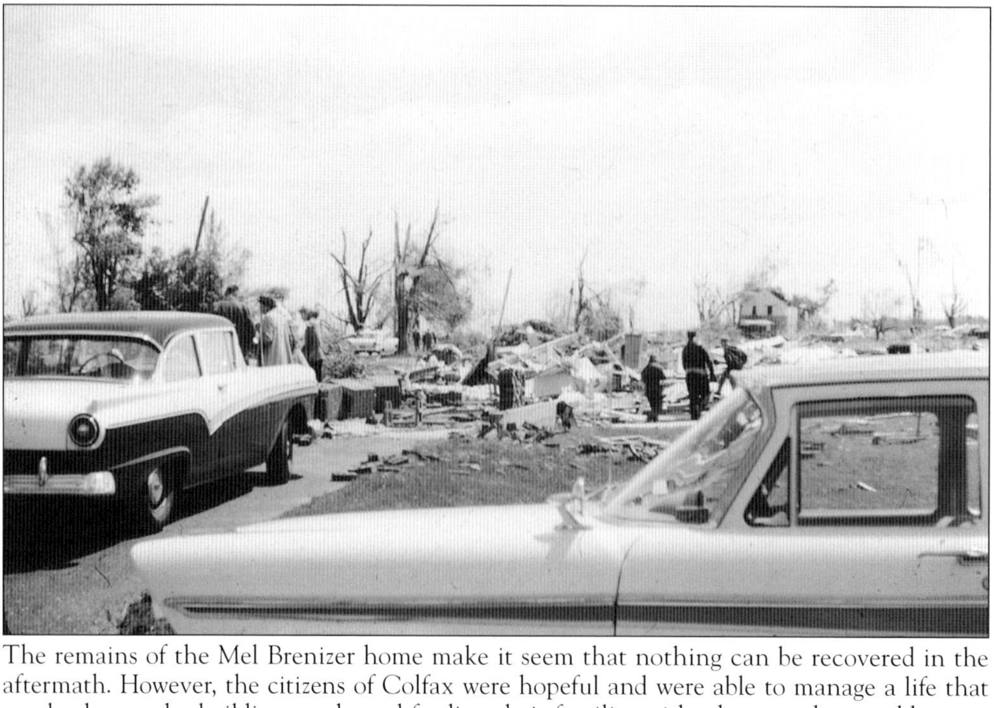

The remains of the Mel Brenizer home make it seem that nothing can be recovered in the aftermath. However, the citizens of Colfax were hopeful and were able to manage a life that revolved around rebuilding, work, and feeding their families with whatever they could scrape together. (Courtesy of Diane Haugle Hodgson.)

A group of men are trying to salvage the corn that once was stored in this corn crib. Another part of the relief process was supplied by the Lake to Lake Dairy Cooperative, which sent 94 heifers to Colfax farmers who had lost cattle in the tornado. (Courtesy of Ron Blakely.)

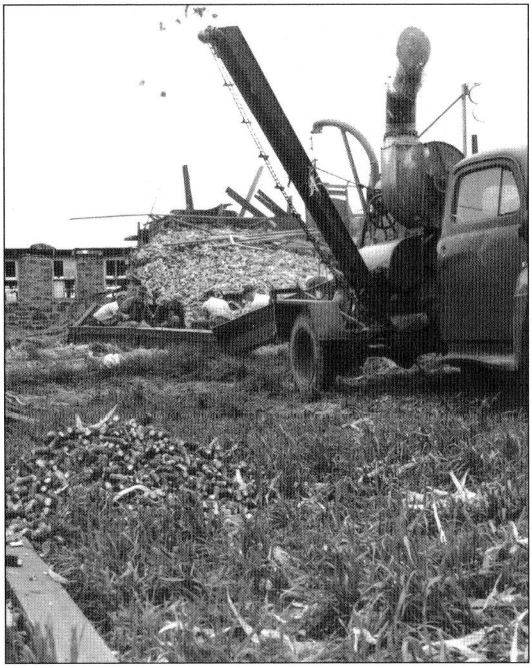

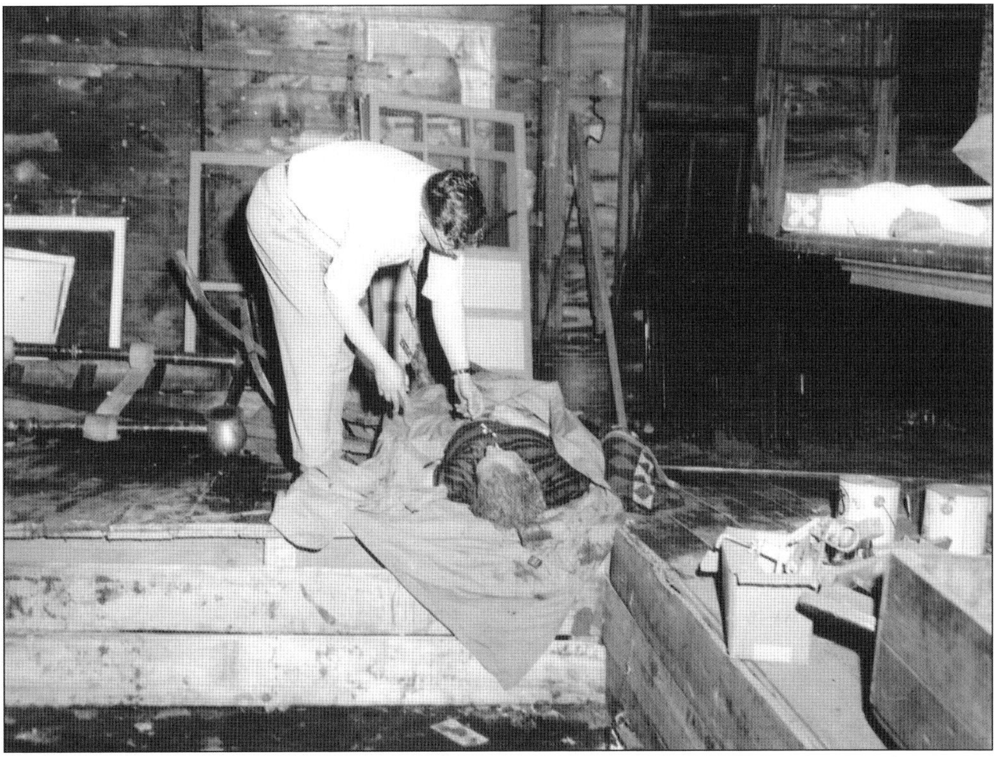

Overall, the tornado claimed the lives of 28 people. One in the Wilson area, two in the Knapp area, three north of Menomonie and Cedar Falls, twelve in Colfax, nine in Chippewa County along Highway N, and one south of Thorp. Here, Fritz Bremer is taking care of Nora Gerber's body, one of the Colfax victims. (Courtesy of the Colfax Public Library.)

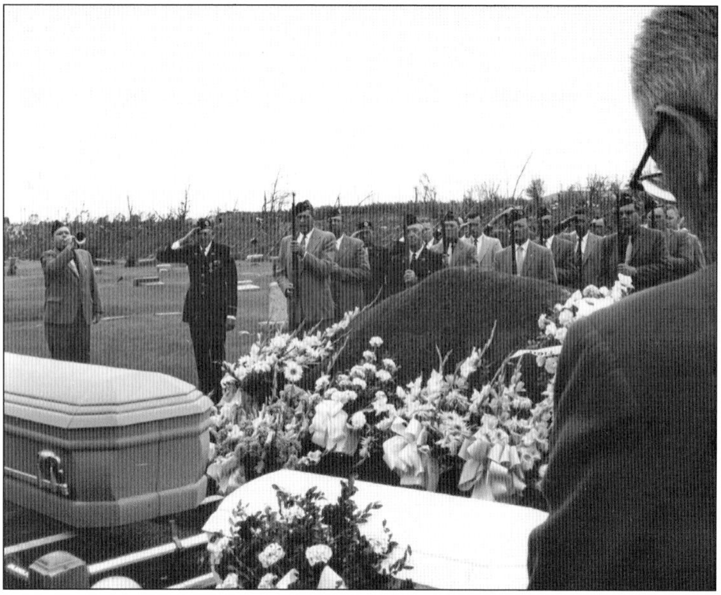

A funeral was held at the Evergreen Cemetery for Erling Lunn and his son Leon, two of the twelve casualties in the village. Some of those attending the funeral are Laverne Hovland, Inky Stene, Austin Rude, Fred Mortenson, Mike Hanson, Garland Mittelstadt, and Leon Dunbar. (Courtesy of Ron Blakely.)

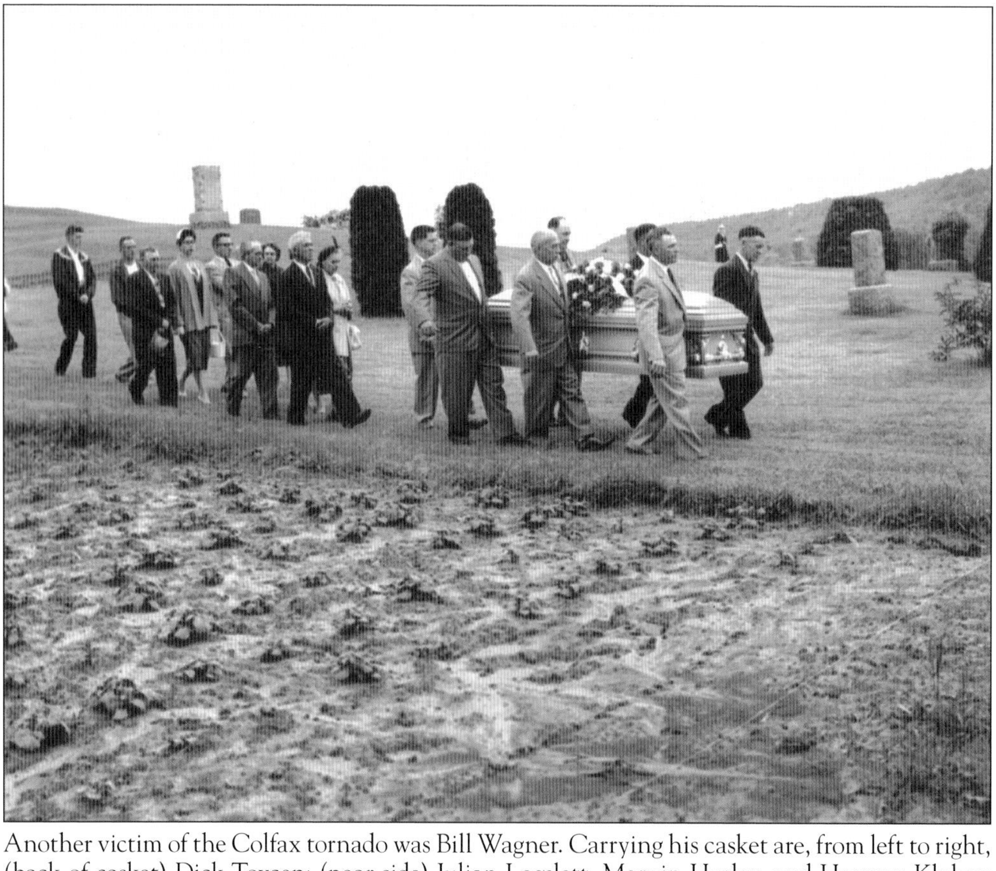

Another victim of the Colfax tornado was Bill Wagner. Carrying his casket are, from left to right, (back of casket) Dick Toycen; (near side) Julian Logslett, Marvin Hurley, and Herman Klukas; (far side) two unidentified and Garfield Gunnufson. The tornado left a 90-mile path through six Wisconsin counties. (Courtesy of Ron Blakely.)

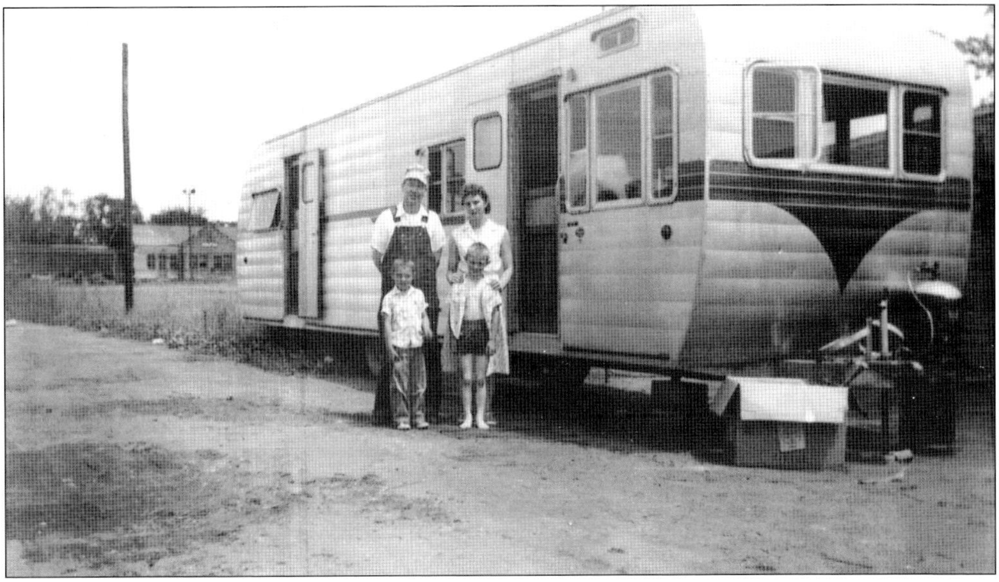

Mobile homes were brought in for families to stay in after the storm while the daunting task of cleanup was taking place. Here, Juel, Doris, Mike, and John Haugle stand in front of their new home during the cleanup process. The Wisconsin Mobile Home Association donated the use of the mobile homes for a month free of charge, with a nominal fee thereafter. (Author's collection.)

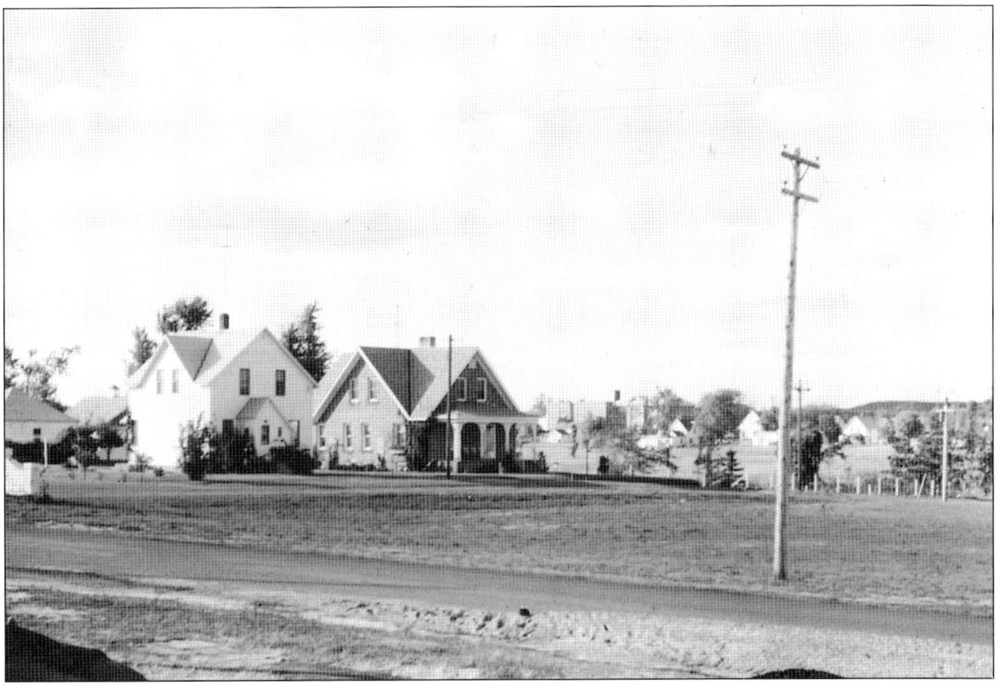

Two years after the tornado, the people of Colfax were back on track to living a normal life. Homes were rebuilt, and things were getting back in order. This photograph was taken looking northwest toward the homes of Nora Wiseman on the right and Jennings and Mattie Page on the left. The huge three-story high school can be seen in the background. (Courtesy of Diane Haugle Hodgson.)

APPRECIATION DAY — JUNE 4, 1960
COLFAX, WISCONSIN

1:00 P. M. — Memorial Service
1:30 P. M. — Doll Buggy and Pet Parade
2:00 P. M. — Grand Parade
4:00 P. M. — Drills by Eau Claire Boys' Drum and Bugle Corps at the Village Park
4:30 P. M. — Tug of War between Barron Whiskered Gents and Boyceville Gents

Free lunch for all at park

EVENING PROGRAM

8:00 P. M. — Country Jamboree with Betty Lee
Memonomie Barbershoppers Chorus and Quartets
Quartet from Hudson

Compliments of
THE COLFAX MESSENGER

You Helped Us

When It Looked Like This

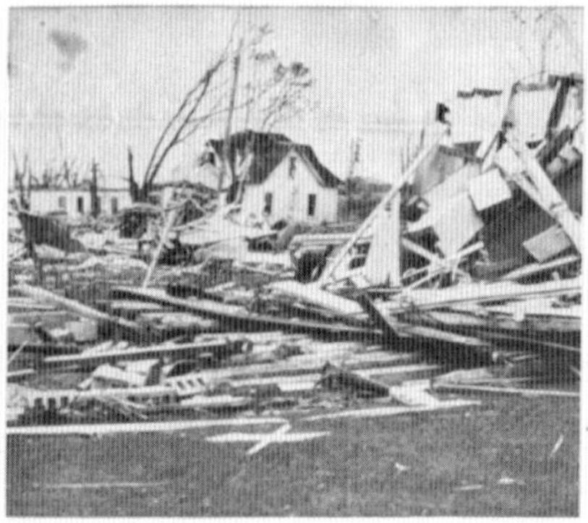

Two years after the tornado, there was an appreciation day to thank everyone who helped during the cleanup and rebuilding. The Woman's Club won an honorable mention for their assistance in the efforts immediately following the storm. (Author's collection.)

For That . . . We Extend Sincere Thanks

Because . . .

Now It Looks Like This

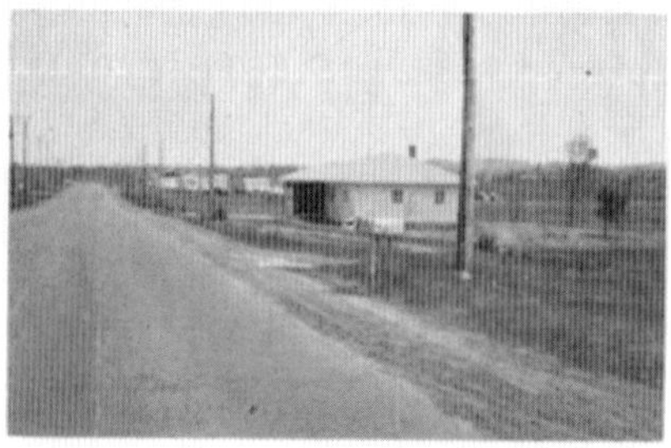

The appreciation day was full of activities for the entire community. There was a parade with pets and dolls, tug of war, barbershop singing, and a memorial service led by Rev. S.M. Moe of Colfax Lutheran Church. The pastor pointed out that of the homes destroyed, 79 had been replaced with new ones. (Author's collection.)

After the disaster, Adina Felland and the Colfax Woman's Club started a tree fund to replace the hundreds of trees that were lost during the storm. Several hundred 10-foot trees of various species were bought with the money raised and planted throughout the damaged parts of the village. (Author's collection.)

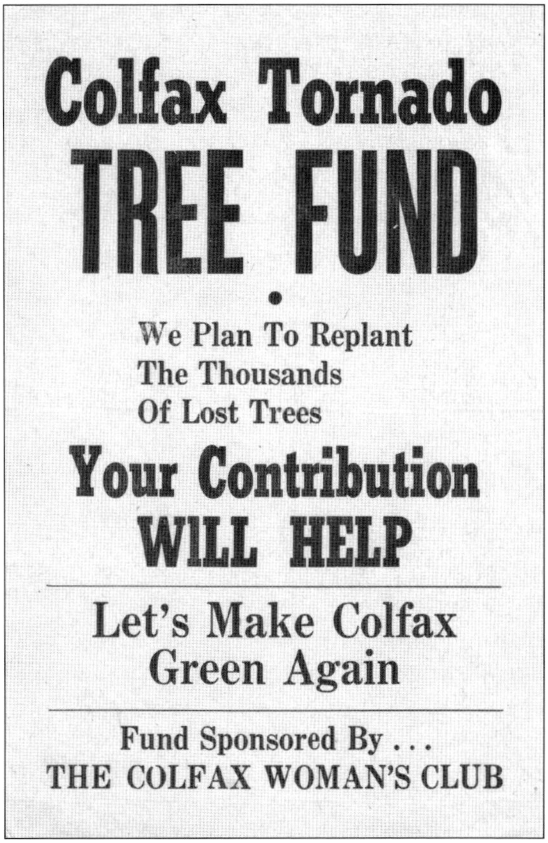

Colfax Tornado
TREE FUND

We Plan To Replant
The Thousands
Of Lost Trees

Your Contribution
WILL HELP

Let's Make Colfax
Green Again

Fund Sponsored By . . .
THE COLFAX WOMAN'S CLUB

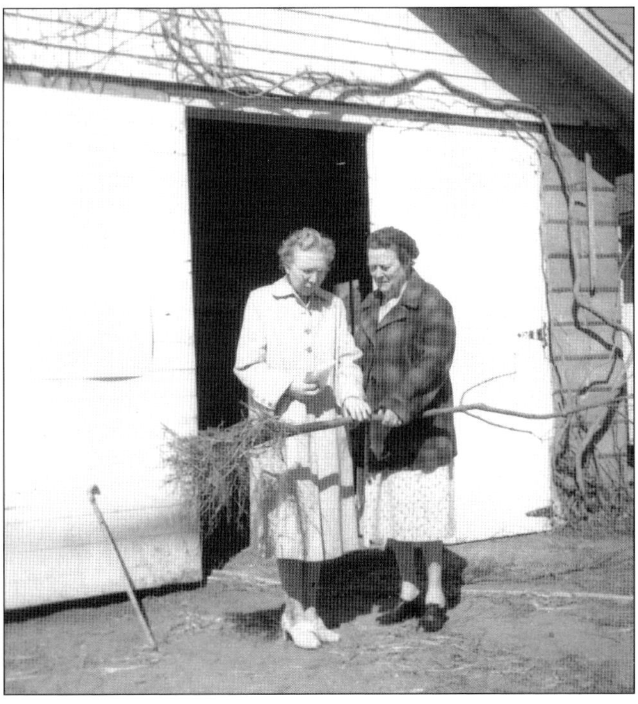

Alice Hawkins (left) and Betty Martin inspect newly purchased trees for the replanting efforts at the home of Doctor Felland. Hundreds of trees were replanted within a year of the tornado, thanks to the generous donations of people from across the state. They served as a reminder of the destruction from the year before and the healing that followed. (Courtesy of the Colfax Woman's Club.)

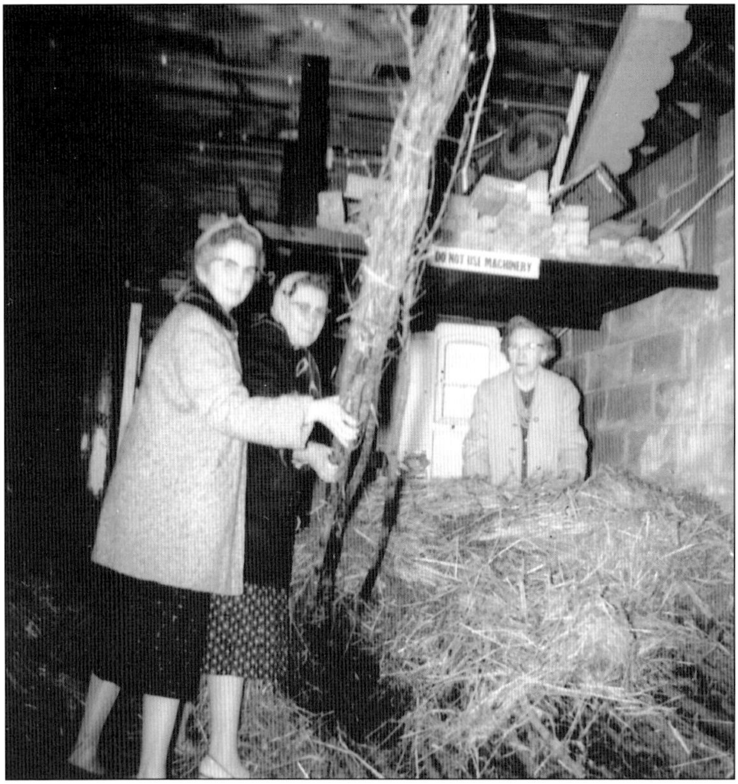

Trees are ready for distribution in this photograph. The committee in charge of the tree replanting was Adina Felland, Edna Hill, and Mary Weeks. Thanks to their generous efforts, Colfax is green again and thriving in spite of losing so much in the tornado. Many of the trees are a current reminder of the rebuilding efforts of a community that would not give up. (Courtesy of Colfax Woman's Club.)

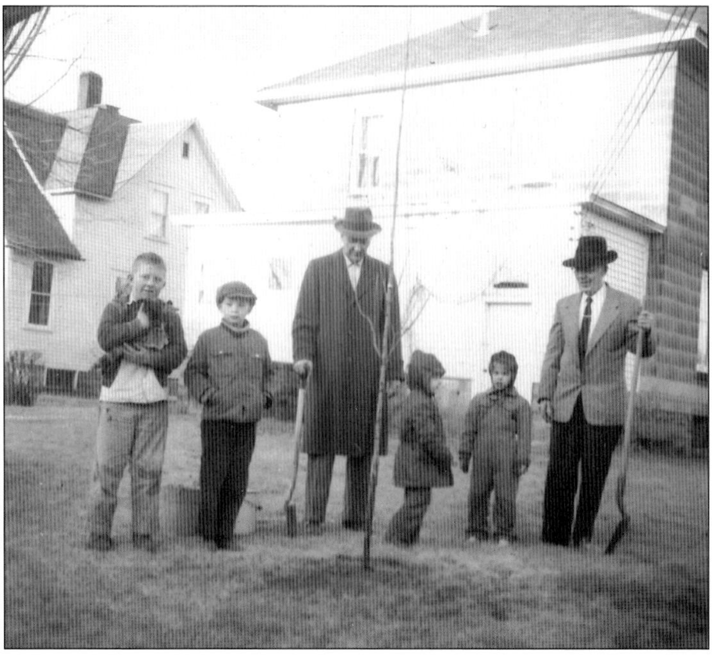

In the effort to "Make Colfax Green Again," a tree was planted at the home of Sam K. Iverson. Chuck Hovland, Lloyd Ziebell, Ken Iverson, Ruth (Ronning) Klawiter, Rondi (Iverson) Demoe, and Sam K. Iverson are pictured here. This tree was named Adina in honor of Doctor Felland's wife, who spearheaded the replanting efforts. (Courtesy of Colfax Woman's Club.)

Three

A Time to Remember, A Time to Honor

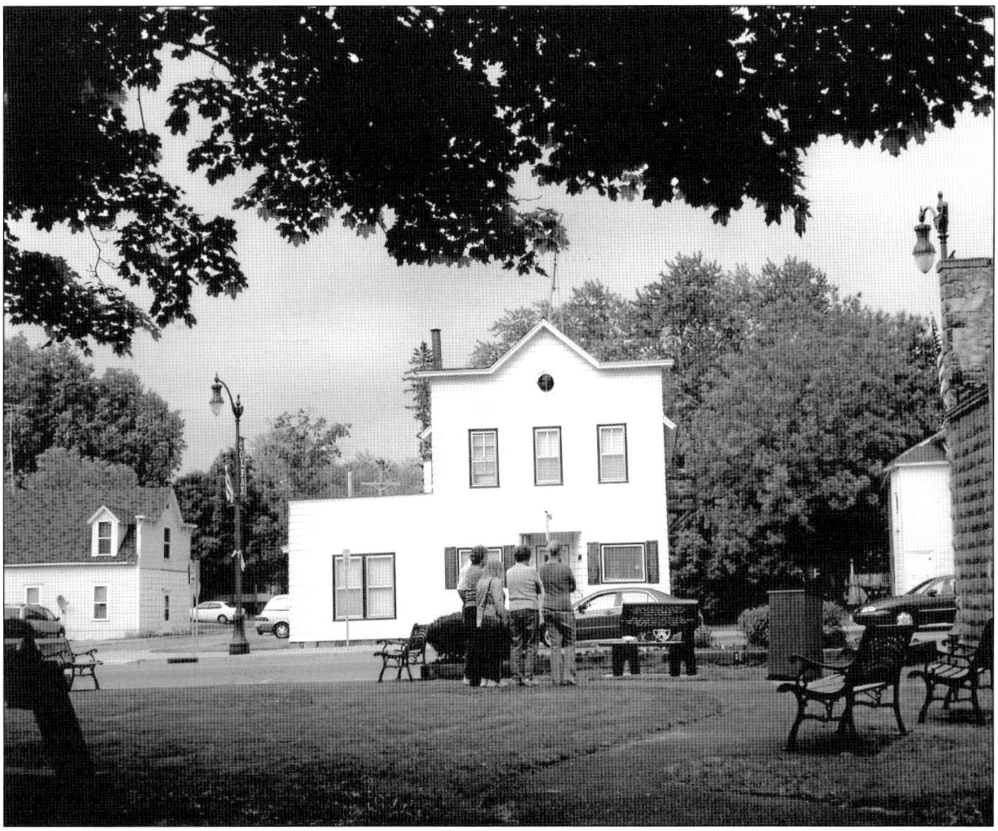

Jean Olson wrote, "the real story of the Colfax Tornado is a message of courage, compassion and hope." This was shown over and over again by the survivors and surrounding community members who stepped in to help when that was the most important task at hand. People worked tirelessly to help the community recover. (Courtesy of Jim Eggert.)

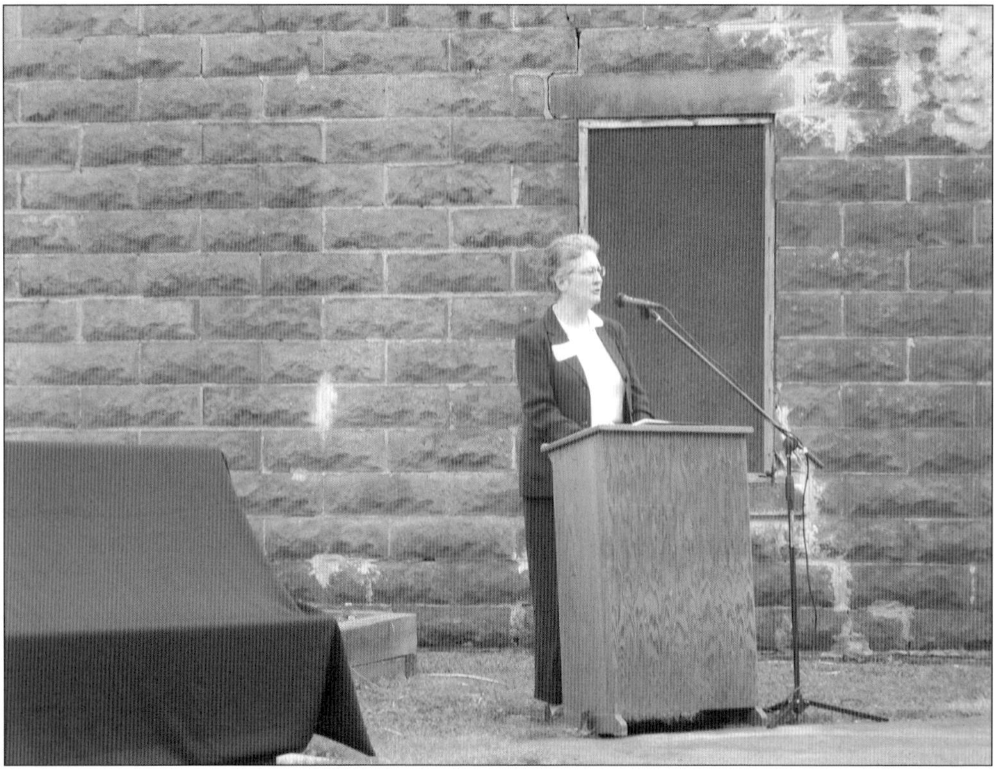

Acting village president and active community member Jean Olson shares comments related to the planning, organizing, and inspiration for the events. Planning for the 50th anniversary commemoration began a year before the anniversary by organizing a committee of local community members, as well as with the help of survivors and their stories, and support from local businesses. (Author's collection.)

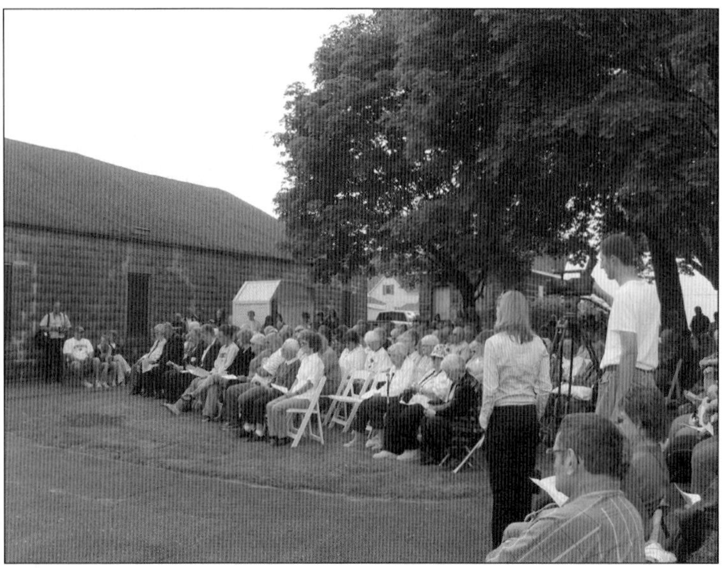

Hundreds of people and local news media were on hand for the commemoration activities. This crowd anxiously awaits the unveiling of the Memorial Bench in Tower Park. The commemoration event was the idea of community member Karen Hendrickson. Hendrickson was a child at the time of the tornado and was severely injured. (Author's collection.)

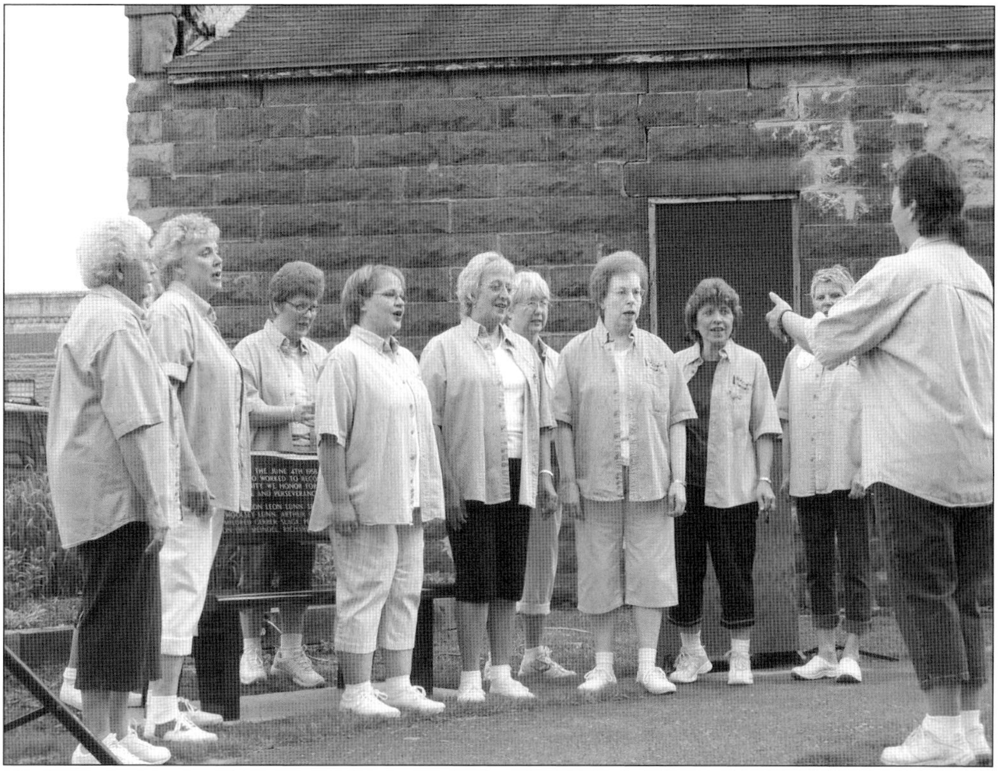

Phyllis Sarauer, Jennifer Davis-Farlow, Karen Geissler, Doreen Lorenzen, Kathy Tape, Pat Eggert, Claudia Hogan, Marian Zwiefelhofer, Mona Thorson, and Dawn Roberts of the local vocal group Sweet Adelines offered "How We Sang Today" as a musical tribute honoring the victims. The song perfectly summed up the events: "Tomorrow is another day / So take my hand my friend / I'm glad we laughed and loved and sang together today." (Author's collection.)

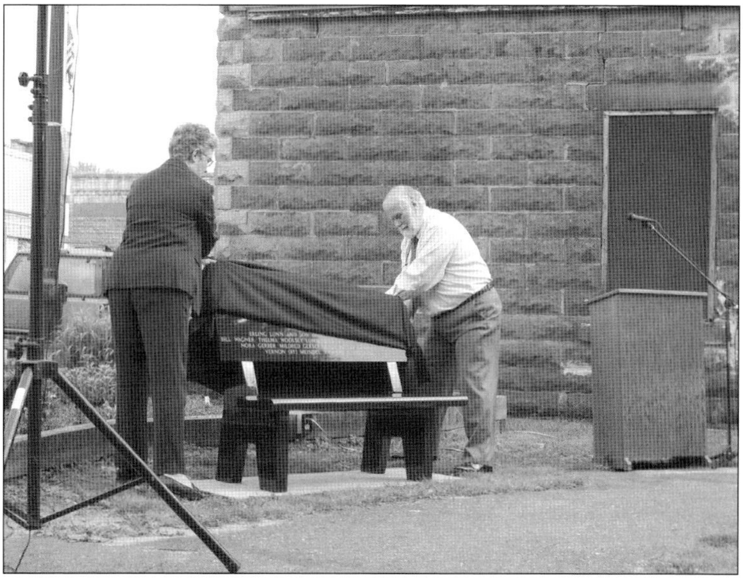

Acting village president Jean Olson and community member Ron Peterson uncover the bench for the crowd gathered in Tower Park. The black granite bench is a centerpiece of the park. Every year on June 4 at 7:07 p.m., Colfax Lutheran Church plays "Amazing Grace" on the carillon to honor the memory of the victims. (Author's collection.)

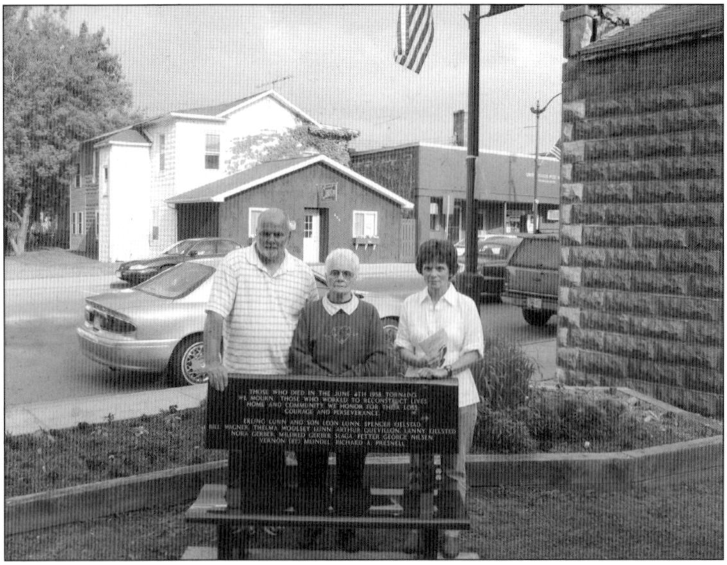

From left to right, Ronald Fjelstad, Ethel (Fjelstad) Nelson, and Emily (Fjelstad) Bowe stand behind the Memorial Bench, which was dedicated to the victims, including Ethel's husband and Ronald and Emily's father, Spencer, who was killed in the tornado at age 38. Hundreds of people, organizations, and businesses donated to make the purchase of the bench possible. (Author's collection.)

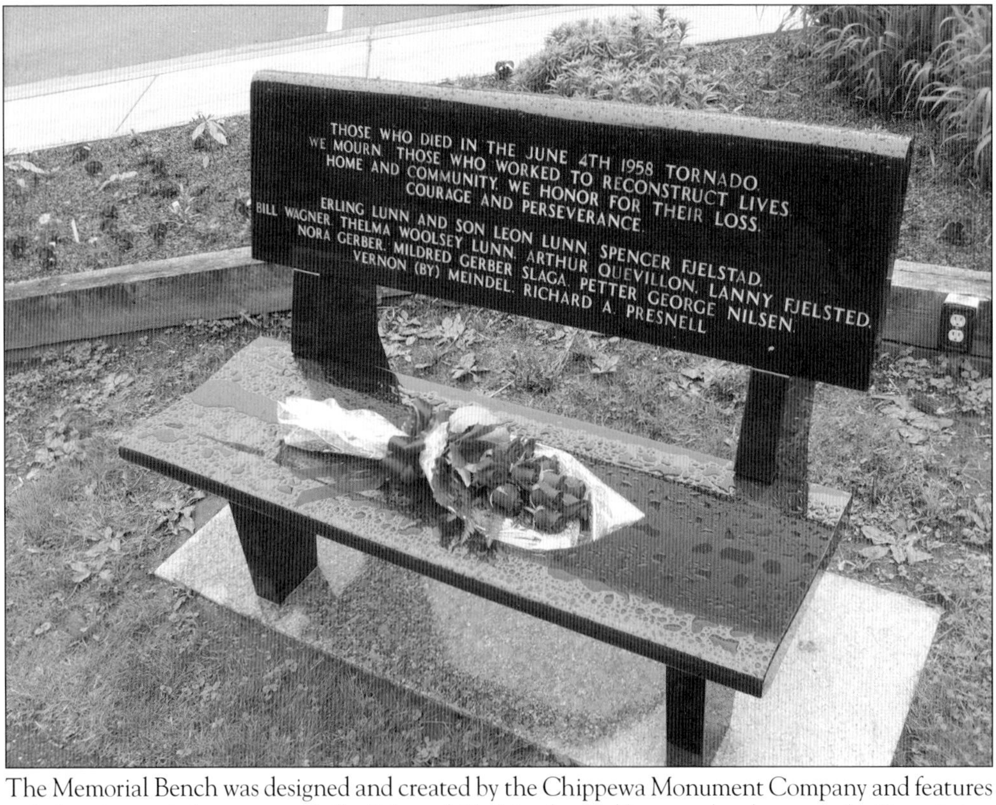

The Memorial Bench was designed and created by the Chippewa Monument Company and features a dedication and the names of all of those killed in the Colfax area by the tornado. Remaining funds were disbursed to purchase floodlights so the bench could be lit, along with "Welcome to Colfax" road signs. (Author's collection.)

Elementary students created artwork to show their understanding of the tornado and to share their thoughts and inspirations through writing. Third-grade students are taught about the history of their community, including the tornado. The stories centered around the tornado capture the interest of the most students. (Author's collection.)

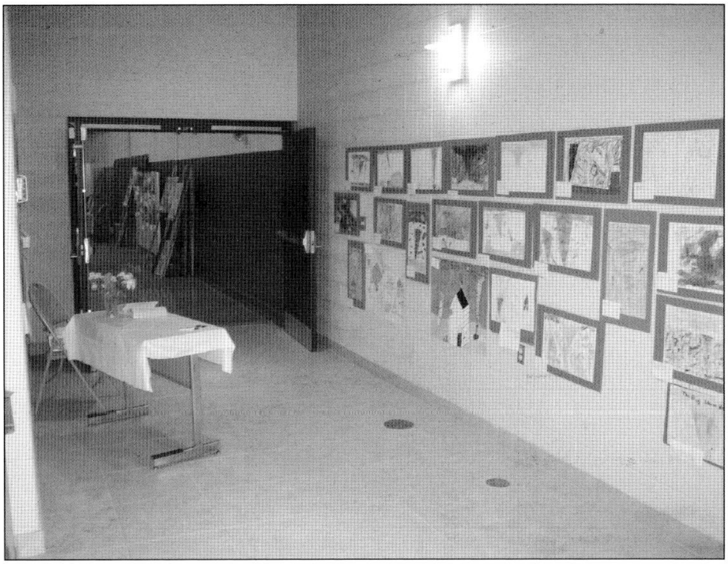

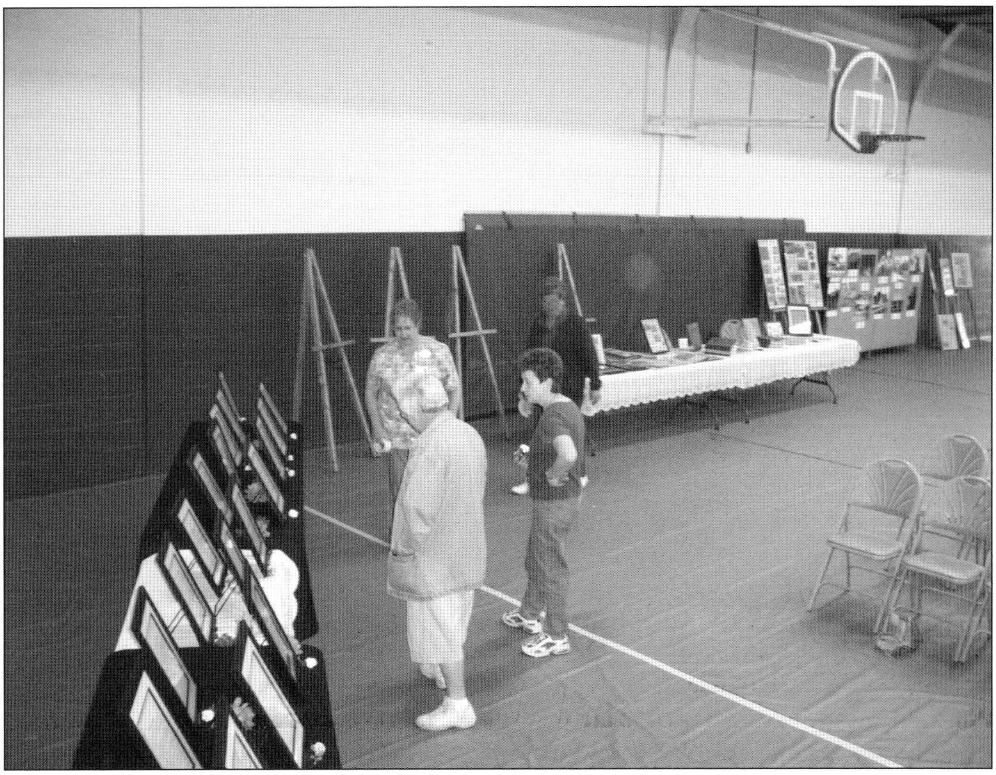

From left to right, anniversary committee members Karen Hendrickson, Julie Harmon, Deb Klukas, and Marlene Johnson inspect the framed obituaries of the 12 Colfax tornado victims. The commemoration was held in their honor, with some family members in attendance. These were given to family members of the victims following the event. A total of 28 people were killed as a result of the tornado. (Author's collection.)

Here is a view of the framed obituaries of the tornado victims in the Colfax High School gymnasium. Those killed in the storm ranged in age from 3 years old to 71. (Author's collection.)

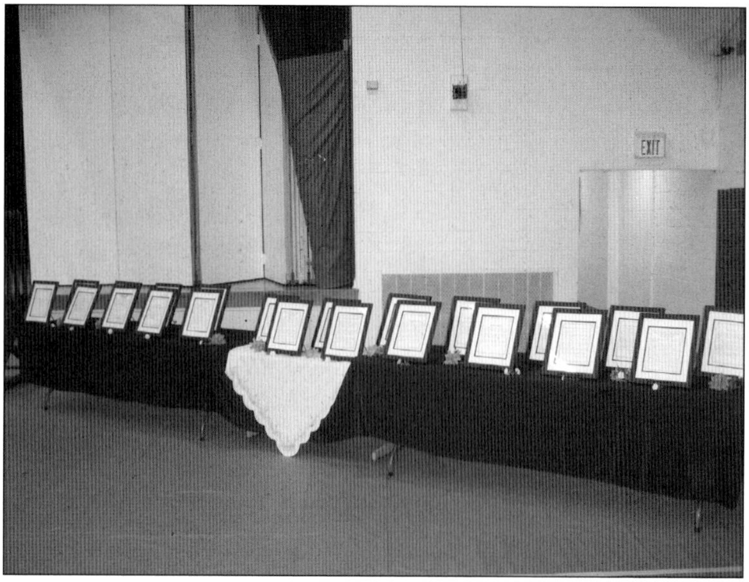

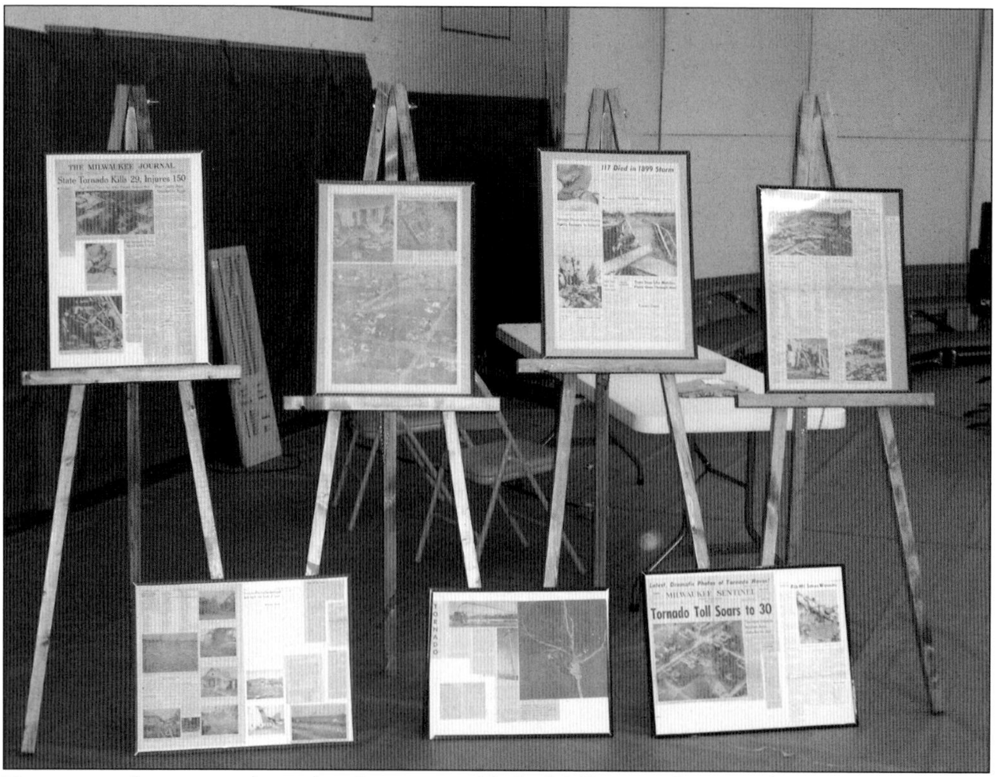

Newspaper clippings and articles that were published following the tornado in local, state, and out-of-state media were on display for the commemoration. The story of the actual tornado, as well as the stories of the victims, survivors, and cleanup efforts, was big news all over Wisconsin. (Author's collection.)

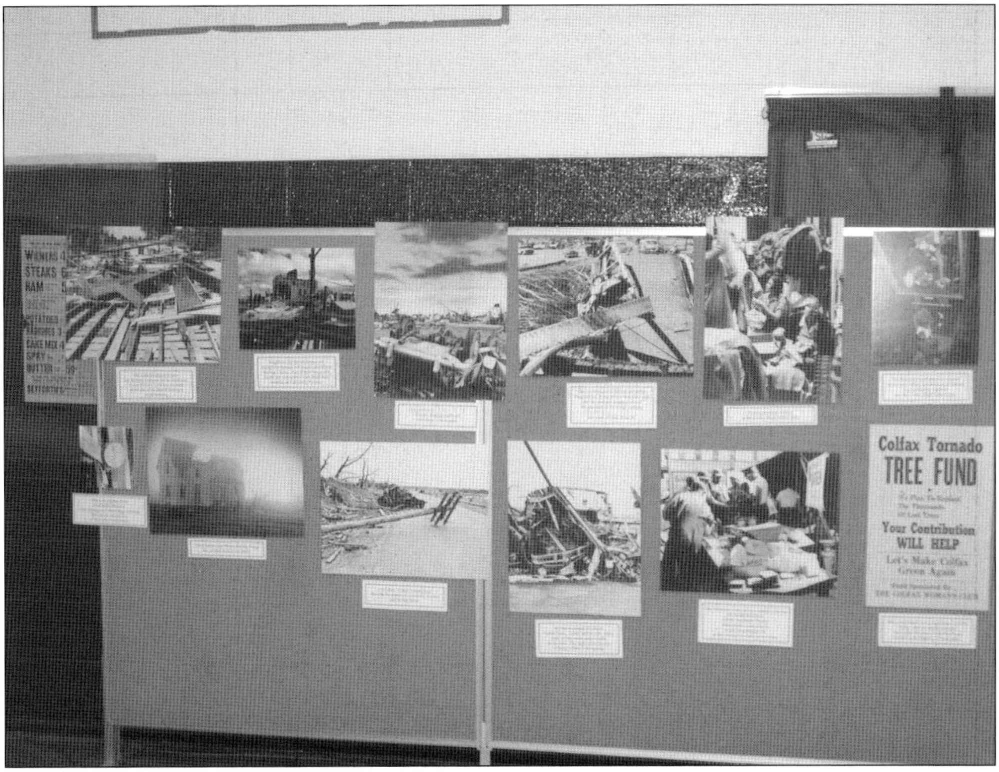

Photographs of the damage left behind by the tornado as well as the cleanup efforts were on display for the 50th anniversary commemoration event. Thanks to the generous support and help from members within the community, many people were able to remember, share stories, and honor those affected by the tornado. (Author's collection.)

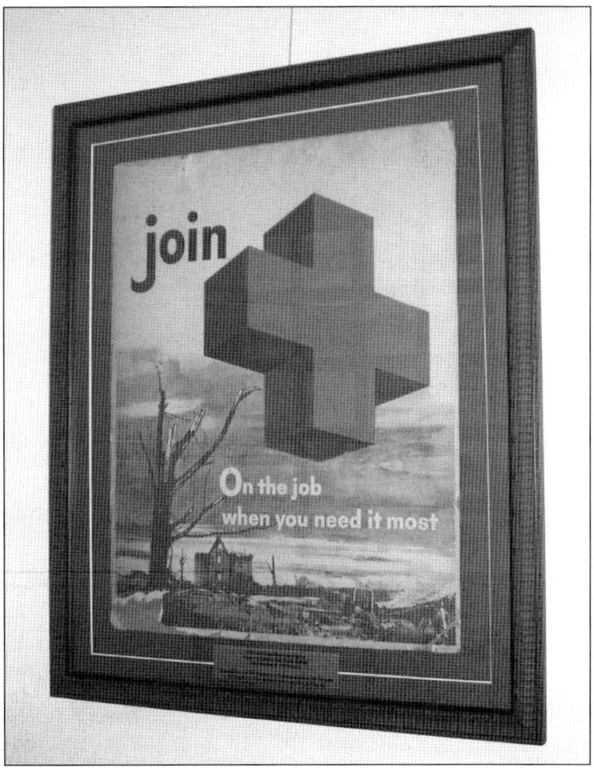

This Red Cross poster was donated to the Colfax Municipal Building Restoration Group by the family of Clarence and Minda Burling. Their home, which was destroyed by the tornado, is pictured on the poster. The poster is currently on display in the Colfax Municipal Building. (Author's collection.)

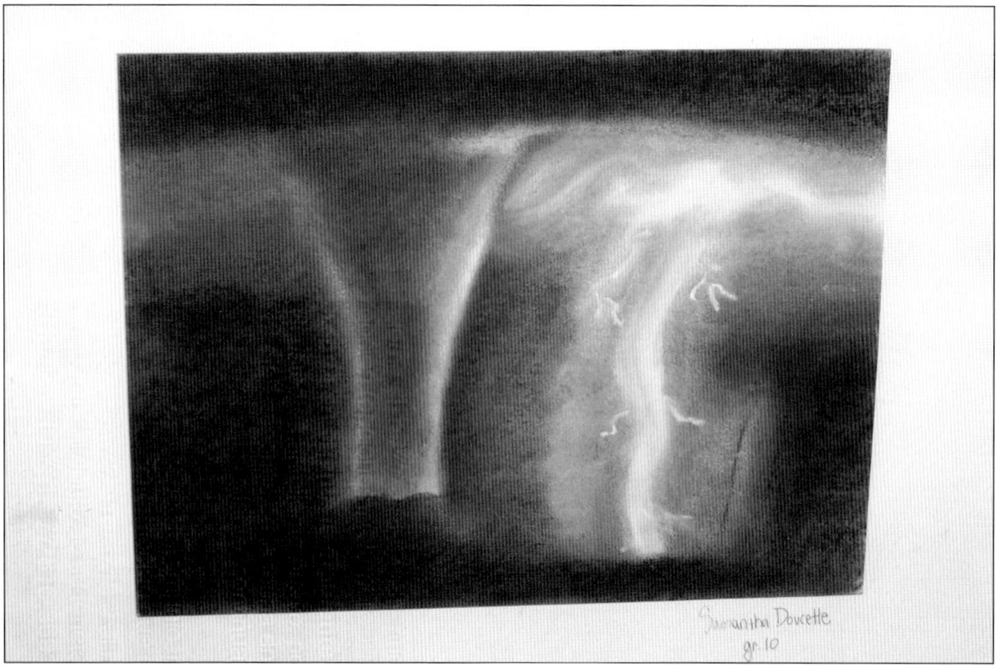

Artwork by high school student Sam Doucette invokes the dark mood and shows the terrifying destructive nature of a tornado. It captures the sense of helplessness of those who would have watched it drop from the sky. Fourth-grade students wrote essays about what they thought the tornado was like. (Author's collection.)

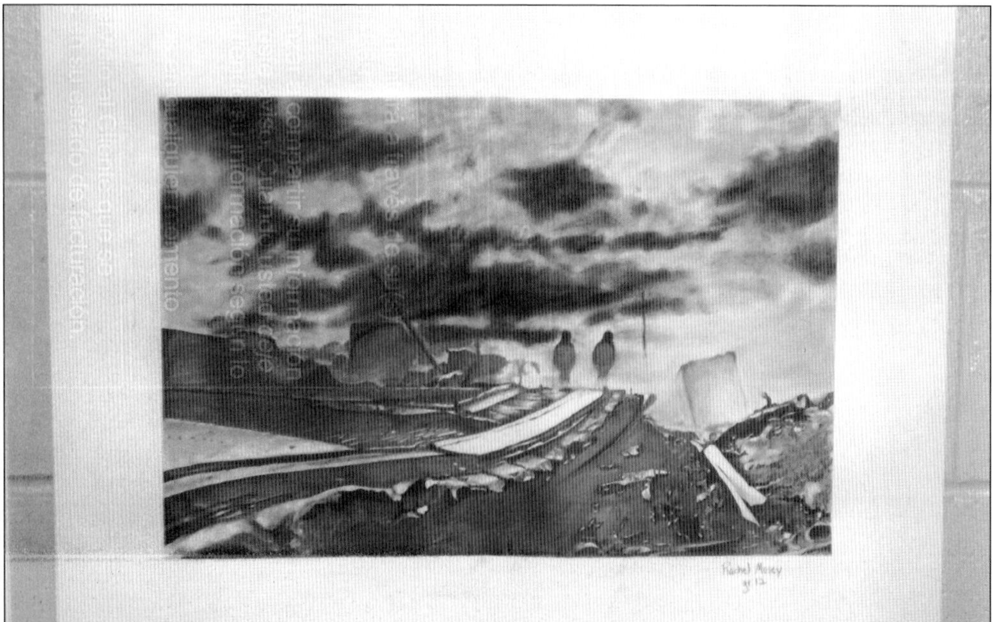

This depiction of the storm by student Rachel Mosey combines the aftermath of the tornado with a glimpse of hope in healing that was to come in the days, weeks, months, and years following. Students submitted over 80 drawings, sculptures, and paintings to observe the anniversary in their own way. (Author's collection.)

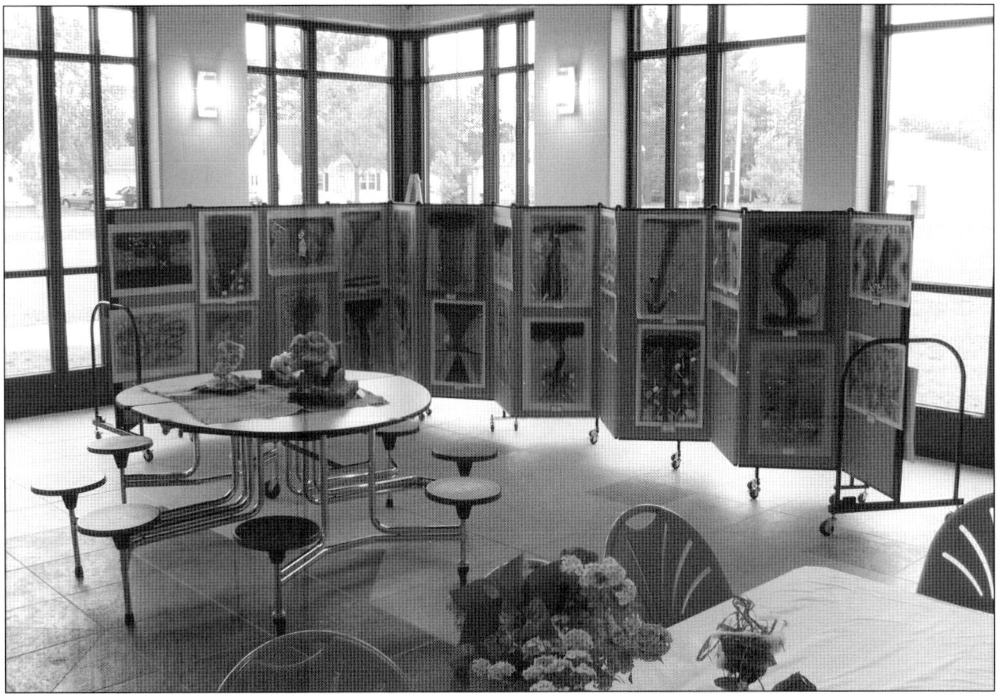

Elementary and high school students created paintings and sculptures in their art classes, which were inspired by the tornado. Students were taught about the tornado and its impact in Colfax so they could understand and appreciate the shock and recovery of their community. These were on display as part of the commemoration event. (Author's collection.)

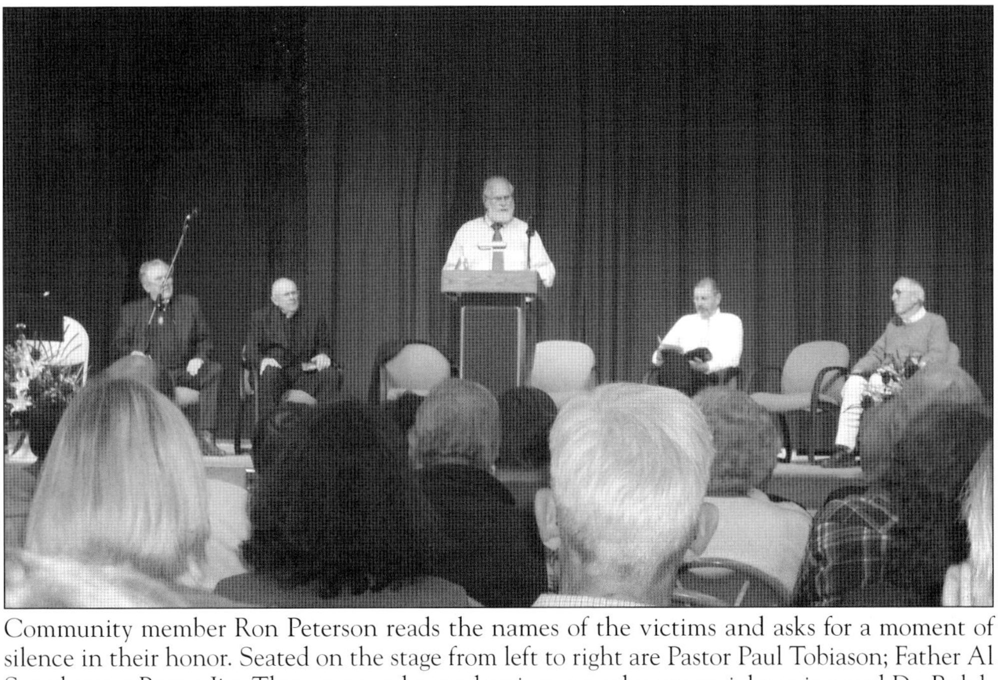

Community member Ron Peterson reads the names of the victims and asks for a moment of silence in their honor. Seated on the stage from left to right are Pastor Paul Tobiason; Father Al Sonnberger; Pastor Jim Thunstrom, who read scripture at the memorial service; and Dr. Ralph Hudson, who shared his own story from the tornado. (Author's collection.)

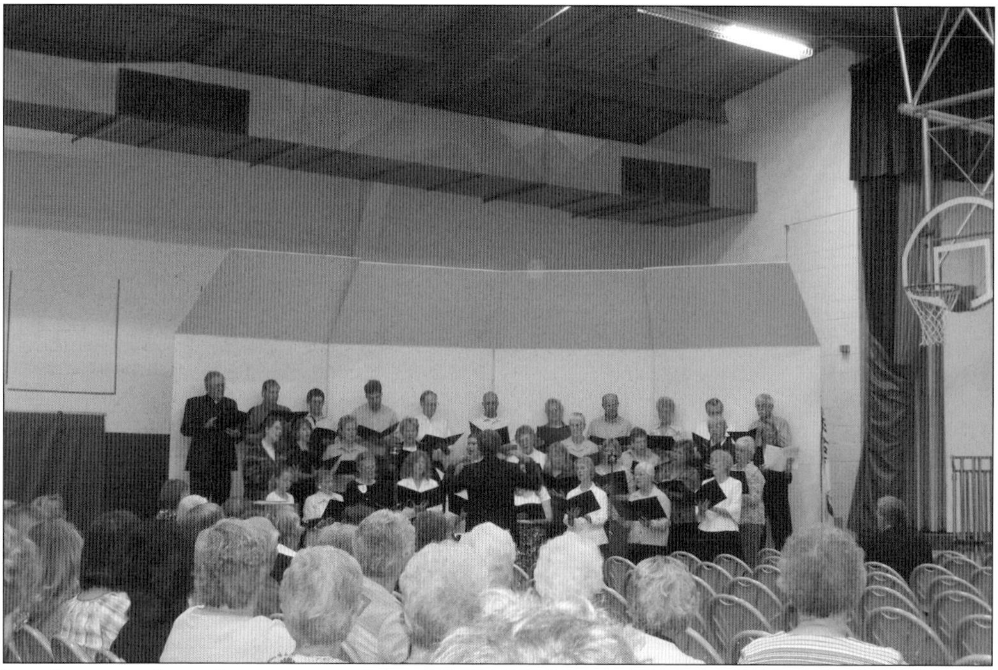

Local citizens formed a community choir that offered an anthem of remembrance, "All Thanks and Praise," at the end of the memorial service. Other offerings related to the anniversary commemoration were DVDs that featured pictures and interviews, buttons, and a Colfax Municipal Building Restoration Group tornado calendar as well as a booklet that published stories from survivors of the tornado. (Author's collection.)

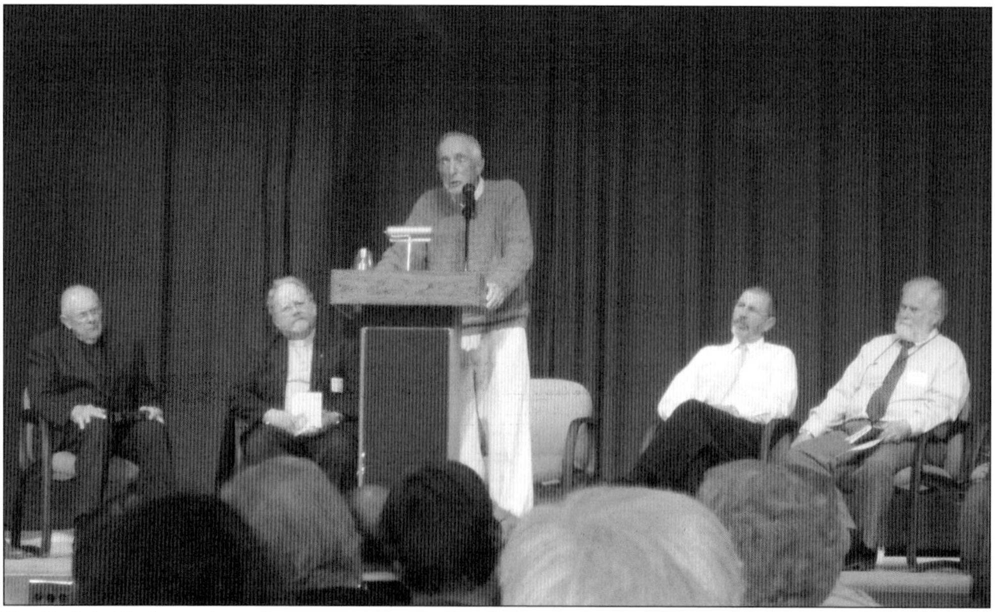

Dr. Ralph Hudson shared emotional remarks about treating the injured from the tornado. His most memorable patient was a baby found in a field with extensive injuries. The baby was Chris Lunn, and due to the excellent care from doctors and nurses and his own inherent resilience, Lunn survived his injuries. (Author's collection.)

Honoring the Victims

From the beginning, there were known fatalities from the storm. As the night and the next day proceeded, there were more names added to that list. Gathered from different sources, here is a list of the victims along with their age and community of origin.

Erling Lunn, 28, Colfax
Leon Lunn, 4, Colfax
Spencer Fjelstad, 38, Colfax
William Wagner, 50, Colfax
Thelma Woolsey Lunn, 21, Great Falls, Montana
Arthur Quevillon, 52, Colfax
Lanny Fjelsted, 16, Colfax
Nora Gerber, 66, Colfax
Mildred (Gerber) Slaga, 39, Pomona, California
Petter George Nilsen, 70, Colfax
Vernon Meindell, 40, Bloomer, Wisconsin
Richard Presnell, 27, Bloomer, Wisconsin

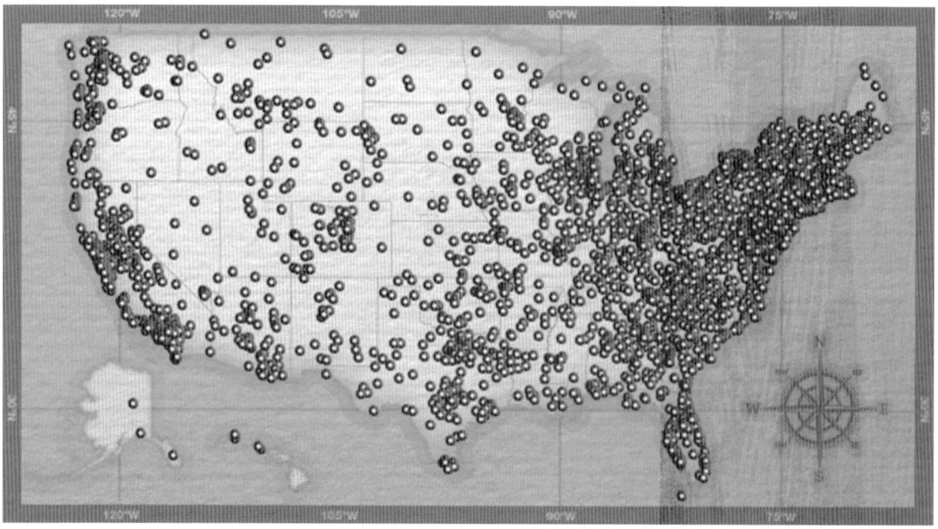

Consistent with our mission to preserve history on a local level, this book was printed in South Carolina on American-made paper and manufactured entirely in the United States. Products carrying the accredited Forest Stewardship Council (FSC) label are printed on 100 percent FSC-certified paper.

MADE IN THE USA